CAPACITY MANAGEMENT

John H. Blackstone, Jr.

Department of Management
University of Georgia

GF60AA
PUBLISHED BY
SOUTH-WESTERN PUBLISHING CO.
CINCINNATI   WEST CHICAGO, IL   CARROLLTON, TX   LIVERMORE, CA

Library of Congress Cataloging-in-Publication Data

Blackstone, John H.
  Capacity management.

  Bibliography: p. 247.
  Includes index.
  1. Industrial capacity—Management. I. Title.
HD69.C3B63 1989 658.5′038   88-61340
ISBN 0-538-80277-4

    3 4 5 6 7 8 M 5 4 3

Printed in the United States of America

To Melissa Swift Blackstone

CONTENTS

FOREWORD

I am honored to have been asked to write a foreword to John Blackstone's text on capacity management. The text actually started about nine years ago as a set of lecture notes for an APICS certification review workshop at the Chattahoochee Valley chapter. From the very beginning, the author attempted to develop in his audience a thorough understanding of the underlying concepts of managing capacity as the scarce resource it is. Over the years since then, John has revised and expanded the original manuscript for use in APICS chapter meetings, regional and national seminars, and undergraduate and graduate-level courses. He has become well known for his expertise in this rapidly changing field.

With each reading of the manuscript, I have developed a deeper understanding of this complex topic. The text provides comprehensive coverage of an often neglected but vitally important area. Literature in the field is fragmented and conflicts with the emergence of the just-in-time and optimized production technology (OPT) philosophies. Our entire field may change as a result of these and other developments.

Almost fifteen years ago, Joe Orlicky wrote a text on material requirements planning (MRP) that has become the most important single resource on material requirements planning to date. Since that time, MRP has evolved from a bill of material explosion technique to a comprehensive manufacturing information system. Orlicky's text was instrumental in providing the knowledge required to promote development and growth of these concepts. Little progress has, however, been made in understanding the capacity problems of manufacturing. Capacity may be far more complex than current thinking suggests. It may be the key to proper management of manufacturing activities. With reduced inventory levels, effective use of system capacity is the competitive edge to increase overall plant output. This text offers students and practitioners the opportunity to develop a thorough understanding of current and promising techniques.

This is the first academic text on capacity management. An academic text provides a comprehensive literature review, an extensive development of basic and advanced concepts and techniques, and numerous supporting exercises and problems. The primary objective of any academic text in production/

operations management should be to produce a person thoroughly grounded in the literature, capable of understanding real-world problems, and capable of developing appropriate solutions to these problems. By these measures, this text is proven.

JAMES F. COX

PREFACE

As this is the first textbook to appear in the capacity management area, I have attempted simultaneously to address the needs of undergraduate and graduate students as well as the needs of practitioners who are studying for APICS certification. In order to maintain readability, all graduate-level material has been placed in appendices following various chapters. Graduate-level exercises have been labeled "Advanced."

The Intended Audience of This Book

This text began as a monograph created in 1981 for undergraduate students in materials management at Auburn University. The materials management sequence is a two-course sequence covering the (then) five APICS certification topics. Although adequate material was available for most areas, I found that there was no paper or set of papers which covered capacity management theory in a logical sequence. I soon began teaching APICS certification short courses, using the monograph as a handout. A number of participants in these short courses later told me they found the monograph to be their most useful study aid in preparing for certification and urged me to publish it.

I use *Capacity Management* as the primary text for a course in materials management, which covers capacity management, production activity control, and just-in-time. Prerequisites for the course include master planning, inventory management, and material requirements planning. I cover all chapters in sequence, supplementing Chapter 7 extensively for production activity control and Chapter 10 extensively for just-in-time.

Capacity Management may also be used as a supplementary text for a broader operations management course, to provide additional detail in the area of capacity management. Useful for this purpose are Chapters 1 through 5, which cover the basic definitional material, rough-cut capacity planning, capacity requirements planning, and input/output control. These chapters provide far greater detail than is usually found in operations management texts.

Few operations management texts have more than cursory coverage of the OPT or synchronized production philosophy. The philosophy is covered in detail in Chapter 9. Depending on the focus of the operations management course, one might also wish to use materials from Chapters 7 and 8 on dispatching and capacity planning for tooling.

Software

Provided free to instructors who adopt the text, the software performs rough-cut capacity planning on IBM PC's and compatibles. There are two versions of the software on the disk, one compiled from FORTRAN source code which requires no special software, and one designed for Lotus 1-2-3.* The Lotus version will run on Version 1A but is too large to run on the student version. Throughout the text are discussions of how to develop microcomputer software to accomplish the task at hand.

Acknowledgments

After some delay and much revision, my original monograph, expanded and amended, is now a textbook. I am grateful for the encouragement given by many former students. Without their encouragement I never would have attempted this text. Comments provided by Jim Wahlers and Archie Lockamy were especially helpful. I am also grateful to Ray Martin of the University of Central Florida for his careful review of the first manuscript. His comments were extremely helpful in identifying advanced material to move to appendices. Ashok Rao of Babson College and Stan Gardiner of Auburn University also provided helpful editorial comments. I would also like to recognize the fine efforts of Wayne Todd, who coded the software provided as ancillary material. Wayne worked long hours to provide code which would be easy to use as well as functionally correct. Finally, I would like to express extreme gratitude to Jim Cox of the University of Georgia, who provided much encouragement to attempt the text and who has been a constant reviewer and critic through both drafts of the manuscript.

JOHN H. BLACKSTONE, JR.

---

*Lotus and 1-2-3 are registered trademarks of the Lotus Development Corporation.

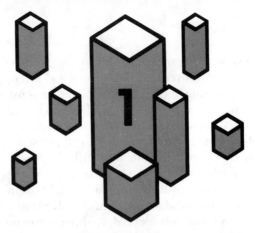

Introduction and Definitions

INTRODUCTION

The *APICS* (American Production and Inventory Control Society) *Certification Program Examination Study Guides* (1) define capacity management as "the function of planning, establishing, measuring, monitoring, and adjusting levels of capacity so that sufficient capacity is available to permit execution of the manufacturing schedules. . . . Capacity planning is the process of measuring the amount of work scheduled and then determining the necessary people, machines, and physical resources needed to accomplish it. Capacity control involves monitoring both work input and production output to ensure that capacity plans are being achieved, and taking corrective action if there are significant variations in input or output" (p. 23).

Good capacity management makes it possible to have the product available when and where the customer demands it. Because the production process usually extends through several stages, from raw materials to component items to subassemblies to finished goods, a delay at any of these stages may mean that the product is not available when it is needed. If one visualizes the production process as a series of pipes through which the product must flow, any condition that hampers free movement through the production pipeline creates a **bottleneck** and causes product delivery to be delayed. Thus, a major aspect of capacity management is the control of actual and potential bottlenecks.

Clearly, another aspect of capacity management is the control of costs. Throughout this text we will consider the cost of having too much capacity (excess wages and capital investment) versus the cost of having too little capacity (excess inventory, delay costs, and lost opportunities).

The function of capacity planning is interrelated with that of production planning. It is useful to view the relationship between these two planning functions over four time ranges, from the very long term to the very short term. In the very long term, say 1 to 10 years, the production plan must consider resource requirements so that the necessary land, facilities, equipment, and trained work force can be made available. Very long term planning is known as **resource requirements planning.** In the medium to long term (1 to 2 years), the **master production schedule (MPS)** must be validated against existing capacity before it is adopted. Within the medium to long term some adjustments to capacity are possible; however, gross discrepancies between the MPS and existing capacity may require that the MPS be revised. The validation of the MPS against existing capacity is often called **rough-cut capacity planning (RCCP)**. The relationships between production planning, resource requirements planning, and rough-cut capacity planning are illustrated in Figure 1.1.

Although the *APICS Dictionary* (2) considers resource requirements planning and rough-cut capacity planning synonymous terms, it is clear from published cases that there are really two long-term capacity planning activities. In this text, *resource requirements planning* will be used to describe an activity that is primarily concerned with plant expansion and the acquisition of major equipment. *Rough-cut capacity planning* will be used to describe the validation of the MPS.

In the medium to short range (3 months to 1 year), a detailed comparison of the material requirements plan to available capacity is performed. This activity, **capacity requirements planning (CRP)**, is usually considerably more detailed than rough-cut planning since it involves exploding the MPS and planning production of all components. Discrepancies between the capacity required by the MPS and available capacity may mean revising the MPS (as a last resort); however, it may be possible to provide additional capacity by means of subcontracting, overtime, or alternative routing.

The relationship between capacity control and production control extends into the very short term through the function of **dispatching**. If dispatching (a production control function) does not recognize capacity limitations, work-in-process inventory (WIP) increases. **Input/output control** is a technique that dispatchers use to manage queues of work by limiting work center input to its capacity and/or adjusting capacity by use of overtime.

JOB SHOPS AND ASSEMBLY LINES

In this section, manufacturing plants are classified into three types: fabrication shops (also known as job shops), assembly shops (also known as assembly lines), or fabrication and assembly shops. Although these classifica-

FIGURE 1.1   AN OVERVIEW OF CAPACITY MANAGEMENT

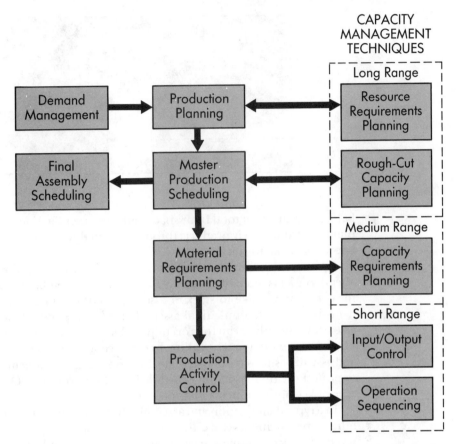

SOURCE: Adapted from *APICS Certification Program Examination Study Guides* (1987), p. 23.

tions are somewhat arbitrary, nevertheless they serve to explain differences in the way various manufacturers manage capacity. However, the reader should be aware that these terms differ quite a bit between industries and often between firms within the same industry, despite APICS efforts to standardize them.

Figure 1.1 shows the planning process for the most common type of manufacturing facility in the United States: a fabrication and assembly shop. A fabrication and assembly shop is a plant which constructs components *and* assembles them into end items. The layout of such a plant is shown in Figure 1.2. Note from Figure 1.2 that there is a set of departments (A–E) which fabricate components, a large area for storage of components (often comprising

FIGURE 1.2   FABRICATION AND ASSEMBLY SHOP

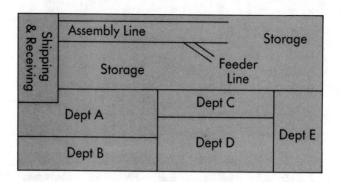

half to two-thirds of total floor space), and an assembly line area. Often such plants distribute their products through regional warehouses. This system is known as **make-to-stock**.

In some cases, orders for end items are satisfied by assembling components after the order is received. This system is known as **assemble-to-order.** Whether the company is make-to-stock or assemble-to-order, a large stock of components is used to decouple final assembly from component fabrication. Final assembly scheduling can thus occur parallel to, and somewhat independently of, master production scheduling, as depicted in Figure 1.1. Most fabrication and assembly shops create **safety stocks** of optional component items in order to protect the final assembly schedule from forecast errors. Otherwise stockouts of key optional items might occur.

In a typical fabrication and assembly shop, the assembly line has the capability of producing several different models. It usually takes quite a long time, several hours or perhaps several days, to change the line from producing model A to producing model B. The **final assembly schedule (FAS)** shows the daily rate of production of model A, the length of the production run, the time required for changeover, and the daily rate for model B. Because of long setup time, production runs for each model tend to be quite large, hundreds and often thousands of units.

Since the components which go into model A are not the same as those going into model B, a coordination problem arises. Suppose A consists of a C and two D's, while B consists of a C and two E's. Suppose further that in one week 2,000 A's are to be made while in another week 2,200 B's are to be made. Components needed for the two weeks, then, are 4,200 C's, 4,000 D's, and 4,400 E's. The D's are due this week, the E's next week. All 4,200 C's may be due this week or 2,000 C's may be due this week and 2,200 next week, depending upon batch-size decisions made in fabrication.

A typical fabrication and assembly shop makes dozens to hundreds of **end items**, each in large batches. Producing each end item requires that large batches of components be fabricated and placed in stock before final assembly begins. In order to maximize profit, the company wishes to minimize the amount of time components are in stock. Therefore careful coordination between the FAS and the MPS is crucial. The coordination problem is complicated by the fact that machines break down, workers get sick, engineers change product designs, and customers change their minds.

Figure 1.3 depicts a typical **just-in-time** (also known as **zero inventory**) assembly line layout. Note that the layout is by product line. Like the make-to-order and assemble-to-order plant, the typical just-in-time assembly line makes numerous products; however, it does not require long changeover (or setup) times. Rather than making all A's one week and all B's the next, the just-in-time line prefers to run ABABAB if equal numbers of the two products are needed. Note that only one unit is run before switching to a new product. Ideally, this lot size of one is carried into fabrication of components, making the component area a product layout (assembly line) rather than a process

FIGURE 1.3   JUST-IN-TIME PLANT CONFIGURATION (PRODUCT LAYOUT)

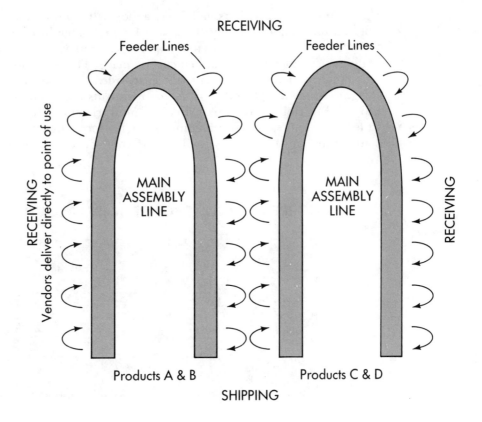

layout (job shop). Thus, instead of having all lathes in one department, lathes are scattered throughout the shop as needed to support fabrication of specific components. The feeder lines which make components are placed close to the point where the assembly line uses the components. Feeder lines terminate at the point on the main line where the component will be used so that assembly workers can pick up new components as they are needed. Fabrication workers can stockpile only a limited number of components; thereafter, they must wait for an assembly worker to claim finished components before any more components can be made. Purchased parts are delivered in small batches and taken directly to assembly or fabrication lines. The result is the elimination of the storeroom and almost all inventory.

Just-in-time plants, thus, have a different type of capacity problem from that depicted in Figure 1.1. Resource requirements planning is still needed to plan new additions to the plant, but rough-cut capacity planning, CRP, and input/output control are replaced by line balancing. The just-in-time plant typically adjusts its output rate once a month so that units are produced at the same rate that they are sold. Line balancing will be discussed in Chapter 10, after capacity management in a process layout has been thoroughly considered.

Figure 1.4 depicts a **job shop**; that is, a shop with a process layout throughout. Layout is not by product line, as in Figure 1.3, but by type of machine. There is no assembly line in a job shop. Such a shop typically produces low-volume, complex products, often custom made. This shop arrangement is also known as **make-to-order** or **engineer-to-order**. This book will use the term *engineer-to-order* rather than *make-to-order* to distinguish it from assemble-to-order. In a job shop there is no final assembly schedule, only a master schedule. Furthermore, capacity planning may be less formalized, since planners do not always know how long it will take to complete certain operations as in

FIGURE 1.4 JOB SHOP (PROCESS LAYOUT)

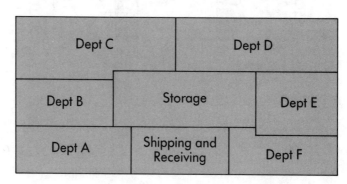

shops where the product is standardized. However, with minor adjustments, a job shop usually manages capacity in a manner similar to that depicted by Figure 1.1.

DEFINITIONS

Before moving to a full-scale discussion of capacity management at the department and plant level, it is necessary to establish the definition of a number of terms and to learn how to measure capacity. Therefore, the remainder of this chapter is devoted to definitions and measurement. In Chapter 2, the discussion of capacity management at the plant level begins.

Capacity Versus Load

Capacity is often defined by picturing a manufacturing facility as a funnel or as a trough. **Capacity** is the rate at which work is withdrawn from the system. **Load** is the volume of work in the system. These concepts are illustrated in Figure 1.5. The funnel depicted is often called *Wight's funnel* after Oliver Wight, a pioneer in capacity management theory. The trough representation, however, more clearly illustrates that management has two controls over the amount of work in a system: input into the system and output from it.

FIGURE 1.5   REPRESENTATION OF CAPACITY AS A RATE OF OUTPUT

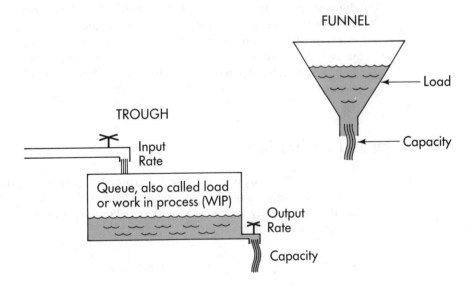

Whenever the input rate exceeds the output rate, the work in the system increases, and vice versa. This seemingly simple concept is often overlooked in complex environments because management, in concentrating on trying to get specific jobs out of the system on time, misses this important point: to be able to get the right work out, one must first get enough work out; that is, capacity planning must precede priority planning.

Units of Measure

The unit of measure selected for capacity planning should be common to the mix of products encountered, e.g., pieces, tons, feet, or standard work hours per time period. It must be a common denominator for all products measured. One of the primary purposes of capacity analysis is to identify bottlenecks; the unit of measure selected should be meaningful in terms of such identification. For an operation producing only one product, a measure such as pieces produced is meaningful. For example, one may learn that a bottling plant fills 10,000 bottles per day. If all bottles contain the same amount of liquid, stating the number of bottles produced would be a useful measure of capacity; and if on a particular day the plant only produced 9,500 bottles, management could be fairly confident that the plant had had a substandard day. But what if the plant fills a variety of bottles, ranging from one pint to two gallons? To state that the plant fills an average of 10,000 bottles a day would not be a very meaningful statistic. On a particular day when only 9,500 bottles were filled one would not know whether output was above or below average. Substantially more information regarding the mix of bottles and the length of time usually required to fill a bottle of each size would be needed. It would be far more meaningful to convert from pieces produced to the standard time required to produce these pieces. If one is told that a plant usually produces 10,000 standard hours of output but produced only 9,500 standard hours today, it would be apparent that output had declined, regardless of the mix of output.

Efficiency and Utilization

It is important to distinguish between *measuring* capacity and *calculating* capacity. In measuring capacity one averages some set of historical data. In calculating capacity, one sets capacity equal to the product of time available, efficiency, and utilization:

$$C = T \times E \times U \qquad (1.1)$$

where C is the capacity available or required, T is the time available, E is the efficiency factor as a proportion, and U is the utilization factor as a proportion.

For example, over the previous four weeks, work center 149 produced outputs of 125 standard hours, 140 standard hours, 132 standard hours, and 135 standard hours. The *measured capacity* of work center 149 would be $(125 + 140 + 132 + 135)/4 = 133$ standard hours. Note that measured capacity is defined as average output, not maximum output. If one were to give work to a work center every week equal to its maximum historical output, the amount of uncompleted work would grow.

Now suppose a factory worked two shifts with five machines staffed on each shift, eight hours a day, five days a week, with no scheduled overtime. Ignoring efficiency and utilization, the factory's calculated capacity would be 400 hours a week. Suppose further that historical machine utilization was 90 percent and historical efficiency was 95 percent. Then calculated capacity would be equal to 342 standard hours of output $(400 \times 0.90 \times 0.95)$. Calculated capacity is also called **rated** or **nominal capacity.**

The *APICS Dictionary* (2) defines **efficiency** as "a measure of how closely predetermined standards are achieved." The reason for considering efficiency in the capacity calculation is to convert from clock hours worked to standard hours produced. Suppose a work center is to produce 24 widgets on a particular day. An engineering report indicates that the standard time to produce one widget is 20 minutes. From this one may determine that it is supposed to take an average worker 480 minutes to produce 24 widgets. Workers are rarely average (and engineering standards are often out-of-date). The use of an efficiency factor based on a work center's actual output in recent periods can be used to determine whether the center should be allowed more or less than 480 minutes to produce the 24 widgets.

Note that the measure of efficiency is extremely sensitive to the experience of the workers present. When a skilled worker is replaced by an apprentice, the efficiency of the work center will drop immediately. Failure to adjust efficiency ratings results in overestimating the capacity of the work center. For this reason, the efficiency rating of a work center should be updated frequently, especially after personnel changes.

Machine utilization measures the fraction of time a machine is in use. The *APICS Dictionary* (2) defines **utilization** as "a measure of how intensively a resource is being used. . . . To calculate machine utilization, the total time charged to creating output (setup and run time) is divided by the total clock hours scheduled to the available for a given period of time." The theoretical maximum utilization is 1, or 100 percent. To achieve this maximum, the machine must never be out of service because of breakdown, operator absenteeism, or lack of parts. Since breakdowns, absenteeism, and lack of work do occasionally occur even under the best management, it is unrealistic to expect a machine to have a utilization of 100 percent. Historical utilization should provide a reasonable estimate of machine utilization, provided that there has been no major shift in product mix, demand level, or the condition of the facility.

CALCULATING UTILIZATION, EFFICIENCY, AND CAPACITY

Consider the following: A work center is composed of three machines staffed for two 8-hour shifts, five days a week. Thus, there are 240 work hours available per week. Records for the past several weeks indicate that break-downs reduced machine usage an average of 12 hours per week. Hours worked were therefore $240 - 12 = 228$ hours. Records also indicate that the work center produced an average of 250.8 standard hours of output. Given these data, the utilization in percent of the work center is determined as follows:

$$Utilization = \frac{Hours\ available\ -\ Hours\ down}{Hours\ available} \times 100 \qquad (1.2)$$

$$= \frac{Hours\ worked}{Hours\ available} \times 100$$

$$= \frac{240\ -\ 12}{240} \times 100$$

$$= 95\%$$

The efficiency in percent of the work center is determined as follows:

$$Efficiency = \frac{Standard\ hours\ produced}{Hours\ worked} \times 100 \qquad (1.3)$$

$$= \frac{250.8}{228} \times 100$$

$$= 110\%$$

Finally, it can be verified that the calculated, or nominal, capacity of the work center is

$$Capacity = Time\ available \times \frac{Time\ worked}{Time\ available} \qquad (1.4)$$

$$\times \frac{Standard\ hours\ produced}{Time\ worked}$$

$$240 \times 0.95 \times 1.10 = 250.8\ standard\ hours\ produced$$

A number of interesting problems can be solved through the application of these simple formulas. The following series of increasingly complex situations are presented to illustrate the use of the capacity formula.

PROBLEM 1.1

Suppose the standard time required to assemble a wagon is 15 minutes. 500 wagons need to be assembled in a 40-hour week. How many assemblers are needed if efficiency and utilization are both equal to 1?

SOLUTION

To solve this problem one must rearrange the capacity formula. Recall from equation 1.1 that the formula for calculating capacity available is $C = T \times E \times U$. In this instance C is 125 standard hours (500 wagons $\times$ 1/4 hour each). Since one must solve for T, the equation becomes:

$$T = \frac{C}{E \times U} \qquad (1.5)$$

Since $E \times U = 1$, the time available should be 125 hours. Given a standard week of 40 hours, 3.125 workers are needed; i.e., three workers with some planned overtime. If overtime is not an option, four workers are needed.

PROBLEM 1.2

Suppose in Problem 1.1 that the efficiency is known to be 0.9 and utilization is known to be 0.8. How many wagon assemblers are needed?

SOLUTION

Using equation 1.5, the formula for time required is now

$$T = \frac{125}{0.9 \times 0.8}$$
$$= \frac{125}{0.72}$$
$$= 174 \ hours \ (rounded \ to \ the \ nearest \ hour)$$

Thus 4.35 workers (174 hours/40 hours per worker), or four workers plus overtime, are needed. If overtime is not an option, five workers are needed.

PROBLEM 1.3

Suppose a scrap factor of 5 percent is added to Problem 1.2. How many person-hours are required?

SOLUTION

The number of parts started is $500/.95 = 526.3 = 527$. The time required is therefore

$$T = \frac{527 \; parts \times 0.25 \; hrs/part}{0.9 \times 0.8}$$

$$= \frac{131.75}{0.72}$$

$$= 183 \; hours \; (rounded \; to \; the \; nearest \; hour)$$

Two mistakes are commonly made in solving this problem. The first is to account for the scrap factor by multiplying by $1 +$ scrap rather than dividing by $1 -$ scrap. When this mistake is made, one would start with 525 units rather than 527. If 525 units have a 5 percent scrap factor, then 26.25 units will be scrapped, and the final lot size will not be quite large enough. The second common mistake is to round to the nearest integer (526.3 to 526). The correct procedure is to take any fractional part up to the next larger integer. Going up to the next larger integer ensures that the full scrap allowance requested is in effect.

PROBLEM 1.4

Suppose in Problem 1.2 that a 5 percent rework allowance is added, that rework requires the same time as the original work, and that there is no scrap allowance.

SOLUTION

When the original 500 units are completed, 25 would be sent for rework. When those 25 were completed, 5 percent of those would need rework, etc. Assuming $0 < r < 1$, this is an infinite sum whose limit is $x = 1/(1 - r)$, where x is a multiplier and r is the rework factor. In other words, you will multiply by $1/0.95$, which is the same as dividing by 0.95. So Problem 1.4 and Problem 1.3 have the same solution. *Important note: This result depends on the assumption that rework requires the same amount of time as the original work.*

PROBLEM 1.5

Suppose that in Problem 1.4 the rework takes 30 minutes rather than the ordinary processing time of 15 minutes.

SOLUTION

Capacity required equals lot size $\times$ time per piece $+$ pieces reworked $\times$ rework time per piece. There are a number of ways to determine the number of pieces reworked. The simplest of these is to multiply lot size by $(x - 1)$, where x is defined as $1/(1 - r)$. In this case

$$\textit{Pieces reworked} = 500 \times (1.0526 - 1)$$
$$= 26.3$$
$$= 27$$

Capacity required, in hours, is

$$C = 500 \times 1/4 + 27 \times 1/2$$
$$= 125 + 13.5$$
$$= 138.5 \ \textit{standard hours}$$

We now must assume that the efficiency and utilization factors for the work center hold for rework as well as for ordinary processing. If the efficiency and utilization factors given in Problem 1.2 are assumed, the solution becomes

$$T = \frac{138.5}{0.72}$$
$$= 187 \ \textit{hours (rounded to the nearest hour)}$$

SUMMARY

This chapter has introduced the definitions of capacity, efficiency, and utilization and demonstrated how to calculate all three of these factors numerically to determine the capacity required, or available, at a single work center. The remainder of the text will explain how to combine single-station calculations in order to plan departments and plants over long-range, medium-range, and short-range horizons.

REFERENCES

1. *APICS Certification Program Examination Study Guides.* Revised Edition for 1988 Exams. Falls Church, Va.: American Production and Inventory Control Society, 1987.
2. *APICS Dictionary.* 6th ed. Falls Church, Va.: American Production and Inventory Control Society, 1987.

EXERCISES

1. Define utilization and efficiency. Show the formula for calculating each.
2. Using the formulas for capacity, utilization, and efficiency, show that capacity is a rate of output.

3. A work center has exhibited the following output for the past six weeks:

Week	Output (standard hours)
1	247
2	224
3	217
4	238
5	227
6	243

What is its measured capacity?

4. Work center 43 makes three whatchamacallits, labeled A, B, and C. Industrial Engineering has determined that the standard time required to build these items is 10.2 hours, 1.8 hours, and 5.3 hours, respectively. The output of work center 43 in units over the past four weeks has been as follows:

Week	A's	B's	C's
1	14	49	22
2	25	5	11
3	8	150	18
4	15	95	17

What is the measured capacity of the work center? Answer first in units, then in standard hours. Comment on the adequacy of units as a measure of capacity in this situation.

5. The production schedule for a certain part calls for 1,000 units to be built for each of the next four weeks. Producing the part requires five operations on five different machines. Assuming that this part is the only part to be built on each of the five machines, determine the number of hours that should be scheduled on each machine. The standard time requirements for each of the five operations are as follows:

Machine Number	Time per Unit (hours)	Utilization (%)	Efficiency (%)
1	0.042	82	113
2	0.086	94	125
3	0.082	91	115
4	0.051	76	104
5	0.050	80	97

6. A machine characteristically loses 0.7 hours each day for maintenance. The assembly department works 8 hours per day. The machine operator is rated as 110 percent efficient. How many actual hours should be allowed to produce a job which requires 20 standard hours of work? Suppose the machine operator goes on vacation and is replaced by an ap-

prentice rated as 80 percent efficient. How many actual hours should be allowed?

7. A plant must make 2,000 pump housings a month, each requiring 0.21 hours of grinding machine time.

   a. Assuming no scrap losses or lost machine time, how many grinding machines should be scheduled for this job if the plant works 8 hours per day for 21 days a month at 100 percent efficiency?

   b. What is the answer if the company gets only 80 percent machine utilization and the operators are 105 percent efficient?

   c. How many housings should go into production if the scrap rate is 0.07? How many machines will be needed, given the utilization and efficiency figures given in *b* and the scrap rate in *c*?

8. In the past 12 weeks, an assembly department has assembled the following:

Part Number	Units Completed/Week
124A7	1,600
125B9	1,200
134A8	1,800
146C4	2,100

   From industrial engineering records, the times required to assemble these units are:

Part Number	Standard Hours/Unit
124A7	0.12
125B9	0.18
134A8	0.08
146C4	0.09

   What is the weekly capacity of the assembly department?

9. The assembly department in Exercise 8 employs 2 workers, 5 days per week, 8 hours per day. During the past 12 weeks, 6 person-days were lost to absenteeism. What is the utilization of the department? What is its efficiency?

APPENDIX 1A
On Capacity
Management Theory

1. INTRODUCTION

A critical decision in the operation of any business is the development of a master schedule, the basic plan of what goods and services are to be produced over the planning horizon. For a manufacturing firm the planning horizon is typically 6 to 18 months. During this period, plant and major equipment are considered to be fixed, but employment levels are variable. In developing a master schedule, it is important to verify that sufficient capacity exists at a few, critical work areas to meet the projected demand. If insufficient capacity exists, lead times grow, due dates are missed, inventories build up, and profit margins deteriorate. The process of verifying that sufficient capacity exists to meet the master schedule is known as rough-cut capacity planning.

A 1982 article by Berry, Schmitt, and Vollmann (2) on information needs for capacity planning cited 61 references, most of which discuss the estimation of required capacity. By contrast, almost no literature exists on the estimation of capacity available. Unfortunately, the issue of how much capacity is *available*, when it is discussed at all, is treated at a very rudimentary level. In this paper it is argued that a more careful definition of available capacity is needed to plan manufacturing operations properly.

From a paper by the author previously published as University of Georgia MIS Working Paper no. 24. Presented is a suggested reformulation of a portion of capacity management theory. The material is not at this time part of the body of knowledge as defined by APICS.

An example of the rudimentary level at which capacity available is discussed is in Lunz (5), who describes a measure he calls the capacity planning performance factor, tracked on a monthly basis for each work center as follows:

1. Compute total hours worked.
2. Compute total actual direct labor hours.
3. Divide step 2 by step 1 to get percentage of direct labor hours.
4. Multiply step 3 above by 8.
5. Divide actual direct labor hours by standard direct labor hours to get an efficiency percentage.
6. Multiply the percentage in step 5 by 4 to realize effective hours.
7. Add an allowance for absenteeism.

Lunz's description fits well with the accepted body of knowledge. It is said to yield the *available capacity in standard hours.* Under this approach, a master schedule is said to be feasible if the number of standard hours required is less than or equal to the number of standard hours available. On the basis of this comparison, many shops estimate an underload or overload which measures the difference between capacity required and capacity available, as described by Wemmerlov (7).

The concept of comparing capacity required to capacity available is often depicted by representing a water trough with a faucet bringing water into the trough and a second faucet taking water out of the trough. The two faucets represent the rate of input and output, respectively. The height of the water in the trough is a measure of load to be processed (in this case, to flow through the output faucet). It is said that if input exceeds output the level of load will rise, but that if output exceeds input the level of load will fall. Implicit in this statement is that if input equals output the level of load will remain constant. This concept is illustrated in Figure 1A.1, taken from what is considered to be one of the most significant articles on capacity management, an article which APICS has reprinted in both of its Capacity Management Reprints series.

Those who have studied queueing theory will recognize immediately that the trough representation is valid only if the rates of input and output are constant. For those who have not studied queueing theory, a brief digression is in order. Suppose a bank teller processed one customer every two minutes, exactly. Suppose further that a customer arrived precisely once every two minutes and that there currently is one customer in service and one in queue behind the customer being served. In this situation the number of customers in the system will always be two, with one arriving just as one departs. Utilization of the teller is 100 percent, i.e., the teller is never idle. Average wait time is two minutes, since each arriving customer finds one customer just entering service.

Average time in the system is four minutes, with zero variance. Now suppose that in this situation both arrival and service times are random variables;

FIGURE 1A.1   LOAD VS. CAPACITY

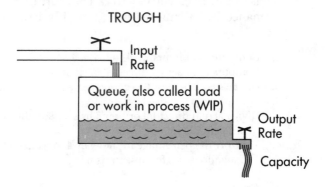

The relationship between the expected waiting time for an arriving customer and server utilization can be depicted as shown in Figure 1A.2, which represents the average time spent in queue for an M/M/1 queueing system. Figure 1A.2 was developed from equation 1A.1 using the values of a/s shown on the x-axis. For a manufacturing operation in which releases of orders to the shop are controlled, arrivals of orders are random variables, but perhaps not Poisson. The probability distribution for service times may not be exponential. To what extent does the type of distribution involved affect the shape of Figure 1A.2? The basic shape of this function is the same whenever both the arrival and service rates are independent random variables, although the point specifically, assume that arrivals are Poisson with 30 arrivals an hour and service is exponential with a mean service time of two minutes. Intuitively, it would seem that the average waiting time should still be two minutes, since the average arrival and service times have not changed. In fact, this is an instance of a queueing system for which the expected long-range waiting time in the queue is infinite. The expected waiting time in the queue, $E(W)$, is found by the formula

$$E(W) = \frac{a}{s(s - a)} \qquad\qquad (1A.1)$$

where a is average arrival rate per time unit and s is average service rate per time unit. It can be shown that equation 1A.1 limits to infinity when a approaches s, i.e., when the arrival rate of customers into the system approaches the rate of customer service.

FIGURE 1A.2   EXPECTED WAITING TIME IN QUEUE*

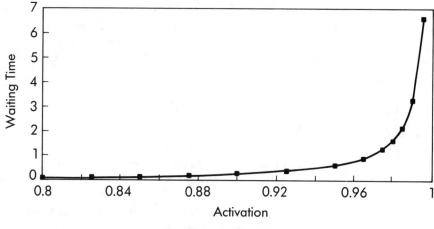

● Waiting Time (hours)

*Exponential arrivals, exponential service time, 1 server.

Look again at the capacity planning performance factor described by Lunz. Note that the method takes no note of the amount of load in the system. Server utilization is accepted in step 3 without asking whether that utilization is too high or too low. It is the contention of the author that omitting the issue of desired utilization has led to excessive work-in-process inventory and excessive lead times throughout most industries.

There are two ways of verifying this contention. The first is to note that under most performance measurement systems a work center is encouraged to work 100 percent of the time it is available. A text that enjoys a tremendous reputation among practitioners devotes several pages to the calculation of the minimum level of backlog required to keep a work center in service virtually all the time (6). If one recognizes that input is a random variable, based on the time other work centers happen to finish, and that output is a random variable, subject to machine downtime and operator absenteeism as well as operator variation, one must realize that an attempt to reach 100 percent utilization will bring one far up the waiting time curve depicted in Figure 1A.2.

A second way to verify the contention that manufacturers are ignoring the relationship between utilization and queue time is simply to note the number of articles devoted to the problem of excessive work-in-process inventory (WIP), excessive lead times, and excessive tardy jobs. Clearly the problem of excessive WIP is pervasive and has been impervious to attempts to correct it. Lack of a cure is a sure sign that the problem is almost universally misunderstood. It is my contention that what is not understood by most practitioners is the impact of attempting to reach 100 percent utilization.

In section 2 of this paper the standard definition of capacity available will be presented. In section 3 a revised definition will be proposed. Section 4 will present the modifications in capacity management practice needed to implement the new definition under a system controlled by a material requirements planning system. Section 5 will discuss the use of the new definitions as performance measures.

2. THE STANDARD DEFINITION OF CAPACITY AVAILABLE

Capacity is defined to be a rate of output per time unit. The unit of measure must be common to all types of output. The only units common to all output are dollars and standard hours. Dollars are occasionally used for long-range capacity studies, but standard hours are the more common measure.

The formula usually given for determining available capacity is

$$Capacity\ available = Hours\ available \times Utilization \times Efficiency \qquad (1A.2)$$

where utilization equals hours worked divided by hours available and efficiency equals standard hours output divided by hours worked.

This equation can be inferred from transparency 10 of the American Production and Inventory Control Society *Capacity Management Training Aid* (1). One can easily verify that by substituting the definitions for utilization and efficiency into equation 1A.2 one obtains standard hours output as the unit of measure for capacity available. One might also note that this is a point estimate with no measure of the precision of the estimate.

In fact, capacity available is a random variable. Hours available is a known constant; the shop is scheduled to work x hours per week. Both efficiency and utilization are random variables. Utilization is random since a machine may be idle because it is broken, because the worker is absent, or because there is no work to do. Efficiency is a random variable since workers work at different paces and even the same worker works at different paces over time.

Efficiency is a fairly straightforward variable. The efficiency of a work center is a function of the skill level of the worker(s). As long as work center staffing is unchanged, efficiency should exhibit only minor variation. When a new worker is being trained, efficiency would be expected to drop and to rise gradually as the worker progresses along the learning curve. With a reasonable estimate of the slope of the learning curve one could produce good estimates of efficiency during the time a worker was becoming skilled.

Utilization is not a well-defined variable. There are really two variables imbedded in utilization. The first is downtime forced by machine breakdown or absenteeism. The second is downtime caused by lack of work. Unfortunately, the two variables have different ideal values. Ideally, downtime forced by breakdown and absenteeism should be zero. It would be good to manage a plant in such a way as to avoid all breakdowns and all stoppages caused by absenteeism. On the other hand, Figure 1A.2 demonstrates that having no downtime due to lack of work is not an ideal. In fact, we may choose to target a substantial amount of downtime due to lack of work in order to gain a small level of WIP and a small lead time.

Thus, the present definition of capacity is inadequate because one cannot set a target level for efficiency and utilization and judge plant performance based on the actualization of those variables. The next section presents an alternative definition which contains variables useful as performance measures.

3. A REVISED DEFINITION OF CAPACITY AVAILABLE

I propose that capacity available be defined in the following fashion:

$$\textit{Capacity available} = \textit{Time available} \times \textit{Efficiency} \\ \times \textit{Availability} \times \textit{Activation} \qquad \textbf{(1A.3)}$$

where availability equals 1 minus the fraction of time down due to machine breakdown and/or absenteeism, activation equals 1 minus the fraction of time down due to lack of work, and efficiency equals standard hours output divided by hours worked.

Note that capacity available is still measured in standard hours of output. In fact, the only change in equation 1A.3 from equation 1A.2 is that utilization has been split into availability and activation. From a management perspective the change is significant because both availability and activation can be used as performance measures. Clearly, ideal availability is 1. Ideal activation is harder to define. One knows that a relationship such as the one illustrated in Figure 1A.2 exists, although one is not sure of the precise shape. If the arrival rate happens to be Poisson and the service rate exponential, Figure 1A.2 holds. In most instances neither is true. In contrast, the arrival rate of gating operations can be controlled, but the arrival rates of later work centers are dependent on the service rates of previous work centers. The service rate may be normal or lognormal, making Figure 1A.2 difficult to estimate analytically. According to Gross and Harris (4), such computations often require "advanced concepts from the theory of complex variables" (p. 297).

However, once the need for a decision on ideal activation is recognized, one could create a chart such as Figure 1A.2 empirically by plotting activation against queue time measured for several weekly periods. Once an estimate of the trade-offs between ideal time, on the one hand, and work-in-process inventory and lead time, on the other, is understood, management is in a position to set a target level of activation for each work center. Target activation should not as a general rule be 1. There may be a few bottlenecks in any shop for which continuous operation is desirable. These work centers will require a large buffer to protect against inevitable fluctuations in preceding work centers. The majority of stations in any shop will not be bottlenecks. It is not possible to balance the workload in the shop to such a degree that many stations are equally loaded. Once one recognizes that not all work centers are bottlenecks, one also recognizes that optimal activation of a non-bottleneck is determined by the level of activity needed to keep the bottlenecks operating all the time. The principle that a bottleneck sets the level of operation for a non-bottleneck was first expressed by Goldratt and Cox in their book *The Goal* (3).

The scheduling logic behind the software known as OPT (for optimized production technology) recognizes the relationship between queue time and activation. OPT places large queues in front of bottlenecks, building extra days of lead time into the schedule, in order to avoid idle time at bottlenecks. However, OPT plans for short queues or no queues at non-bottlenecks, in order to reduce the lead time. OPT users have to be *trained* to accept idle time at non-bottlenecks as inevitable and beneficial. *The Goal* (3) was written to foster this change in thinking and to try to convince people that an activation of 1 at a non-bottleneck is counterproductive.

4. USE OF THE ACTIVATION CONCEPT IN A MATERIAL REQUIREMENTS PLANNING SYSTEM

Material requirements planning (MRP) is an information system which is used to plan the purchase and manufacture of component items to support the manufacture of end products. MRP is insensitive to capacity (it assumes capacity to be infinite). Thus for MRP to work well, some form of capacity management external to the system must be provided. Rough-cut capacity planning is one of those external factors. It is possible for an MRP system having rough-cut capabilities to determine the level of activation of a work center necessary to meet the schedule, provided that efficiency and availability assumptions are correct.

The material requirements planning system should have a file which is known as the work center master file. In this file are two fields, utilization and planned queue. There is no requirement that these two fields be consistent. Indeed, unless utilization is split into availability and activation, there is no way to determine that the two fields are consistent. A chronic problem with MRP systems is that the actual queue at many work centers exceeds the planned queue. Indeed, there is an entire technique, called input/output control, which has the sole purpose of trying to keep the actual queue length down to that of the planned queue (8).

It is important to recognize that input/output control cannot achieve significant reductions in work-in-process inventory and lead time if the system is operated so as to try to keep all work centers busy all the time. It is therefore important to convey to managers the concept of *activation* of a work center. Unless the lead time estimates (i.e., the planned queue time estimates, since lead time equals queue time plus operation time) are consistent with work center activation, the MRP system will contain improper lead time data and thus will cause orders to be released at the wrong time.

One difficulty in conveying the importance of activation to managers is that the level of work in a work center fluctuates a great deal. One might picture the level of work in a work center as water depth measured by a stick in the ocean; the water level fluctuates as each wave crests and troughs. It is easy to lose the concept of mean or average height because of all the variation. However, it is the average water height (capacity required) which determines activation in the long run. One can picture the effect of average water height as being like the tide. If activation is high, the tide is high and fluctuation is around a high point on the stick. If activation is low, the tide is out and the stick may at times be entirely out of the water. Unfortunately, high material tides don't leave watermarks as tides on the beach do, and many managers have not yet grasped the picture of the effect high activation levels have on both lead time and work-in-process inventory.

5. THE USE OF ACTIVATION AND AVAILABILITY AS PERFORMANCE MEASURES

Another advantage of separating the traditional concept of utilization into activation and availability is that both are useful performance measures. Clearly, desired availability is 1. Most American plants do not have good preventive maintenance. Most plants recognize they must institute good preventive maintenance to become world-class manufacturers, especially if the plant plans to implement just-in-time manufacturing. Using availability as a performance measure for the success of preventive maintenance programs is advantageous.

Using activation as a performance measure is also helpful. For one thing, managers must determine which work centers are bottlenecks and should have high activations. Identifying bottlenecks can lead to increased output in two ways. First, bottlenecks may be managed better (e.g., by placing a quality inspector in front of the bottleneck to prevent wasting time on an already defective product). Second, one may choose an alternative route for some products to avoid the bottleneck.

Another advantage of using activation as a performance measure is that it ensures that rough-cut capacity planning (RCCP) is done correctly. If the plant is managed in order to attain the activation levels used in RCCP, the actual queues should resemble planned queues and due dates should be met. Using activation as a performance measure forces managers to recognize that increasing input to a shop has a price. Consider the following example.

Suppose marketing has discovered an opportunity to make a substantial sale provided delivery can be expedited. In the average firm, the order would be accepted. Expediting the order usually leads to some overtime, but the order probably isn't built entirely on overtime. The firm incurs hidden costs as activation increases. Work-in-process inventory goes up. More due dates than usual are missed. The firm may, in fact, lose a substantial amount of money on the order because of expediting costs and late costs on other orders.

If activation is used as a performance measure, the production manager has an incentive to insist that overtime be increased to the point *that activation does not change.* One desires activation to be stable at both bottleneck and non-bottleneck work centers, since changing activation will also change lead time (actual queue time). As Figure 1A.2 demonstrates, for low values of activation queue time changes very little. The hidden costs should now be avoided, replaced by explicit overtime costs. The firm is likely to make a more rational decision regarding order acceptance and/or order pricing.

SUMMARY

This paper has proposed modifying the measurement of capacity available to make explicit recognition of the fact that it is a random variable. This recognition is necessary so that managers will understand that there is a trade-off between keeping workers and equipment busy and having long lead times and lots of inventory, on the one hand, and having some idle workers and equipment but short lead times and little inventory, on the other. Because managers do not recognize that trade-off, they make poor decisions regarding how much work a plant can really handle during a given time period. Although this concept can be taught without resorting to a course in queueing theory, the use of simulation models may be necessary to demonstrate that curves such as Figure 1A.2 exist and must be included in planning operations.

APPENDIX 1A REFERENCES

1. American Production and Inventory Control Society. *Capacity Management Training Aid.* Falls Church, Va.: APICS, n.d.
2. Berry, William L., Thomas G. Schmitt, and Thomas E. Vollmann. "Capacity Planning Techniques for Manufacturing Control Systems: Information Requirements and Operational Features." *Journal of Operations Management* 3, no. 1 (November 1982): 13-25.

3. Goldratt, Eliyahu, and Jeff Cox. *The Goal.* Croton-on-Hudson, N.Y.: North River Press, 1984.

4. Gross, Donald, and Carl M. Harris. *Fundamentals of Queueing Theory.* New York: John Wiley & Sons, 1974.

5. Lunz, Alfred G. "The Missing Factors—The Real Keys to Effective Capacity Requirements Planning and Control." *Production and Inventory Management* 22, no. 2 (Second Quarter 1981): 1-11.

6. Plossl, George W. *Production and Inventory Control Applications.* Atlanta: George Plossl Educational Services, 1983. Pp. 130-133.

7. Wemmerlov, Urban. "A Note on Capacity Planning." *Production and Inventory Management* 21, no. 3 (Third Quarter 1980): 85-89.

8. Wight, Oliver. "Input/Output Control: A Real Handle on Lead Time." *APICS Capacity Planning and Control Reprints.* Falls Church, Va.: American Production and Inventory Control Society, 1975. Pp. 87-108.

Production Planning and Master Production Scheduling

In Chapter 1 it was noted that a company should produce a production plan extending 5 to 10 years into the future and a master production schedule extending 6 to 18 months into the future. This chapter discusses the development of a production plan, a master production schedule, and a final assembly schedule for a hypothetical company, War Eagle Hoists, Inc. War Eagle Hoists has been deliberately created as an assemble-to-order fabrication and assembly shop having a seasonal business. This environment was chosen because it represents the situation most commonly encountered in American manufacturing. Through an examination of War Eagle's products and procedures, this chapter briefly presents the concepts of production planning, master production scheduling, and final assembly scheduling. The interested reader should consult Berry, Vollmann, and Whybark (1) or Plossl (2).

WAR EAGLE HOISTS

War Eagle Hoists builds 432 models of industrial hoist. The typical industrial hoist is shown in Figure 2.1. Connected to a steel I-beam, which is normally part of the support structure of an industrial building, the hoist is used to lift heavy objects such as steel plates, blocks of aluminum, chucks, vises, etc. Although the basic pattern of a War Eagle hoist is always the same, each hoist has a number of options. There are four drum sizes, four motor sizes (2, 4, 6, and 8 hp), three gear ratios (3:1, 4:1, and 5:1), two cable sizes (0.75″ and 1″),

FIGURE 2.1   TYPICAL INDUSTRIAL HOIST

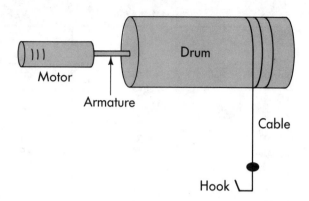

two cable lengths (25′ and 50′), three hook sizes, and three colors for the motor housing and drum (yellow, red, and green). The four drum sizes are predetermined by the cable diameter and length. All other options can be selected independently by the purchaser, yielding $4 \times 3 \times 2 \times 2 \times 3 \times 3 = 432$ possible hoists. Although War Eagle sells all 432 hoists, some combinations are more popular than others. For example, the larger motors are usually found in combination with the larger cable diameter and the largest hook.

War Eagle's business comes from two sources, replacement hoists for existing buildings and hoists for new construction. Because more construction is done during the summer and fall than in other seasons, War Eagle finds that its business is seasonal. Orders from a single customer rarely exceed a dozen hoists. A single customer may order different hoists for the same building, because different lifting capabilities may be needed in different departments. Customers expect to be able to receive a hoist built to their specifications within 3 weeks.

The typical War Eagle hoist sells for $500. War Eagle sells about 2,100 hoists per year. Average demand for an individual hoist is less than 5 per year. Popularity varies widely, with some combinations selling 50 units per year and others selling less than one unit per year. Although average demand is 40 hoists per week, actual demand varies from fewer than 20 hoists per week during some winter weeks to as many as 60 hoists per week during the summer. Actual sales for the 52 weeks of 1987 are shown in Table 2.1.

War Eagle fabricates its own motors. One department does the winding, a second department creates the housing, and a third mills the armature. There is also a motor assembly department which joins the winding and housing (the armature is joined at the winding department). War Eagle mills its own gears from stampings, requiring a stamping department, which stamps circular blanks, and a milling department. The milling department is the same department that mills armatures. A sheet metal department produces the

TABLE 2.1   TOTAL SALES BY WEEK FOR WAR EAGLE HOISTS, 1987

WEEK	DEMAND	WEEK	DEMAND
1	39	27	39
2	28	28	52
3	45	29	59
4	29	30	51
5	27	31	57
6	41	32	60
7	33	33	21
8	31	34	54
9	19	35	54
10	15	36	44
11	40	37	48
12	35	38	34
13	39	39	44
14	52	40	23
15	39	41	19
16	31	42	31
17	43	43	42
18	42	44	47
19	36	45	38
20	16	46	41
21	52	47	40
22	60	48	45
23	33	49	59
24	45	50	26
25	71	51	48
26	26	52	44

drum and the motor housing. Painting is done in the sheet metal department. The cable and hook are purchased. Assembling the cable to the hook occurs in the final assembly area, where the motor, gear, drum, and hook and cable assemblies are all joined to create the final hoist. The final assembly area contains a shear, which is used to cut the cable to the proper length after the hook has been attached. A layout of the War Eagle Hoists plant is shown in Figure 2.2.

Lead times for the various manufactured and purchased items are as follows:

    Final assembly: 2 weeks
    Motor assembly: 1 week
    Motor winding: 2 weeks
    Motor housing: 2 weeks
    Gear machining: 3 weeks
    Armature machining: 3 weeks
    Drum fabrication: 4 weeks

FIGURE 2.2   LAYOUT OF WAR EAGLE HOISTS

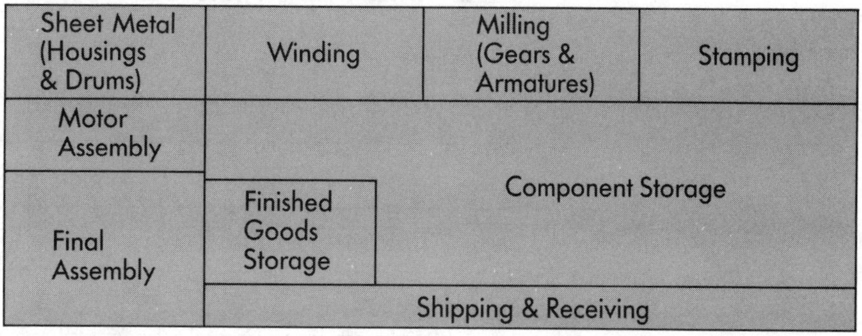

Sheet Metal (Housings & Drums)	Winding	Milling (Gears & Armatures)	Stamping
Motor Assembly	Component Storage		
Final Assembly	Finished Goods Storage	Component Storage	
	Shipping & Receiving		

Purchase of cable: 12 weeks
Purchase of hook: 6 weeks
Purchase of copper wire for winding: 20 weeks
Purchase of magnet for motor: 15 weeks
Purchase of sheet metal (drum and motor housing): 18 weeks
Purchase of stainless steel for armature and gears: 12 weeks

As is shown in Figure 2.3, the critical path lead time for a hoist is 26 weeks. The critical path involves purchase of copper wire, winding assembly, motor assembly, final assembly, and a one-week allowance for delivery by a commercial parcel service for small orders and by contract carrier for large orders. Both carriers guarantee delivery within one week anywhere in the contiguous 48 states. The next longest path, totaling 25 weeks, involves sheet metal purchase, drum fabrication, final assembly, and delivery.

Two aspects of planning at War Eagle Hoists are dictated by the lead time constraints. First, War Eagle must be an assemble-to-order plant. Since customers expect delivery in 3 weeks and total lead time is 26 weeks, War Eagle cannot operate except as an assemble-to-order operation. Second, the minimum planning horizon for a master production schedule is 26 weeks, the critical path lead time. A full-year MPS horizon would provide for better planning provided an accurate forecast can be obtained.

In order for the final assembly to be planned independently of the fabrication operation, all modules going into final assembly must be kept in stock at all times: 12 motors (4 hp ratings in each of 3 colors), 12 drums, 3 hooks, 2 cable diameters, and 3 sets of gears. These 32 items form the basis for planning the master production schedule; i.e., the MPS is designed to keep all 32 major modules in stock at all times.

Actual final assembly requires less than one day. However, certain aspects of final assembly require setup. For example, there is room for only one roll of

FIGURE 2.3 OPERATION PROCESS CHART WITH CRITICAL PATH LEAD TIMES FOR WAR EAGLE HOISTS

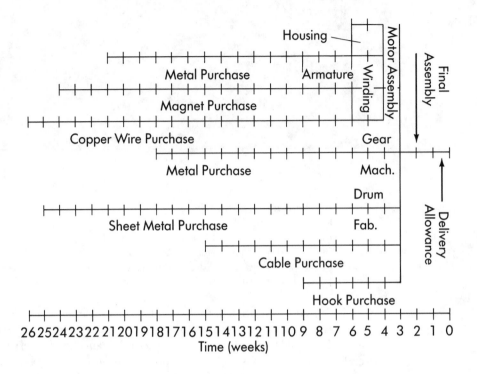

cable in the hook assembly area. Changing from the roll of 0.75″ cable to the roll of 1″ cable requires half an hour. Thus, the final assembly scheduler likes to batch together sets of like hoists. If an order for a hoist using a 6-hp motor, painted red, having a 50′ section of 0.75″ cable, a #2 hook, and a 4:1 gear ratio, were received today, War Eagle might not be able to schedule that order today. Perhaps the hook assembly area is set up for 1″ cable. Perhaps other areas of the final assembly require setup (for example, an adjustment might have to be made when a change is made from 3:1 gear ratio to 4:1 gear ratio). The two-week final assembly lead time is made to allow the final assembly scheduler time to consolidate orders in order to minimize setup time in final assembly.

To minimize the number of components that have to be produced, the same magnet and armature are used in all four motor sizes, the same grade stainless steel is used in gears and armatures, and the same sheet metal is used in all four drums. There are two types of copper wire used in the motors. The small motors (2 and 4 hp) use a cylindrical copper wire; the larger motors (6 and 8 hp) use a flat copper wire.

FORECASTING AT WAR EAGLE HOISTS

War Eagle makes no attempt to forecast the demand for individual hoists. Since some of the 432 combinations sell less than one unit per year, trying to forecast the timing of demand for a given hoist would be futile. Rather, War Eagle forecasts demand for the 32 major modules two months out, demand for hoists divided into those using small (2 and 4 hp) and those using large (6 and 8 hp) motors six months out, and demand for all hoists beyond six months. Forecasts are updated on a weekly basis.

The 32 major modules are forecast two months out because the longest critical path manufacturing lead time, the time needed for drum fabrication, final assembly, and delivery, is 7 weeks. The gears, motor windings, and motor housings have a 6-week lead time. Thus an 8-week forecast is sufficient to guarantee a continuous availability of manufactured parts. The reader may have noted from Figure 2.3 that both hook purchase and armature fabrication have a 9-week critical path from inception to delivery. However, since the armature is the same on all motors and since hook size is closely related to motor size, the forecast extending six months by motor size is sufficient.

Since hooks are a relatively inexpensive item, War Eagle chooses to carry a safety stock of hooks to avoid having to extend the period for which 32 modules must be forecast. As forecasts extend over a longer period it is preferable to aggregate demand into larger groupings to maintain forecast accuracy.

Forecasts from two to six months out are aggregated on the basis of motor size in order to facilitate purchase of copper wire. Recall that the 2 and 4 hp motors use a cylindrical copper wire in the winding, the 6 and 8 hp motors a flat copper wire. This division is unnecessary for purchasing magnets, stainless steel, and sheet metal since the same material is used in all hoists.

DEVELOPING A FINAL ASSEMBLY SCHEDULE

The final assembly department employs two workers year-round, having a maximum production capability of 40 hoists a week unless overtime is worked. During weeks 21–32 a local college student is hired for the period that school is not in session. Because the student lacks experience, adding this third worker raises the maximum production capability of final assembly to 55 hoists, not 60.

The final assembly scheduling process occurs in two phases. In the first phase, the scheduler assigns a motor to a given week. In the second phase, the scheduler sequences the motors for a given week.

During phase 1, the final assembly scheduler matches capacity with orders week by week and keeps track of the number of hoists available to promise (ATP):

Week	18	19	20	21	22	23
Capacity	40	40	40	55	55	55
Orders	40	37	25	12	0	0
ATP	0	3	15	43	55	55

The ATP row is used to establish final delivery dates on orders. Since War Eagle guarantees delivery in three weeks, the scheduler sees any demand that exceeds capacity three weeks before the delivery date. The scheduler checks to see if capacity exists (a positive ATP quantity in weeks 1 or 2). If it does, the scheduler will attempt to level the production by pulling work forward into week 1 or week 2. The scheduler attempts to maintain production at five units under maximum capacity in order to leave room for emergency orders. The scheduler next attempts to level production without overtime, scheduling overtime only as a last resort. The entire scheduling algorithm is depicted in Figure 2.4.

Table 2.2 summarizes the final assembly schedule for 1987. This schedule simply recaps the final set of weekly decisions made by the scheduler and never existed as a single schedule. In the first week of the year the scheduler saw firm demands for 39, 28, and 45 units for weeks 1, 2, and 3, respectively. Following her instruction to level the load, she moved 7 units from week 3 to week 2, producing an assembly schedule of 39, 35, and 38 units. Units which are built early may be held in stock or shipped early, depending on customer preference. Note that the shop has a storage area for finished hoists awaiting shipment.

At the beginning of week 12, the scheduler found demands of 35, 39, and 52 for weeks 12, 13, and 14, respectively. She therefore scheduled 40, 40, and 46 units of production, building 6 units on overtime during week 14. The scheduler is permitted to build up to 10 units per week using overtime, provided that the units cannot be built in the preceding two weeks without overtime.

Phase 2 of the final assembly scheduling process is to create the sequence in which the hoists are to be assembled. As mentioned previously, this decision is made in order to batch similar hoists together and to minimize setups. Occasionally, excessive setups reduce the capacity of the assembly area to less than 40 hoists per week without overtime. Loss of capacity due to excessive setups is another reason why the scheduler is instructed to attempt to balance the load so that all weeks are *below* capacity.

War Eagle has considered using inventory to provide more capacity flexibility, stocking some of the more popular items and operating in part on a make-to-stock basis. Consider from Table 2.2 weeks 40–41 and weeks 48–49. During weeks 40–41, as a result of purely random fluctuations, the final assembly area was well below capacity. At that time the scheduler might have

FIGURE 2.4 PROCEDURE TO ASSIGN AN ORDER TO THE FINAL ASSEMBLY SCHEDULE

Let D_k be accumulated Demand, week k.
  C_k be maximum normal Capacity, week k.
  O_k be overtime Capacity, week k.
Then the algorithm is:

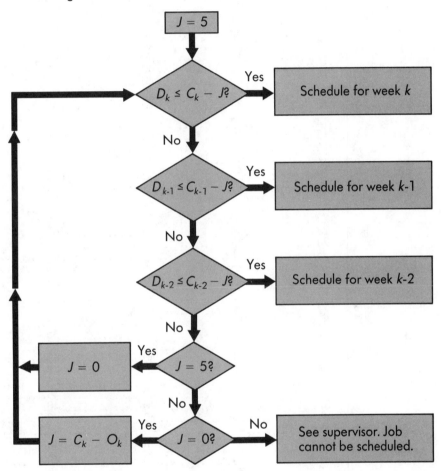

ordered 10 extra units to be built during each of the two weeks and placed these 20 units in stock, knowing that sooner or later a demand would exceed final assembly capacity. As it happened, the excess demand did show up in weeks 48 and 49, when 45 and 59 units, respectively, were ordered. The problem is that since War Eagle has 432 models, it is possible that none of the 104 units ordered in weeks 48 and 49 would match the 20 excess units. To avoid overtime

TABLE 2.2 FINAL ASSEMBLY SCHEDULE FOR 1987

WEEK	DEMAND	NORMAL CAPACITY	OVERTIME CAPACITY	UNITS ASSEMBLED
1	39	40	48	39
2	28	40	48	35
3	45	40	48	38
4	29	40	48	29
5	27	40	48	33
6	41	40	48	35
7	33	40	48	33
8	31	40	48	31
9	19	40	48	19
10	15	40	48	20
11	40	40	48	35
12	35	40	48	40
13	39	40	48	40
14	52	40	48	46
15	39	40	48	39
16	31	40	48	36
17	43	40	48	40
18	42	40	48	40
19	36	40	48	36
20	16	40	48	33
21	52	55	65	40
22	60	55	65	55
23	33	55	65	49
24	45	55	65	50
25	71	55	65	50
26	26	55	65	26
27	39	55	65	50
28	52	55	65	50
29	59	55	65	50
30	51	55	65	55
31	57	55	65	55
32	60	55	65	58
33	21	40	48	40
34	54	40	48	41
35	54	40	48	48
36	44	40	48	44
37	48	40	48	48
38	34	40	48	38
39	44	40	48	40
40	23	40	48	23
41	19	40	48	19
42	31	40	48	40
43	42	40	48	40
44	47	40	48	40
45	38	40	48	39
46	41	40	48	40
47	40	40	48	48
48	45	40	48	48
49	59	40	48	48
50	26	40	48	38
51	48	40	48	40
52	44	40	48	40
Total	**1,995**			**1,995**

completely, all 20 units would have to be among the 104 units ordered, a highly unlikely posssibility. For this reason War Eagle has decided to remain a pure make-to-order operation for now, although the possibility of stocking some of the more popular models is still under consideration.

DEVELOPING A MASTER PRODUCTION SCHEDULE

The master production schedule (MPS) for War Eagle Hoists is developed around the 32 modules which, in various combinations, make up the 432 possible hoist configurations. The 32 modules are 12 motor size and color combinations, 12 drum size and color combinations, 3 gear ratios, 3 hooks, and 2 cable diameters. Since the cable and hooks are purchased, the MPS is built around motors, drums, and gears. The department having the most severely limited capacity is the winding department. Plans for this department strongly influence planning in other departments.

Winding Department An electric motor consists of a length of copper wire wound around a central magnet. As electric current passes through the copper wire, the magnet rotates, turning with it an armature which can be harnessed for work. A winding is the central part of the motor, i.e., the magnet, armature and copper coil. The winding is produced on a machine which holds the magnet, armature, and a small frame in place. The winding machine turns the entire core, precisely winding the copper wire around the core. As the machine turns the core, the operator must feed an insulating material, usually heavy paper, under the wire to prevent successive turns from causing a short circuit. After every few turns the operator must stop the process and securely tape the winding in place.

At War Eagle, four hours are needed to complete a single winding. Thus, each operator can produce ten windings in a 5-day workweek. There are four winding machines and four operators. Without overtime, the winding department has a capacity of 2,080 windings per 52-week year. In developing an MPS for 1988, War Eagle management noted that 1987 sales were 2,087 units and assumed that 1988 sales would be the same. The management also knew that there were 80 windings in stock, 20 each of the four motor sizes. These 80 windings are considered safety stock and are to be maintained. Deciding to use overtime only for emergencies, War Eagle planned a level production of windings, as shown in Table 2.3 and Figure 2.5. In Figure 2.5 the cumulative demand for windings is compared to the cumulative production. Note that in weeks 35–40, the line for cumulative demand is above the line for cumulative production. This condition would render the MPS infeasible were it not for the 80 windings held as safety stock. Table 2.3 shows that in week 37 cumulative demand exceeds cumulative production by 26 units. Since this excess demand can be covered by safety stock, the MPS is feasible.

TABLE 2.3   MPS FOR WINDINGS

WEEK	DEMAND	CUMULATIVE DEMAND	PRODUCTION	CUMULATIVE PRODUCTION	INVENTORY
1	39	39	40	40	81
2	28	67	40	80	93
3	45	112	40	120	88
4	29	141	40	160	99
5	27	168	40	200	112
6	41	209	40	240	111
7	33	242	40	280	118
8	31	273	40	320	127
9	19	292	40	360	148
10	15	307	40	400	173
11	40	347	40	440	173
12	35	382	40	480	178
13	39	421	40	520	179
14	52	473	40	560	167
15	39	512	40	600	168
16	31	543	40	640	177
17	43	586	40	680	174
18	42	628	40	720	172
19	36	664	40	760	176
20	16	680	40	800	200
21	52	732	40	840	188
22	60	792	40	880	168
23	33	825	40	920	175
24	45	870	40	960	170
25	71	941	40	1,000	139
26	26	967	40	1,040	153
27	39	1,006	40	1,080	154
28	52	1,058	40	1,120	142
29	59	1,117	40	1,160	123
30	51	1,168	40	1,200	112
31	57	1,225	40	1,240	95
32	60	1,285	40	1,280	75
33	21	1,306	40	1,320	94
34	54	1,360	40	1,360	80
35	54	1,414	40	1,400	66
36	44	1,458	40	1,440	62
37	48	1,506	40	1,480	54
38	34	1,540	40	1,520	60
39	44	1,584	40	1,560	56
40	23	1,607	40	1,600	73
41	19	1,626	40	1,640	94
42	31	1,657	40	1,680	103
43	42	1,699	40	1,720	101
44	47	1,746	40	1,760	94
45	38	1,784	40	1,800	96
46	41	1,825	40	1,840	95
47	40	1,865	40	1,880	95
48	45	1,910	40	1,920	90
49	59	1,969	40	1,960	71
50	26	1,995	40	2,000	85
51	48	2,043	40	2,040	82
52	44	2,087	40	2,080	75

FIGURE 2.5   GRAPHICAL REPRESENTATION OF MPS FOR WINDINGS

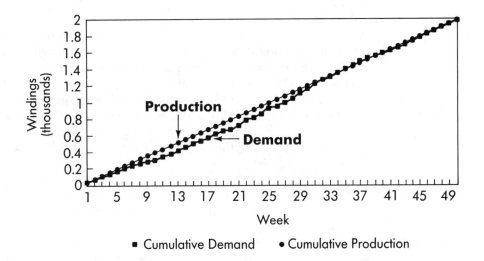

• Cumulative Demand   • Cumulative Production

Of the total demand for motors, 25 percent is for 2 hp, 25 percent for 4 hp, 30 percent for 6 hp, and 20 percent for 8 hp. Thus the MPS of 40 windings per week is split into ten 2-hp units, ten 4-hp units, twelve 6-hp units and eight 8-hp units. Of the four winding machine operators, one works exclusively on 2-hp units, one on 4-hp units, and one on 6-hp units; the fourth operator makes eight 8-hp units and two 6-hp units a week. Since both of the small windings take the same-size cylindrical wire and both of the large windings take the same-size flat wire, there is very little setup involved in having one worker switch from 6-hp to 8-hp units.

War Eagle tries to handle short-term imbalances out of safety stock. Thus, if in one week demand was for fifteen 2-hp units and only five 4-hp units, the extra demand would be taken from safety stock. At the end of the week there would still be 80 units in safety stock, but instead of having twenty 2-hp units and twenty 4-hp units there would be only fifteen 2-hp units and twenty-five 4-hp units.

Note from Table 2.3 that with the winter trough in demand the inventory of windings grows to 200 units in week 20 before dwindling to 54 in week 37. During the trough period, the mix of motors produced will not be altered unless a sustained shift in demand mix is detected. However, during the period when inventory is dwindling, the winding mix may have to be altered if safety stock for a particular unit gets very low. Fortunately, War Eagle engineers had the foresight to use the same armature, magnet, and housing for all four motors, so it is possible to change the mix of units in the winding department without disrupting schedules in the purchasing department, the milling department, or the sheet metal department.

Milling Department   The milling department consists of one milling machine, which is used to mill armatures and gear sets. It requires 20 minutes to mill an armature, 25 minutes to mill a gear set, 60 minutes to set up from armature to gear set, and 30 minutes to set up when the gear-set size is changed. Thus, if precisely 40 armatures and 40 gear sets were produced each week, the time required at the milling department would be 800 minutes for armatures, 1,000 minutes for gears, 120 minutes for major setup (from armatures to gears and, at the end of the week, from gears back to armatures), and 60 minutes for two minor setups. Total time required is 1,980 minutes. Time available in a 40-hour week is 2,400 minutes.

It is necessary to mill 40 armatures a week, since the armatures are needed by the winding department. However, the gears are not needed until final assembly. Using the 420 minutes that are otherwise idle, the milling department can produce up to 56 gear sets in a week.

Safety stock of armatures and gears has been set at 40 units and 90 units, respectively. The 40 armatures provide the winding department with a one-week supply. At the beginning of each week, the milling department produces 40 new armatures which will be used in the winding department the following week. The milling department follows a pure demand chase schedule on gears. A demand chase strategy attempts to produce what is demanded each period in order to minimize inventory. The 90 finished gears held as safety stock, 30 sets each of the three ratios, provide a sufficient supply for final assembly. Since the milling department knows in advance how many gears of each type final assembly will use, the milling department builds exactly the number of components used, provided that number does not exceed 56. Based on an assumption that the 1988 demand pattern will follow the 1987 demand pattern, a master production schedule for gears was developed and is shown in Table 2.4.

Stamping Department   The stamping department has the capacity to provide many more blanks than are needed. The stamping department operator, who is told by the MRP system what the milling department's demand is, stamps out the proper number of blanks early in each week, while the milling department is milling armatures. The proper blanks are thus available when needed by the milling department. The stamping department operator is a multifunction worker, able to fill in for absentees in all other departments. Because War Eagle has a low rate of absenteeism, this procedure has caused no problems.

Sheet Metal Department   The sheet metal department consists of two workers, one who makes and paints motor housings and one who makes and

TABLE 2.4   MPS FOR GEARS

WEEK	DEMAND	PRODUCTION	INVENTORY
1	39	39	90
2	28	28	90
3	45	45	90
4	29	29	90
5	27	27	90
6	41	41	90
7	33	33	90
8	31	31	90
9	19	19	90
10	15	15	90
11	40	40	90
12	35	35	90
13	39	39	90
14	52	52	90
15	39	39	90
16	31	31	90
17	43	43	90
18	42	42	90
19	36	36	90
20	16	40	114
21	52	44	106
22	60	44	90
23	33	45	102
24	45	50	107
25	71	54	90
26	26	40	104
27	39	40	105
28	52	45	98
29	59	55	94
30	51	55	98
31	57	55	96
32	60	55	91
33	21	30	100
34	54	44	90
35	54	54	90
36	44	44	90
37	48	48	90
38	34	34	90
39	44	44	90
40	23	23	90
41	19	19	90
42	31	31	90
43	42	42	90
44	47	47	90
45	38	38	90
46	41	41	90
47	40	40	90
48	45	50	95
49	59	54	90
50	26	26	90
51	48	48	90
52	44	44	90

paints drums. The drum worker has a capacity of 65 units per week, the housing worker a capacity of 70. Painting is done at the end of the week, when the schedule for final assembly and motor assembly for the next week is absolutely firm. This process ensures that the proper color mix is always available.

In order to simplify the planning process, the sheet metal department uses the same aggregate schedule as the milling department. Since all motor housings are identical, the MPS for housings is complete. For drums, the MPS must be split into drum sizes. Past demand proportions for drum sizes 1, 2, 3, and 4 have been 15, 25, 30, and 30 percent, respectively. Setup time for changes in drum size is 6 hours, run time is 30 minutes. Drum lot sizes are set equal to demand over the next 4 weeks. Each size is run once in each 4-week period. Drum inventory averages approximately 120 units—80 units of cycle stock plus 40 units of safety stock.

Motor Assembly   The motor assembly department consists of one operator who assembles the winding in the motor housing and tests the motor. The operator has a capacity of 80 units per week. The schedule for the motor assembly operator is the final assembly schedule one week in the future, ensuring that the final assembly department has the correct mix of motors at the beginning of each week. No safety stock of finished motors is held. If units are added to the final assembly schedule at the last minute, the motor assembler produces the required motor and takes it directly to final assembly.

DEVELOPING A PRODUCTION PLAN FOR WAR EAGLE HOISTS

War Eagle plans a major marketing campaign during the end of 1988 which is projected to raise total demand to 2,500 units in 1989 and level off at 3,000 units in 1990. This plan will require the addition of one winding machine and operator each year and one milling machine and operator. One additional final assembly operator will have to be added in 1989; because demand is seasonal, the summer assembly worker will still be necessary.

SUMMARY

This chapter has presented one case, a hypothetical fabrication and assembly operation, in order to demonstrate how long-term, intermediate-term, and short-term capacity planning fit together. The example of War Eagle Hoists will be used later in the text when numeric computations are required to illustrate a technique.

REFERENCES

1. Berry, William, Thomas Vollmann, and D. Clay Whybark. *Master Production Scheduling: Principles and Practice.* Falls Church, Va.: American Production and Inventory Control Society, 1979.
2. Plossl, George W. *Production and Inventory Control Applications.* Atlanta: George Plossl Educational Services, 1983.

DISCUSSION QUESTIONS

1. Given present staffing levels, discuss the safety stock policy employed at War Eagle Hoists. Are the windings, armatures, etc., held as safety stock needed? If they are needed, are the levels reasonable?
2. Discuss the addition of a fifth winding machine and operator during 1988. What are the arguments for and against such a move? Given five winding operators, prepare an MPS for windings for 1988. The MPS should be at an aggregate level, ignoring the four motor types.
3. Trace the critical path lead time for a typical hoist. What impact does this large lead time have on forecasting, inventory, and customer service levels? What could be done to reduce the critical path lead time?
4. Why does War Eagle use the same armature and housing for all four motor sizes? Discuss which aspects of the planning system would need to be changed if each motor size had a unique armature and housing. What is the overall impact on inventory of using standard components across numerous products?

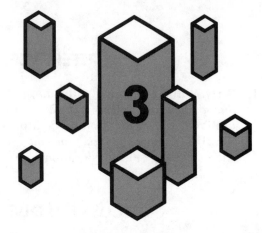

Long-Term Capacity Planning Activities

Capacity planning and control techniques for job shops are usually separated into four categories representing the four time horizons considered—resource requirements planning, rough-cut capacity planning, capacity requirements planning, and input/output control. Within a material requirements planning (MRP) system the typical sequence is to create a master schedule, use rough-cut capacity planning (RCCP) to verify the master schedule, and then feed the results into MRP, from which it moves to capacity requirements planning (CRP), as illustrated in Figure 3.1. When a planned order from the MRP system is released to the shop floor, detailed scheduling and dispatching must be performed. This chapter covers resource requirements planning and rough-cut capacity planning. Capacity requirements planning in Chapter 4, input/output control in Chapter 5, operations scheduling in Chapter 6, and dispatching in Chapter 7 complete the sequence.

RESOURCE REQUIREMENTS PLANNING

Resource requirements planning decisions are among the most difficult and potentially disastrous decisions a company can make. To illustrate the problems inherent in long-term capacity planning, one need only look at the problems caused by the OPEC cartel's raising of oil prices in the 1970s. The electric power industry, faced with no growth for the first time in history, found it necessary to scrap a number of billion-dollar nuclear power plants already under construction. The automobile industry, having an excess of

FIGURE 3.1   AN OVERVIEW OF CAPACITY MANAGEMENT

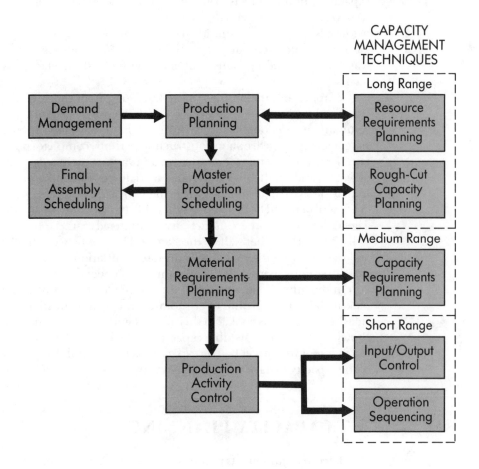

capacity to produce big cars and insufficient capacity to produce small cars, lost a tremendous amount of the market to European and Japanese car makers who could deliver fuel-efficient cars. The oil industry, finding itself with insufficient drilling equipment, greatly expanded drilling capacity, only to find itself with much idle equipment when the combination of newly discovered oil and energy conservation measures brought the real price of oil down to pre-1970 levels.

Whenever a company experiences a substantial increase in unit sales, it must answer the question, "Is this increase permanent?" If the increase is not permanent, the company should provide additional output by subcontracting, thereby avoiding a permanent addition to capacity. If, on the other hand, the increase is permanent, the company will make more money by adding capacity. The dilemma is to know in advance what will happen. In 1980 there were very few people who thought that the price of gasoline would ever drop below $1 per gallon again. Most, in fact, were predicting that the price of gasoline would eventually level off closer to $3 per gallon. Almost everyone was wrong, including many companies with well-funded forecasting departments.

Complicating the problem of making long-term capacity planning decisions is the long lead time needed to add to physical plant. Very often the company must choose a site, acquire the land, have environmental impact statements approved, obtain construction permits, complete construction, obtain permits to operate (and, often, to add various chemicals to nearby bodies of water), and finally hire and train a work force. The entire process may take from 5 to 15 years, the latter figure being typical of the electric power industry. What will demand be in 5 years? Will oil still flow from the Middle East? Will a breakthrough in superconductivity have altered markets? How many people will have AIDS? What will be the state of relations between the United States and the Soviet Union? What will the rate of inflation be? Lacking answers to these questions, perfect decisions cannot be made.

On the other hand, decisions must be made. The scope of such decision making falls in the realms of economics and of strategic planning, well outside the scope of this book. On this matter I will simply say that experience has shown that the more flexible capacity is, the better. Detroit would have lost much less of its market had its capacity been in flexible units, enabling some of the capacity to have switched fairly rapidly to the production of small cars.

ROUGH-CUT CAPACITY PLANNING

Material requirements planning (MRP) uses a master production schedule (MPS) of end items to determine the quantity and timing of component part production. MRP is capacity insensitive; it implicitly assumes that sufficient capacity is available to produce components at the time they are needed. The following discussion assumes that the reader is familiar with the basics of MRP. Those who are unfamiliar with this technique should first read Orlicky (4), Chapters 1–4.

A problem commonly encountered in operating an MRP system is that the MPS on which it is based has been overstated, ordering more production to be released than the shop can complete. An overstated master schedule causes raw materials and work-in-process (WIP) inventories to increase because more materials are purchased and released to the shop than are needed. It also causes a buildup of queues on the shop floor, and lead times increase as jobs wait to be processed. With the increase in lead times, forecast accuracy over the lead time diminishes, because forecasts are more accurate for shorter periods than for longer ones. Thus, validating the master schedule with respect to capacity is an extremely important step in MRP. This validation exercise has been termed rough-cut capacity planning. There is no general agreement on the level of detail that should be incorporated in the MPS validation.

Plossl and Welch (5) describe the role rough-cut capacity planning plays in the overall MRP system:

> The logical sequence is important. It should follow these steps:
> - Develop a production plan and the necessary resource planning for long-range use.
> - Translate this into a master production schedule and evaluate it for realism by rough-cut capacity planning.
> - Develop detailed material requirements information from the master production schedule covering both released orders and planned orders to be issued in the future.
> - Improve the detailed planning of capacity requirements using both planned and released order information.
> - Develop input/output controls to insure that actual work center outputs are adequate or to highlight deficiencies so that capacity on the master schedule can be adjusted.

Berry, Vollmann, and Whybark (2) provide a description of the process of rough-cut capacity planning:

> Rough-cut capacity planning is an activity that involves an analysis of the master production schedule to determine the implied capacity requirements for critical manufacturing facilities. Such an analysis is performed less frequently than CRP, e.g., monthly or quarterly, often using less complex data, e.g., bills of labor rather than time-phased requirements and routing file data. Typically, this analysis serves as the basis for negotiations between marketing and production in making adjustments to the MPS. It is also useful in indicating the strategy to be followed in making capacity adjustments, e.g., subcontracting vs. alternate routing vs. overtime vs. work force level adjustments. *Although the rough-cut capacity planning procedures used by the eight firms in this monograph varied considerably, nearly all firms performed such an analysis on a regular basis* [emphasis added].
>
> The rough-cut capacity planning analysis provides information in a timely fashion that can be of value in discussions among top-level marketing, finance, and production managers. That is, rough-cut procedures can be utilized quickly and inexpensively to examine capacity limitations and to evaluate tradeoffs for a variety of alternative solutions. While rough-cut capacity planning procedures are not as accurate as CRP information, they are sufficiently accurate to focus on the tradeoffs and to guide the aggregate level decisions. [p. 15]

THE BILL OF LABOR APPROACH

A good definition of rough-cut capacity planning, using the **bill of labor (BOL)** approach (also known as **bill of resources** or **bill of capacity**), is given in Conlon (3):

> The bill of labor is a listing by item number of the amount of labor required by a major labor category to produce that item or group of part numbers. It is not intended to be a routing, but merely a means of estimating the capacity requirements for a particular item. The bill of labor (BOL) may be compiled for every distinct item or for groups of similar items, and extended by the scheduled quantities to determine capacity requirements.

An example will be introduced to illustrate the concept of the bill of labor approach. This example will also be used later in the text to illustrate several different techniques. This example involves three end items (a total of eight part numbers), built at four work centers. The size was selected to be large enough to provide some richness of detail yet small enough to be completely comprehended. The problem is based on War Eagle Hoists, the hypothetical company described in Chapter 2.

EXAMPLE 3.1:
THE BILL OF LABOR APPROACH

The firm produces three end items:

100	Complete hoist
200	Motor winding only
300	Hoist lacking winding

The **bill of material** for parts 100, 200, and 300 is shown in Figure 3.2. Part 100, a complete hoist, is the entire figure. Part 200, a motor winding, is shown in the boxed area. Part 300, a hoist lacking winding, is all of Figure 3.2 except the boxed area. The bill of material is set up this way because windings are manufactured on a level production basis (stocked in the off-peak season and removed from stock during the peak season) while all other items are built on a demand chase basis and are not stocked. For simplicity, a number of minor parts have been omitted from the bill of material. A part number ending in P is a purchased item.

Capacity planning must be done in the milling, winding, and sheet metal departments. Because there is ample capacity in stamping and motor assembly, these departments are ignored during the rough-cut phase. Final assembly is also ignored during the rough-cut phase, since it is planned by the final assembly schedule, not by the master production schedule. For the rough-cut capacity check, the following data on utilization and efficiency apply:

FIGURE 3.2 SIMPLIFIED BILL OF MATERIAL FOR A HOIST

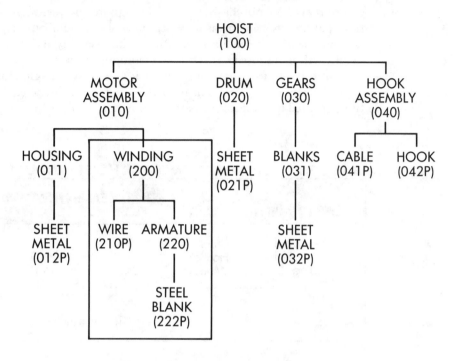

Department	Utilization	Efficiency
Sheet Metal	0.98	0.95
Winding	0.99	1.02
Milling	0.95	1.05

Rough-cut capacity planning also requires data on the standard time required to complete a master scheduled item and all its components. Consider the following **summarized bill of material** for a hoist:

Manufactured	Purchased
Motor assembly	Sheet metal
Drum	Wire
Gears	Sheet steel
Hook assembly	Cable
Motor housing	Hook
Motor winding	
Armature	
Gear blanks	

The summarized bill of material is divided into manufactured and purchased parts. The purchased parts will be ignored in the rough-cut planning phase; although some firms have begun to plan vendor capacity, War Eagle does not make such calculations. Also, motor assembly and stamping of gear blanks will be ignored, since these operations are handled in work centers known to have more than ample capacity given War Eagle Hoists' current level of operation. The remaining parts, departments involved, and standard time required to produce the part are shown in Table 3.1.

TABLE 3.1 STANDARD TIMES FOR HOIST PRODUCTION

DEPARTMENT	PART	RUN TIME/ PIECE	SETUP TIME/ LOT	LOT SIZE
Sheet Metal	Drum	30	4	5
Sheet Metal	Housing	35	0	1
Winding	Winding	240	0	10
Milling	Gear	25	120	55
Milling	Armature	20	60	40

Time in minutes

A bill of labor gives the times required to produce a part and all component items in various work centers. The bill of labor for all parts will now be derived. Note that the bill of labor will have the general form of Table 3.2. The body of the bill of labor contains standard operation times; in this example all times are given in minutes. Using the summary bill of material and the standard times, one can determine how much time it requires to build a single unit of a given part. An implicit assumption of the bill of labor approach is that

TABLE 3.2 THE FORM OF A BILL OF LABOR

DEPARTMENT	TIME REQUIRED FOR PART NUMBER				
	PN1	PN2	PN3	PN4	PN5
WC1	___	___	___	___	___
WC2	___	___	___	___	___
WC3	___	___	___	___	___
WC4	___	___	___	___	___

whenever the part is built, all components must also be built. Thus, building one lot of 40 windings requires that 40 armatures also be built. The standard time data give run time per piece and setup time per lot. To obtain operation time per piece, one must set

$$Operation\ time/piece = Run\ time/piece + Setup\ time/piece \qquad (3.1)$$
$$= Run\ time/piece + \frac{Setup\ time/lot}{Average\ lot\ size}$$

Rough-cut capacity planning is always an approximation. If the actual lot sizes vary from the average lot size, the operation time estimate will be a somewhat rougher approximation than if a single lot size is always used. Often, common sense must be used to yield a bill of labor which produces usable results. Consider the milling department, in which one machine is used to mill armatures and gears. Determining the operation time for an armature is easy. From Table 3.1, run time per piece is 20 minutes. Setup time per lot is 60 minutes. The lot size is 40. Using equation 3.1, operation time is therefore 21.5 minutes.

Determining the correct setup time per piece for gears is more difficult. First, there are major and minor setups. Second, the lot size varies from week to week. The major and minor setups can be treated fairly easily. Recall from Chapter 2 that switching from armatures to gears requires 60 minutes. Switching from one gear size to another requires 30 minutes. Since one lot of armatures plus one lot of each gear size is made each week, there will be one major and two minor setups involved in producing gears. Total setup time is therefore 120 minutes [60 + (2 × 30)]. To get setup time per piece one divides 120 by the lot size. But gears are made lot-for-lot. Based on the 1987 MPS for gears (Table 2.4), production may vary from 15 units to 55 units. Rough-cut capacity planning can accept only one setup per lot figure.

At first glance it might seem that the best approach would be to use an average lot size. While this approach is not completely erroneous, it does have one drawback: setup time is *overestimated* when production approaches capacity. This overestimation of setup time can show an apparent need for overtime when the need really does not exist. In this instance, War Eagle knows that 55 gear sets can be produced in a week without overtime. They therefore selected 2.2 minutes (120/55) as a better estimate of setup time per piece. This approach results in a greater underestimation of time required when production is very light. However, since the worker must be available for an entire shift in any event, the underestimation is of no consequence.

Many commonsense adjustments to setup time such as the one just illustrated may be necessary to create a usable bill of labor. There are now enough data in hand to complete the bill of labor for the three critical work centers. Part 100, a complete hoist, requires the following parts to be fabricated:

Department	Part	Minutes
Sheet Metal	Housing	35
Sheet Metal	Drum	39
Winding	Winding	240
Milling	Armature	21.5
Milling	Gear set	27.2

Thus, the bill of labor for the complete hoist can be found by combining times which occur in the same department, yielding:

Department	Minutes
Sheet Metal	74
Winding	240
Milling	48.7

Since parts 200 and 300 are subsets of part 100, all bills of labor can easily be derived as shown in Table 3.3.

TABLE 3.3   BILLS OF LABOR FOR WAR EAGLE HOISTS

DEPARTMENT	TIME REQUIRED FOR PART NUMBER		
	100	200	300
Sheet Metal	74	0	74
Winding	240	240	0
Milling	48.7	21.5	27.2
	Time in minutes		

To complete the rough-cut capacity planning process, War Eagle develops a master production schedule for parts 100, 200, and 300. Because 40 windings must be produced every week, the following algorithm is employed:

Production of hoists (X)	100's	200's	300's
$X < 40$	X	$40 - X$	0
$X = 40$	40	0	0
$X > 40$	40	0	$X - 40$

Table 3.4 shows production of 100's, 200's, and 300's by week. Table 3.5 aggregates the production by quarter.

Calculation of the rough-cut capacity requirements will now be demonstrated using Table 3.3 and Table 3.5. From Table 3.5 one finds that first-

TABLE 3.4 WEEKLY MASTER SCHEDULE FOR WAR EAGLE HOISTS, 1988

WEEK	DEMAND	PARTS 100's	200's	300's
1	39	39	1	0
2	28	28	12	0
3	45	40	0	5
4	29	29	11	0
5	27	27	13	0
6	41	40	0	1
7	33	33	7	0
8	31	31	9	0
9	19	19	21	0
10	15	15	25	0
11	40	40	0	0
12	35	35	5	0
13	39	39	1	0
14	52	40	0	12
15	39	39	1	0
16	31	31	9	0
17	43	40	0	3
18	42	40	0	2
19	36	36	4	0
20	16	16	24	0
21	52	40	0	12
22	60	40	0	20
23	33	33	7	0
24	45	40	0	0
25	71	40	0	31
26	26	26	14	0
27	39	39	1	0
28	52	40	0	12
29	59	40	0	19
30	51	40	0	11
31	57	40	0	17
32	60	40	0	20
33	21	21	19	0
34	54	40	0	14
35	54	40	0	14
36	44	40	0	4
37	48	40	0	8
38	34	34	6	0
39	44	40	0	4
40	23	23	17	0
41	19	19	21	0
42	31	31	9	0
43	42	40	0	2
44	47	40	0	7
45	38	38	2	0

TABLE 3.4   (CONTINUED)

			PARTS	
WEEK	**DEMAND**	**100's**	**200's**	**300's**
46	41	40	0	1
47	40	40	0	0
48	45	40	0	5
49	59	40	0	19
50	26	26	14	0
51	48	40	0	8
52	44	40	0	4

TABLE 3.5   QUARTERLY MASTER SCHEDULE FOR WAR EAGLE HOISTS, 1988

PART	Q1	Q2	Q3	Q4
100	415	461	494	457
200	105	59	26	63
300	6	85	123	46

quarter production of 100's (complete hoist) is 415 units. From Table 3.3 one finds that in the sheet metal department, 74 minutes are required to build one complete hoist. Therefore, the standard time required by the sheet metal department to build 415 hoists in quarter 1 is 415 × 74 = 30,710 minutes. One can also note that 105 part 200's (windings) are to be built in the first quarter; however, windings require no time in the sheet metal department. Finally, Table 3.5 indicates there are six part 300's to be built in the first quarter, and these also require 74 minutes in the sheet metal department. The standard time required to build 300's is thus 6 × 74 = 444 minutes. The total time required in the sheet metal department during quarter 1 is thus 31,154 standard minutes.

This set of calculations must be performed 12 times, once for each of the three work centers for each of the four quarters. One more set of calculations will be fully examined, this time using the milling department during quarter 3. From Table 3.5, the master schedule for parts 100, 200, and 300 for quarter 3 is 494, 26, and 123 units, respectively. From Table 3.3, the time required to build a single unit of 100, 200, or 300 in the milling department is 48.7, 21.5, or 27.2 minutes, respectively. Thus, the time required in the milling department during quarter 3 is $(494 \times 48.7) + (26 \times 21.5) + (123 \times 27.2) = 27{,}962.4$ standard minutes.

At this point the reader should be able to calculate the rough-cut capacity requirements for any work center for any quarter. The full set of rough-cut capacity requirements in minutes is as follows:

Department	Q1	Q2	Q3	Q4
Sheet Metal	31,154	40,404	45,658	37,222
Winding	124,800	124,800	124,800	124,800
Milling	22,631	26,031	27,962	24,862

In matrix notation, Table 3.3 is a three-row-by-three-column (3×3) matrix. Note that the master schedule, Table 3.5, is a three-row-by-four-column (3×4) matrix. Students familiar with matrix multiplication will have recognized the process used to obtain the rough-cut requirements as a matrix multiplication. Appendix 3A describes how to perform matrix multiplication using an electronic spreadsheet. Details of how to use IBM-PC compatible software provided with the Instructor's Manual to perform rough-cut computations appear in an appendix at the back of the book.

In general, assume there are n master scheduled items. Let the master schedule amount for product i in week j be denoted M_{ij}. Let the bill of labor amount for product i in work center k be denoted L_{ik}. Then the formula for the capacity required in work center k for week j is

$$Capacity\ required = \sum_{i=1}^{n} M_{ij} L_{ik} \qquad (3.2)$$

The capacity available for each quarter of 1988 is found by first multiplying 2,400 minutes per week by 13 weeks by the number of workers in each department. Sheet metal has 2 workers, winding 4, and milling 1. Then multiply the total minutes available by *utilization* and *efficiency* to convert from clock minutes available to standard minutes which can be produced:

Department	Minutes Available	× Utilization	× Efficiency	= Capacity
Sheet Metal	62,400	0.98	0.95	58,094
Winding	124,800	0.99	1.02	126,023
Milling	31,200	0.95	1.05	31,122

Most commercial software packages have the ability to display the rough-cut capacity planning as graphic output, in a form such as that in Figure 3.3. This graphical representation makes it much easier to spot occasions in which capacity required exceeds capacity available.

FIGURE 3.3   TWO EXAMPLES OF RCCP AS GRAPHIC OUTPUT

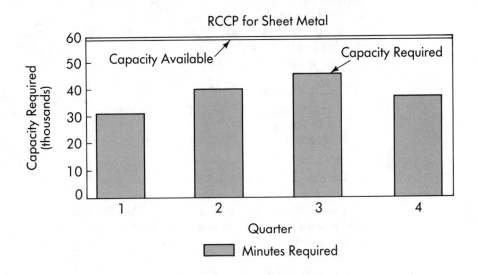

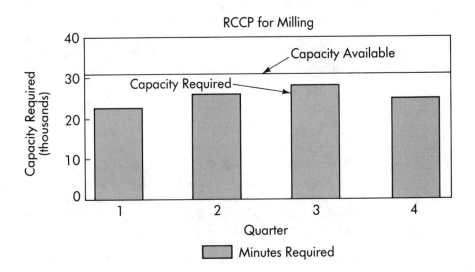

DEFINITION OF WORK CENTER

It should be noted at this point that the sheet metal department should not be classified as one work center for capacity planning purposes. There are two workers in the sheet metal department. One works exclusively on drums, the other exclusively on motor housings. The problem with lumping two such workers together is that it is possible for the work center to have sufficient capacity *on average* while one of the workers is overloaded and the other underloaded. War Eagle is not experiencing problems with this definition at present since ample capacity exists for both workers given the present schedule. Poor work center definition is a common reason for poor capacity planning performance.

HOW MUCH CAPACITY AVAILABLE IS ENOUGH?

Traditional capacity management techniques indicate that a work center is not overloaded when capacity available equals capacity required. The use of Wight's funnel (see Figure 1.5) as an analogy in this case can be misleading. The funnel concept says that if input equals output, load stays the same. While this is true for input rates and output rates which are constants, it is misleading if the input and output rates are random variables. Consider a simple example. Suppose a work center has two units in queue, that it takes 100 time units to produce a part, and a new part arrives every 100 time units. Then the number in the system is always two units. Each arriving unit finds one unit exiting and one unit just going into service. Each unit must wait for the unit in front of it to be processed. Time at the work center is 200 units for the part (including the operation time for the part itself).

The paper presented in Appendix 1A argues that for random arrival and service times the queue grows ever larger when the arrival rate equals the service rate. In order to explore this notion further, a simple simulation is described. Complete simulation results are shown in Appendix 3B. This simulation has a single server and a queue of customers awaiting service. As a benchmark case, the initial queue is 2. Arrivals and service completions are considered to be constant, each occurring 100 time units apart. A model of this sort, in which no uncertainty is included, is called a **deterministic model**. The simulation run for five replications of 1,000 customers passing through the queue finds an average time in system of 199.9, with a standard deviation of 3.161. The result is not 200 units with a standard deviation of 0 because the first customer in queue when the simulation started went into service immediately and completed in 100 time units.

The model is next run with arrivals and service completions each being random variables having a uniform distribution over the range [0,200]. For those not familiar with statistics, this simply means that when an arrival (or a service completion) occurs, the next arrival (completion) may be anywhere from 0 to 200, with each of the 200 unit intervals being equally likely. This model is chosen in order to create a situation in which there was a great deal of variation in both the service time and the time between arrivals. The paper in Appendix 1A argues that this model should result in a very long queue, one tending to grow infinitely large if allowed to exist for an infinite period. In this model, simulated through five replications of 1,000 entities each time, the average time in the system is found to be 1,789 units rather than the 200 predicted by the deterministic model.

It is unlikely that a service time would be distributed from 0 to 200 units with every choice being equally likely. Service times are more likely to be bell shaped. If the worker is experienced and does not suffer delays from machine or tool breakages, the variation of service time should be small. Does the queue tend to grow infinitely if the variation in service time is small? In order to test this, the simulation is modified so that the service time is normally distributed (bell shaped) with a mean of 100 and a standard deviation of 15. Recall that 68 percent of the normal distribution lies within one standard deviation of the mean, 95 percent within two standard deviations. Thus, in the simulation, 68 percent of all service times are on the interval [85,115] and 95 percent are on the interval [70,130]. In most situations, arrival times are less easily controlled than service times and hence exhibit larger variation. Recognizing this, time between arrivals is set to a uniform distribution on the interval [50,150]. The arrival rate is chosen so that the mean equals the mean service rate and so that the variation is greater than the variation of service time but only half of the rate used for the high variance case. This model, also simulated for five replications of 1,000 units each, results in a mean time in system of 691 units, almost 3.5 times larger than that predicted by the deterministic model.

The model presented in Appendix 1A also suggests that if a situation is allowed to persist in which the arrival rate equals the service rate, the queue in front of the work center will grow longer over time. In order to test the applicability of this notion to manufacturing situations, the simulation model having normally distributed service times and uniform arrivals is run once with 20,000 entities passing through the server. The mean is found to be 2,932, over four times larger than that found when only 1,000 entities passed. Also, the queue length is observed every 100,000 units of simulated time (corresponding to approximately 1,000 units passing through the system). Figure 3.4 presents the results of these observations. Note that the queue does continually lengthen, although, as with all random processes, the queue length fluctuates quite a bit. Thus, one may conclude that a random arrival rate equal to the service rate will cause the queue to grow indefinitely, even with moderate variation in service times.

What relevance has Figure 3.4 to capacity management? Clearly, the procedure of verifying that capacity available is equal to or less than capacity required is not proper, since it results in long queues when capacity available *equals* capacity required. As a general rule, capacity available must be *greater than* capacity required in order to avoid the problem of queues which grow indefinitely. Like all general rules, this rule has exceptions. The winding area of War Eagle Hoists is an exception. Since the winding area follows a level production strategy, producing 40 windings each week, the pattern of job arrivals is entirely predictable. Assuming no absenteeism or machine breakdowns, the service pattern is also predictable. Thus, the winding area of War

FIGURE 3.4   NUMBER IN QUEUE AT SELECTED TIMES*

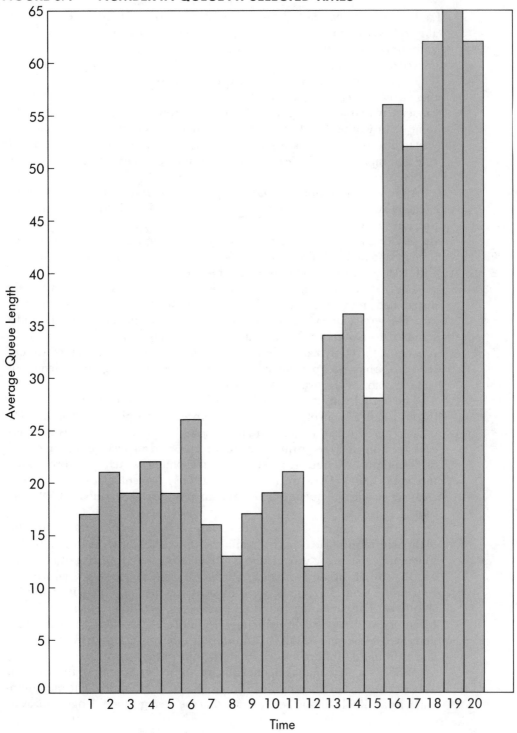

* One replication, 20,000 entities, arrivals uniform [50,150], service normal [100,15].

Eagle Hoists fits the deterministic model quite well, and War Eagle should be able to load the work center until capacity required equals capacity available without causing a buildup of work awaiting processing. Similarly, if a job arrived only when the previous job finished service, the queue could not grow. There are many *gateway* work centers to which work is released directly. For these work centers, it is possible to aim for capacity requirements that equal capacity available. For many work centers, however, work arrives only when some other work center has finished. For these work centers there is often no way to directly control the arrival stream. For such work centers, the general rule that capacity available must be greater than capacity required should be observed.

An obvious question is, *how much greater* than capacity required must capacity available be? In order to address this question, the queueing simulation is rerun with arrival rates that are 95 percent, 98 percent, and 99 percent of the service rate to determine the resulting average queue length and average time in system. In all three simulations, the model is run for one replication with 20,000 entities moving through the queue.

The first run of the model is set with an arrival pattern which is uniformly distributed on the interval [55,155]. Note that this distribution has a mean of 105. The service rate remains normally distributed with a mean of 100 and a standard deviation of 15. Thus, one would expect the server to be busy a fraction equal to 100/105, or 95.24 percent. In the simulation, the server was observed to be busy 95.5 percent of the time; there was an average queue length of 0.917 and an average wait of 96 time units.

The second run has an arrival pattern which is uniform on the interval [52,152], with a mean of 102, creating an expected busy percentage of 100/102, or 98.04 percent. In the actual run the observed busy percentage was 98.3 percent, creating an average queue length of 2.935 and an average wait in queue of 299 time units. The third run has an arrival pattern which is uniform on the interval [51,101]. This run had an actual busy percentage of 99.3 percent, creating an average queue of 5.916 and an average wait in queue of 596 time units.

The important thing to note from this set of simulations is that as the ratio of capacity required to capacity available approaches 1, the queue length gets longer in a systematic way. There is a trade-off between the cost of idle time and the cost of inventory needed to avoid idle time. There is no general rule concerning what the ratio between capacity required and capacity available should be. The choice depends on the relative costs of idle capacity and extra inventory. In this example, reducing idle time by 1 percentage point, from 1.7 percent to 0.7 percent, results in a doubling of the queue length from 2.9 to 5.9 and a similar doubling of the time in the system (lead time).

Proper capacity management calls for an understanding of the trade-off between the cost of idle time and the cost of excess inventory. The maximum capacity available should be chosen so that the average queue length and average wait in queue are in keeping with the data used to set lead time for parts passing through the work center. The manager should also understand that as the ratio of capacity required to capacity available approaches 1, the length of the queue tends to fluctuate a good bit. Figure 3.5 shows the queue length at selected points in time during the run having an arrival rate equal to 99 percent of the service rate. The observations are taken on approximately every thousandth unit through the system, so there should be virtually no correlation between one observation of queue length and the next. Note that in fact the queue length fluctuates quite a bit, achieving a maximum of 27 units. One of the liabilities of attempting a utilization as high as 99 percent is that the maximum queue length can get quite long. When 27 jobs are in queue, an arriving job will surely be quite late leaving a work center, especially if lead times are based on the average length (about 6). Furthermore, since arrivals continue to come in at 99 percent of the service rate, it can take quite a long period of time to reduce the excess load.

FIGURE 3.5   AVERAGE QUEUE LENGTH AT SELECTED TIMES*

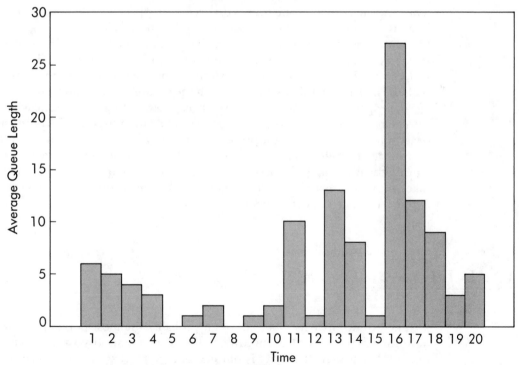

* Arrivals uniform, service normal, 90% server utilization.

The maximum queue length observed in the run having 98 percent utilization was 20. The maximum queue length observed in the run having 95 percent utilization was 8. Perhaps as much attention should be paid to the maximum queue length as to the average queue length in deciding what the maximum ratio of capacity required to capacity available should be. How much is it worth to reduce the maximum queue at a work center from 20 units to 8 units? It could be worth quite a bit, since the number of tardy jobs will be reduced dramatically. It is quite possible that the value of the late costs avoided and the value of the inventory eliminated will more than offset the value of the idle time. In many businesses, direct labor is 10 percent of costs. By having the worker idle 5 percent of the time rather than 1 percent of the time, costs might be increased by 4 percent of 10 percent, or 0.04 percent. As will be shown later in the text, even this cost increase may be nonexistent. If the work center in question is not a true bottleneck, there may be no cost to having some idle time.

Thus, the answer to the question of how much capacity is needed is that management should first decide what the ratio of capacity required to capacity available should be for every work center. Then the amount of needed capacity can be easily determined.

There is one *major* problem with the procedure discussed in this section. The problem is that most current cost accounting packages do not attribute late costs back to the station that caused a job to be late. Thus, although the ideal ratio of capacity required to capacity available may well be 95 percent, the accounting system will say that the manager (or supervisor) is doing a better job if the station is busy 100 percent of the time. The problem lies not with the material in this section, but with the failure of the accounting package to properly value on-time performance, a view dating from a time when direct labor accounted for 75 percent of costs rather than 10 percent. A number of accountants are aware of the problem, and there is a slow movement toward creating a more relevant cost accounting and performance measurement system. In the interim, good capacity management will require the courage to take on the system and to demonstrate that idle time is not universally evil. Perhaps the material contained in this section will help.

VARIATIONS OF THE ROUGH-CUT APPROACH

The bill of labor method, although probably the most popular RCCP technique, is not the only technique. In the next sections, two variations are presented. The first alternative is simpler, but less precise; the second is more detailed, but it is useful only in a limited domain.

Capacity Planning Using Overall Factors (CPOF)

Two variations of the rough-cut approach are discussed by Berry, Schmitt, and Vollmann (1). The first technique is called capacity planning using overall factors (CPOF). With CPOF one multiplies the master production schedule by the total time required to build a part (including components). Summing these results gives the total number of labor hours required in the plant. One then prorates total plant labor to the individual work centers using historical percentages. Example 3.1 will be used to illustrate this technique. Assume that the minutes worked in 1987 were as follows:

Department	Q1	Q2	Q3	Q4	Total
Sheet Metal	31,154	40,404	45,658	37,222	154,438
Winding	124,800	124,800	124,800	124,800	499,200
Milling	22,631	26,031	27,962	24,862	101,486

Summing the total labor minutes worked in 1987, one finds that in the three critical departments, War Eagle Hoists worked a total of 755,124 minutes. The proportion used for prorating total plant labor for each department is found by dividing total department minutes by total plant minutes. Thus, for the sheet metal department, the proportion, rounded to 6 decimals, is 154,438/775,124 = 0.204520. For winding and milling, respectively, the proportions are 0.66183 and 0.134396. Note that the three proportions sum to 1.

Recall that the master production schedule is:

Part	Q1	Q2	Q3	Q4
100	415	461	494	457
200	105	59	26	63
300	6	85	123	46

The final set of input data needed is the total time required to build a unit in the three critical work centers. These data can be obtained by summing the bill of labor. Recall from Table 3.3 that the bills of labor are

Department	Part 100	Part 200	Part 300
Sheet Metal	74	0	74
Winding	240	240	0
Milling	48.7	21.5	27.2
Total time in plant (minutes)	**362.7**	**261.5**	**101.2**

To obtain the total plant labor required in the plant, multiply the time for each part by the master schedule quantity for that part. For example, multiplying 415 units of part 100 by 362.7 minutes per unit yields 150,521 minutes in the plant for part 100 in quarter 1. Each of the following items is obtained by a single multiplication:

Part	Q1	Q2	Q3	Q4
100	150,521	167,205	179,174	165,754
200	27,458	15,429	6,799	16,475
300	607	8,602	12,448	4,655
Total	**178,585**	**191,235**	**198,420**	**186,884**

One must now apportion the total time needed for the plant to the various work centers. Multiplying the percentage factors by total plant time per week gives the rough-cut capacity plan, shown in Table 3.6.

TABLE 3.6   ROUGH-CUT CAPACITY PLAN USING CPOF

DEPARTMENT	PRORATION FACTOR	Q1	Q2	Q3	Q4
Sheet Metal	20.4520%	36,524	39,111	40,581	38,222
Winding	66.1083%	118,060	126,422	131,172	123,546
Milling	13.4396%	24,001	25,701	26,667	25,117
Total plant labor (minutes)		**178,585**	**191,235**	**198,235**	**186,884**

The CPOF approach utilizes fewer data than the bill of labor approach, but it is insensitive to shifts in product mix. This statement explains both why CPOF has been used and why it should not be used now that microcomputers are commonplace. In the era before microcomputers (which began to be used for business purposes about 1981), performing all the multiplications required by the bill of labor approach was a cumbersome process. The CPOF approach is much simpler than the bill of labor approach, requiring only that each proration factor in Table 3.6 be multiplied by the total labor quantity for each quarter, i.e., one multiplication per cell rather than several. For many situations, CPOF was perhaps the only practical solution.

Unfortunately, CPOF's insensitivity to product-mix shifts can lead to problems, as Figure 3.6 illustrates. From an examination of Figure 3.6 one would conclude that the winding department has insufficient capacity during quarter 3. In reality, the winding department has exactly the same load in all four quarters, 40 windings per week, every week. What has happened is that the shift in product mix has altered the total number of hours, with the additional hours in the summer really occurring in the sheet metal and milling departments, both of which operate on a demand chase strategy. However, since CPOF applies the same proration factor for all four quarters, the shift in

FIGURE 3.6   RCCP FOR WINDING DEPARTMENT USING CPOF

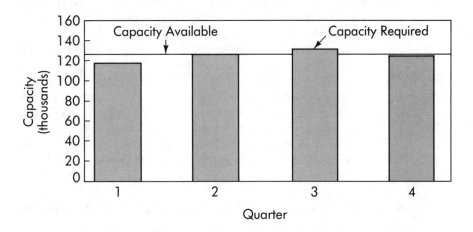

product mix during the summer peak results in a misleading capacity requirement figure.

Note that the bill of labor approach captures the changing product mix since each product has its own bill of labor. For that reason, the bill of labor approach is strongly recommended over the CPOF approach. Now that electronic spreadsheets, are available, the bill of labor approach is just as simple to perform as CPOF. Thus, CPOF, while a useful technique only a few years ago, is clearly outdated and soon will be discussed only as an extinct technique of minor historical interest.

The Resource Profile Approach

The second variation of the rough-cut approach discussed by Berry et al. (1) is the resource profile technique. Though not as detailed as CRP, the resource profile technique is the most detailed rough-cut approach. Both the bill of labor approach and the CPOF approach implicitly assume that all components are built in the same time bracket as the end item; neither considers lead-time offsets. The resource profile technique, on the other hand, *time phases* the labor requirements. Each bill of labor must be time phased for the resource profile approach to be used.

In Example 3.1 part 200, a winding, requires both an armature, which must be milled and moved to the winding department, and the winding itself. In developing a bill of labor for part 200, one includes the time required to mill the armature and wind the winding but does not offset for lead time. Thus, the bill of labor for a winding shows 240 minutes for the actual winding and 21.5 minutes for the armature, both in the same time period. In developing a resource profile, one offsets for lead time. In this case, the armature is normally milled the week prior to the winding. Thus, if part 200 is due in week t, the labor on the winding occurs in week t and the labor on the armature occurs in week $t - 1$.

For part 100, a complete hoist, the procedure is more complex. If the master schedule indicates that part 100 is due in week t, then to meet schedule the hoist must be assembled in week t. To assemble the hoist in week t, motor assembly must be completed in week $t - 1$, as must drum fabrication and gear milling. To assemble the motor in week $t - 1$, the winding and motor housing must be completed in week $t - 2$. Finally, to finish the winding in week $t - 2$ requires that the armature be milled in week $t - 3$. A time-phased list of activities for a complete hoist is set up as shown in Table 3.7

TABLE 3.7   CREATION OF RESOURCE PROFILE FOR PART 100, COMPLETE HOIST

DEPARTMENT	$t - 3$	$t - 2$	$t - 1$	t
Final Assembly				Hoist Assembly
Motor Assembly			Motor Assembly	
Sheet Metal		Motor Housing	Drum Fabrication	
Winding		Winding		
Milling	Armature		Gear	

To complete the resource profile for a hoist, one substitutes the standard time for each operation for the operation description shown in Table 3.7. A similar resource profile has to be created for each end item.

Once the resource profile is created, one multiplies the resource profile by the master schedule to obtain the rough-cut requirements. This multiplication is not a simple matrix multiplication like that in the bill of labor approach. Rather, the procedure must keep careful track of the hours accumulated in each period. The resource profile approach is always implemented on a computer because of the tediousness of the calculations. The resource profile algorithm has been implemented in two programs furnished on the diskette accompanying the Instructor's Manual, one a Lotus spreadsheet, the other a FORTRAN program. Use of the worksheets is explained in an appendix at the back of this text. The interested reader may usefully examine either implementation to deduce the algorithm. For advanced students, implementing the algorithm from scratch using a microcomputer is a reasonable exercise.

To illustrate how the resource profile algorithm is produced, note that the resource profile for part 100 in Table 3.7 has four time periods. Although parts 200 and 300 can be profiled in fewer time periods, all parts must have a resource profile equal in size to the resource profile of the part with the longest lead time. Although neither of the assembly operations is included in rough-cut calculations, part 100 must be described using a four-week horizon to provide a proper lead-time offset for the fabrication operations. To perform the rough-cut calculation for work center i during week 1 one must perform 12 multiplications:

1. MPS, part 100, week 1 $\times$ Resource Profile, part 100, week t
2. MPS, part 200, week 1 $\times$ Resource Profile, part 200, week t
3. MPS, part 300, week 1 $\times$ Resource Profile, part 300, week t
4. MPS, part 100, week 2 $\times$ Resource Profile, part 100, week $t - 1$
5. MPS, part 200, week 2 $\times$ Resource Profile, part 200, week $t - 1$
6. MPS, part 300, week 2 $\times$ Resource Profile, part 300, week $t - 1$
7. MPS, part 100, week 3 $\times$ Resource Profile, part 100, week $t - 2$
8. MPS, part 200, week 3 $\times$ Resource Profile, part 200, week $t - 2$
9. MPS, part 300, week 3 $\times$ Resource Profile, part 300, week $t - 2$
10. MPS, part 100, week 4 $\times$ Resource Profile, part 100, week $t - 3$
11. MPS, part 200, week 4 $\times$ Resource Profile, part 200, week $t - 3$
12. MPS, part 300, week 4 $\times$ Resource Profile, part 300, week $t - 3$

The twelve multiplicative products are then summed to find the amount of time that should be required at work center i during week 1. To complete the resource profile, a similar set of twelve multiplications must be performed for each work center for each week.

Obviously, the resource profile approach requires more computational effort than the bill of labor approach. Is there a return for the additional effort of creating the resource profiles and performing the extra computations? There may be, but only if lead times are quite long and the shop uses a lot-for-lot policy in establishing lot sizes.

EXAMPLE 3.2:
THE EFFECT OF LOT SIZING

To illustrate the effect lot sizing has on the accuracy of the resource profile approach, consider the following example. Suppose that a product, which for the purposes of this discussion will be called a whatsit, has two operations, A and B, performed in departments 1 and 2. Suppose further that the bill of labor, the resource profile, and the master production schedule for the coming four weeks are as follows:

Bill of Labor		Resource Profile		
Department	*Minutes*	*Department*	*Week 1*	*Week 2*
1	20	1	20	0
2	30	2	0	30

Master Production Schedule

	Week 1	Week 2	Week 3	Week 4
Number of Whatsits	100	200	250	100

The rough-cut capacity plans produced by the bill of labor and resource profile approaches are as shown in Tables 3.8 and 3.9, respectively.

Note the difference in requirements for work center 1 in Tables 3.8 and 3.9. Table 3.9 has offset the requirement by a one-week lead time, resulting in a time of 0 for period 4, since no requirement for period 5 is yet visible. Periods 1, 2, and 3 represent requirements placed on the work center one week earlier by the resource profile than by the bill of labor approach. Finally, note that the total hours are 2,000 fewer using the resource profile approach, since the resource profile approach assumes the components for the 100 whatsits due in week 1 have already been built.

When demand peaks occur, such as in week 3 of the master schedule, it is important to reflect the timing of the impact of the peak on various work centers. The resource profile does this, *provided that the quantity of operation A in week t − 1 always coincides with the master schedule amount of whatsits in week t.* Suppose, however, that the lot size for operation A is 700, so that

TABLE 3.8   CAPACITY REQUIREMENTS USING THE BILL OF LABOR

WORK CENTERS	PERIODS 1	2	3	4	TOTAL
WC1	2,000	4,000	5,000	2,000	**13,000**
WC2	3,000	6,000	7,500	3,000	**19,500**

Capacity required in minutes

TABLE 3.9   CAPACITY REQUIREMENTS USING RESOURCE PROFILES

WORK CENTERS	PERIODS 1	2	3	4	TOTAL
WC1	4,000	5,000	2,000	0	**11,000**
WC2	3,000	6,000	7,500	3,000	**19,500**

Capacity required in minutes

incomplete whatsits are stocked after operation A. Then both the bill of labor and the resource profile approach are wrong. At some point during the four weeks, work center A will produce 700 incomplete whatsits requiring 14,000 time units. The timing of this demand will depend on the number of incomplete whatsits currently in stock.

Since both the bill of labor and the resource profile results are incorrect when any lot-sizing rule other than lot-for-lot is used, the bill of labor approach with time buckets as large as practical is recommended (i.e., monthly or quarterly buckets). For companies having lot-for-lot lot sizing throughout all operations, the resource profile approach using small (e.g., weekly) buckets will provide quite a bit of additional information.

SUMMARY

In this chapter three approaches to rough-cut capacity planning have been examined. The least detailed approach, capacity planning using overall factors (CPOF), is quickly computed but is insensitive to shifts in product mix. A second approach, bill of labor, involves multiplying two matrices, the bill of labor and the master production schedule. This approach picks up shifts in product mix but does not consider lead-time offsets. The third approach, resource profile, takes lead-time offsets into account. Both the bill of labor approach and the resource profile approach implicitly assume a lot-for-lot policy for setting lot sizes. If some other technique, such as economic order quantity (EOQ), is used, either approach is a very rough estimate. In any event, rough-cut capacity plans should be used only to determine if sufficient capacity exists over broad time frames, such as a month or a quarter. It is of particular importance that the planned activation of resources (i.e., the ratio of capacity required to capacity available) be consistent with the planned queue length for the work center. In almost all instances the capacity available must be somewhat greater than the capacity required to obtain a reasonable queue length.

REFERENCES

1. Berry, William L., Thomas G. Schmitt, and Thomas E. Vollmann. "Capacity Planning Techniques for Manufacturing Control Systems: Information Requirements and Operational Features." *Journal of Operations Management* 3, no. 1 (September 1982):13–26.

2. Berry, William L., Thomas E. Vollmann, and D. Clay Whybark. *Master Production Scheduling: Principles and Practice*. Falls Church, Va.: American Production and Inventory Control Society, 1979.

3. Conlon, J. R. "Is Your Master Production Schedule Feasible?" *APICS Master Production Scheduling Reprints*. Falls Church, Va.: American Production and Inventory Control Society, 1977.

4. Orlicky, Joseph. *Material Requirements Planning*. New York: McGraw-Hill Book Co., 1976.

5. Plossl, George, and Everett Welch. *The Role of Top Management in the Control of Inventory*. Reston, Va.: Reston Publishing Co., 1979.

EXERCISES

1. Describe the differences between the bill of labor approach and CPOF. Which approach would be preferable for an analyst limited to a hand-held calculator? Is there a clear preference if a microcomputer is available to the analyst?

2. Describe the differences between the bill of labor approach and the resource profile approach. Which approach requires the most data? Which approach would be preferable for a company running an MRP system utilizing the economic order quantity lot-sizing technique? Using the lot-for-lot lot-sizing technique?

3. For a given plant the bill of labor (in hours per part) at bottleneck work centers is as follows:

Work Center	Part A	Part B
WC149	2.4	1.6
WC103	1.7	3.0
WC56	1.5	1.9

The master production schedule, by quarter, for the next year is:

	Q1	Q2	Q3	Q4
Part A	1,500	1,000	1,000	1,900
Part B	1,200	1,200	1,200	1,400

Using the bill of labor approach, determine the number of hours required in work centers 149, 103, and 56 for each quarter.

4. A plant consists of four departments, A, B, C, and D, whose historical proportions of total plant direct labor have been 0.35, 0.22, 0.28, and 0.15, respectively. The plant makes three major product families, F1, F2, and F3, requiring total labor of 25, 22, and 29 hours, respectively. The MPS for the coming year is as follows:

	Q1	Q2	Q3	Q4
F1	2,000	2,500	2,500	3,000
F2	4,000	4,000	4,500	5,000
F3	3,000	3,500	3,000	4,000

Compute required capacity using the CPOF approach.

5. Assume that in Exercise 3, part A is routed WC149 → WC56 → WC103 with a one-week lead time at each work center. Part B is routed WC103 → WC149 → WC56 with a two-week lead time at each center. Assume there is an order for part A currently at center 56 (100 units) and an order of the same size at center 103. There is one order for part B, size 100, at each of the three centers. The MPS for the next eight week is as follows:

	W1	W2	W3	W4	W5	W6	W7	W8
Part A	100	100	100	100	150	150	150	150
Part B	100	100	100	100	100	100	100	100

The underlined orders have been released to the floor and are located as shown above. Determine the capacity needed using the resource profile approach.

6. In this exercise you will be given a bill of materials, a set of routings, and a master production schedule. From this you are to determine (a) a summarized bill of material, (b) a bill of labor, and (c) capacity requirements for the coming year using the bill of labor approach.

Bill of Materials

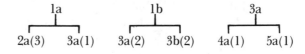

Routings

Part 1a		Lot Size: 100		Parts 3a & 3b		Lot Size: 500
WC	Setup Hrs	Run Hrs/Piece		WC	Setup Hrs	Run Hrs/Piece
1	5	.03		1	11	.02
2	8	.10		2	9	.06

Part 1b		Lot Size: 100		Part 4a		Lot Size: 500
WC	Setup Hrs	Run Hrs/Piece		WC	Setup Hrs	Run Hrs/Piece
1	7	.12		1	4	.06
2	4	.06		2	3	.04

Part 2a		Lot Size: 500	Part 5a		Lot Size: 500
WC	Setup Hrs	Run Hrs/Piece	WC	Setup Hrs	Run Hrs/Piece
1	3	.03	1	5	.03
2	6	.02	2	7	.03

Master Production Schedule for Quarter

	Q1	Q2	Q3	Q4
Part 1a	200	300	300	400
Part 1b	500	400	400	300

7. *Advanced.* Exercise 7 is a much more detailed version of Exercise 6. It should be attempted only by those using the software accompanying the Instructor's Manual. Given the following data, complete both the bill of labor and resource profile approaches to rough-cut capacity planning. For the resource profile approach assume that the component is completed at the same time the end item is completed.

End Items	Components
101	201
102	203
103	205
104	302
105	304

Bill of Materials

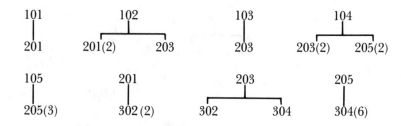

Routings

Part 101	Lot Size 250	Lead Time 5	Part 105	Lot Size 250	Lead Time 5
WC	Setup Hrs	Run Hrs/Piece	WC	Setup Hrs	Run Hrs/Piece
2	3	.05	2	8	.03
5	11	.1	4	2	.05

WC	Setup Hrs	Run Hrs/Piece	WC	Setup Hrs	Run Hrs/Piece
3	2	.03	1	1	.01
1	1	.01	5	7	.05
4	6	.04	3	5	.06

Part 102	Lot Size 150	Lead Time 3	Part 201	Lot Size 1000	Lead Time 3
WC	Setup Hrs	Run Hrs/Piece	WC	Setup Hrs	Run Hrs/Piece
1	2	.03	2	4	.005
3	7	.13	1	4	.007
5	3	.06	5	12	.02

Part 103	Lot Size 200	Lead Time 4	Part 203	Lot Size 1000	Lead Time 2
WC	Setup Hrs	Run Hrs/Piece	WC	Setup Hrs	Run Hrs/Piece
4	4	.08	1	6	.006
2	2	.06	4	14	.03
5	4	.06			
1	9	.08			

Part 104	Lot Size 100	Lead Time 2	Part 205	Lot Size 2000	Lead Time 3
WC	Setup Hrs	Run Hrs/Piece	WC	Setup Hrs	Run Hrs/Piece
2	6	.05	1	2	.003
4	3	.04	2	4	.006
			3	6	.009

Master Production Schedule for Week

End Item	1	2	3	4	5	6	7	8	9	10	11	12	13
101	250	0	0	250	0	250	0	0	250	0	250	0	250
102	150	150	0	150	0	150	150	0	150	0	150	150	0
103	200	200	200	200	200	200	200	200	200	200	200	200	200
104	100	0	100	0	100	0	100	0	100	0	100	0	100
105	0	200	0	200	0	200	0	200	0	200	0	200	0

APPENDIX 3A
Multiplying Matrices in Lotus 1-2-3

Both the *bill of labor* and the *master production schedule* (MPS) are rows and columns of numbers having a rectangular appearance. Such a set of numbers is called a *matrix*. Assume that the bill of labor contains M rows and N columns and that the master production schedule contains N rows and P columns.

Then the bill of labor can be described as an $M \times N$ matrix and the MPS as an $N \times P$ matrix. Note that M is the number of work centers, N is the number of end items in the master schedule, and P is the number of time periods in the master schedule.

To multiply two matrices the inner dimensions must match. The bill of labor can be multiplied by the master schedule because such an operation is $(M \times N) \times (N \times P)$. Note that the inner dimensions are N and N and the outer dimensions are M and P. The multiplication succeeds because the inner dimensions are the same ($N = N$). The resulting product will occupy a matrix having the size of the outer dimensions ($M \times P$ in this case).

For example, if the bill of labor has 5 rows and 4 columns and the MPS has 4 rows and 8 columns, the resulting rough-cut requirements matrix will have 5 rows and 8 columns. It is important to understand how the dimensions work because Lotus must be provided with the proper dimensions and orientation of the matrices. Lotus checks for proper dimensions and will give an error message if the dimensions supplied to it are improper.

LOTUS VERSION 2, THE DATA MATRIX MULTIPLY COMMAND SEQUENCE

The procedure described in this section works only in Lotus Version 2 and later versions. To begin the process, enter the bill of labor and master production schedule on a blank Lotus worksheet. Be sure both are oriented properly. The bill of labor should have work centers for rows and part numbers for columns. The master schedule should have part numbers for rows and time periods for columns. Enter the command sequence / DATA MATRIX MULTIPLY. Lotus will query for the location of the first matrix. Highlight the square representing the time values contained in the bill of labor (i.e., the body but not the margins) and press ENTER. Lotus will next query for the location of the second matrix. Highlight the body of the MPS but not the margins (i.e., highlight the production numbers but not the part or time period numbers). Finally, Lotus queries for the location of the result. Highlight a blank portion of the worksheet having dimension M by P where M is the number of rows in the bill of labor and P is the number of columns in the master schedule. Lotus will multiply the matrices and place the answer at the indicated spot.

It is important to note that if any of the values in the bill of labor and/or master schedule are subsequently changed, the rough-cut requirements (product) matrix is *not automatically recalculated* even if the worksheet is recalculated. To get new values for the rough-cut requirements, the / DATA MATRIX MULTIPLY command sequence must be repeated. If automatic recalculation is desired, the matrix multiplication can be defined as in the next section.

VERSION 1A

Version 1A of Lotus lacks the DATA MATRIX MULTIPLY command. This section describes a procedure for multiplying matrices manually. The procedure also works with Version 2 and has the benefit of being automatically recalculated whenever the worksheet is recalculated. The procedure will be explained by using a specific example, shown in Figure 3A.1.*

Note from Figure 3A.1 that the bill of labor has work center numbers as row margins and part numbers as column margins while the master schedule has part numbers as row margins and time period numbers as column margins. The bill of labor and master schedule may be any size but they must always be oriented as above. Further, the part numbers in the bill of labor must

---

*For those who prefer not to create a model from scratch, a diskette with a functioning implementation of this technique is contained in John H. Blackstone, Jr., *P/OM Spreadsheet Templates for Lotus 1-2-3*, Random House College Software, 1986.

FIGURE 3A.1   PLACEMENT OF RCCP

	A	B	C	D	E	F	G	H
1								
2								
3								
4		Bill of Labor				Master Production Schedule		
5		Part					Period	
6	WC	1	2		Part	1	2	3
7	1	2	4		1	100	200	300
8	2	3	5		2	200	400	600
9	3	8	3					
10								
11								
12			Rough-Cut Capacity Plan					
13				Period				
14		WC	1	2	3			
15		1	(1,1)	(1,2)	(1,3)			
16		2	(2,1)	(2,2)	(2,3)			
17		3	(3,1)	(3,2)	(3,3)			
18								
19								
20								

always be in the same sequence as the part numbers in the master schedule, and exactly the same set of part numbers must appear in each. In this case the set of part numbers is (part 1, part 2).

Also note from Figure 3A.1 that the rough-cut capacity plan is to be a 3×3 matrix since the bill of labor has three rows and the master schedule has 3 columns. Each of the nine cells of the rough-cut capacity plan can be identified as (i,j), where i represents the row number and j represents the column number. Consider how the value of cell $(1,1)$ is calculated.

Cell $(1,1)$ represents the time needed by work center 1 in the first period. In the first period the master schedule calls for 100 part 1's and 200 part 2's. Work center 1 requires 2 time units to make part 1, and 4 time units to make part 2. The time required in period 1 by work center 1 is thus $(100 \times 2) + (200 \times 4) = 1,000$). Similarly, the value for cell $(3,2)$ is $(200 \times 8) + (400 \times 3) = 2,800$.

The formula required to calculate cell $(1,1)$ will now be described. Please refer to Figure 3A.2, noting carefully the row of letters running across the top

FIGURE 3A.2   DEFINING THE FORMULA

C11: F$4*$B4 + F$5*$C4

	A	B	C	D	E	F	G	H
1								
2								
3								
4		Bill of Labor				Master Production Schedule		
5		Part					Period	
6	WC	1	2		Part	1	2	3
7	1	2	4		1	100	200	300
8	2	3	5		2	200	400	600
9	3	8	3					
10								
11				Rough-Cut Capacity Plan				
12				Period				
13			WC	1	2	3		
14			1	1000				
15			2					
16			3					
17								
18								
19								
20								

of the worksheet and the column of numbers running down the far-left side. Note that the first period of the master schedule is contained in column F and that the first row of the bill of labor is contained in row 4. To obtain the value for cell (1,1) of the master schedule, which in the worksheet is cell C11, one must multiply cell F4 by cell B4 and cell F5 by cell C4. Note that the formula for cell C11 is typed "F$4*$B4 + F$5*$C4". The formula is always entered in this fashion in order to set up for a COPY command.

The general formula always looks like the formula for cell C11. There is one term for each part number. In entering the formula, a $ appears before the *number* of the cell reference from the master schedule and before the *letter* of the cell reference from the bill of labor.

Now copy the formula for cell (1,1) to the rest of the matrix. The appearance of the worksheet at the end of the COPY command sequence and at the end of the resulting recalculation are shown in Figures 3A.3 and 3A.4 respectively.

FIGURE 3A.3 COPYING THE FORMULA

	A	B	C	D	E	F	G	H
1								
2								
3								
4		Bill of Labor				Master Production Schedule		
5		Part				Period		
6	WC	1	2		Part	1	2	3
7	1	2	4		1	100	200	300
8	2	3	5		2	200	400	600
9	3	8	3					
10								
11								
12				Rough-Cut Capacity Plan				
13				Period				
14			WC	1	2	3		
15			1	1000				
16			2					
17			3					
18								
19								
20								

FIGURE 3A.4 THE FINAL RESULT

	A	B	C	D	E	F	G	H
1								
2								
3								
4		Bill of Labor				Master Production Schedule		
5		Part				Period		
6	WC	1	2		Part	1	2	3
7	1	2	4		1	100	200	300
8	2	3	5		2	200	400	600
9	3	8	3					
10								
11								
12				Rough-Cut Capacity Plan				
13				Period				
14			WC	1	2	3		
15			1	1000	2000	3000		
16			2	1300	2600	3900		
17			3	1400	2800	4200		
18								
19								
20								

APPENDIX 3B
Simulation Results

This appendix contains the output files from the simulation runs discussed in Chapter 3. All runs were made in the GEMS language. GEMS, an acronym for generalized manufacturing simulator, is a powerful language for generalized simulations and especially for manufacturing simulations.

SIMULATION #1

The first set of output is the case with deterministic arrivals and service completions.

General Information on the Run
Run Name: Deterministic case
This run completed at: 100000.0000000
The maximum number of entries in the lists was   5

Time and Associated Network Cost Statistics   This section shows mean, standard deviation, and minimum and maximum values of time in the entire system.

BOX NUM.	STAT. TYPE	NO. OF OBS.	MEAN	STD. DEV.	MIN.	MAX.
3	INTV	5000	199.900	3.161	100.000	200.000

Queue Box Statistics   This section presents statistics on the queue length, waiting time, etc.

QUE. NUM.	STAT. TYPE	MEAN	STD. DEV.	MIN. MEAN	MAX. MEAN
2	NUMB BUSY SERVER	1.000	.000	1.000	1.000
2	QUEUE LENGTH	1.000	.000	1.000	1.000
2	WAITING TIME	99.900	.035	99.900	99.900
2	BUSY %	100.000	.000	100.000	100.000
2	ENTITIES PASSED	1000.000	.000	1000.000	1000.000
2	MAX QUEUE LENGTH	2.000	.000	2.000	2.000
2	NO. NONZERO WAIT	1000.000	.000	1000.000	1000.000

FINAL STATUS: Q-LENGTH   0 IDLE SERVERS   0

SIMULATION #2

This set of results has the arrival rate equal to the service rate (one arrival and one service completed every 100 time units on the average) with the arrival rate distributed uniformly (50,150) and the service rate normally distributed having a mean of 100 and a standard deviation of 15.

General Information on the Run

Run Name: Arrivals uniform [50,150], service normal [100,15]
This run completed at: 100835.1000000
The maximum number of entries in the lists was   16

Time and Associated Network Cost Statistics

BOX NUM.	STAT. TYPE	NO. OF OBS.	MEAN	STD. DEV.	MIN.	MAX.
3	INTV	5000	690.511	402.302	60.244	1704.582

Queue Box Statistics

QUE. NUM.	STAT. TYPE	MEAN	STD. DEV. MEAN	MIN. MEAN	MAX.
2	NUMB BUSY SERVER	.996	.005	.988	1.000
2	QUEUE LENGTH	5.903	1.466	3.824	7.911
2	WAITING TIME	589.592	144.768	381.187	783.819
2	BUSY %	99.597	.451	98.819	100.000
2	ENTITIES PASSED	1000.000	.000	1000.000	1000.000

2	MAX QUEUE				
	LENGTH	13.200	3.271	9.000	18.000
2	NO. NONZERO				
	WAIT	989.200	16.903	967.000	1008.000

FINAL STATUS: Q-LENGTH   4 IDLE SERVERS   0

This segment presents the queue length at stated times. This particular chart is based on five independent simulations, each having 1,000 entities pass through the queue. Note the tendency of the queue to lengthen as time passes.

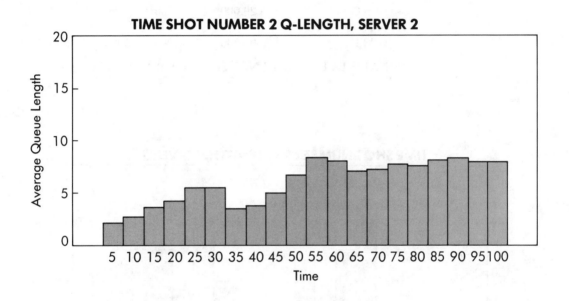

TIME SHOT NUMBER 2 Q-LENGTH, SERVER 2

SIMULATION #3

The study continues with one simulation having 5,000 entities pass to see if the trend toward longer queues continues.

General Information on the Run
    Run Name: Arrivals uniform [50,150], service normal [100,15]
    This run completed at: 502298.2000000
    The maximum number of entries in the lists was   33

Time and Associated Network Cost Statistics

BOX NUM.	STAT. TYPE	NO. OF OBS.	MEAN	STD. DEV.	MIN.	MAX.
3	INTV	5000	1887.153	648.281	81.736	3069.227

Queue Box Statistics

QUE. NUM.	STAT. TYPE	MEAN	STD. DEV. OBS.	MIN. OBS.	MAX.
2	NUMB BUSY SERVER	1.000	.022	.000	1.000
2	QUEUE LENGTH	17.822	6.449	.000	29.000
2	WAITING TIME	1783.947	649.629	.000	2956.102
2	BUSY %	99.952	.000	99.952	99.952
2	ENTITIES PASSED	5000.000	.000	5000.000	5000.000
2	MAX QUEUE LENGTH	29.000	.000	29.000	29.000
2	NO. NONZERO WAIT	5008.000	.000	5008.000	5008.000

FINAL STATUS: Q-LENGTH 17 IDLE SERVERS 0

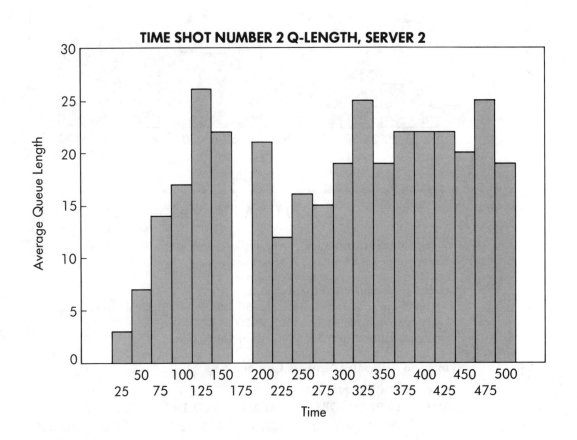

TIME SHOT NUMBER 2 Q-LENGTH, SERVER 2

Note that the queue length is much longer than in the case in which 1,000 entities were processed. However, there seems to be a leveling off of the queue length at approximately 20 entities. A longer run is indicated.

SIMULATION #4

In this run the number of entities processed is increased to 20,000.

General Information on the Run

Run Name: Arrivals uniform [50,150] service normal [100,15]
This run completed at: 2001306.0000000
The maximum number of entries in the lists was   73

Time and Associated Network Cost Statistics

BOX NUM.	STAT. TYPE	NO. OF OBS.	MEAN	STD. DEV.	MIN.	MAX.
3	INTV	20000	2932.489	1616.549	81.736	6826.875

Queue Box Statistics

QUE. NUM.	STAT. TYPE	MEAN	STD. DEV. OBS.	MIN. OBS.	MAX.
2	NUMB BUSY SERVER	1.000	.011	.000	1.000
2	QUEUE LENGTH	28.408	16.275	.000	69.000
2	WAITING TIME	2833.424	1617.627	.000	6737.000
2	BUSY %	99.988	.000	99.988	99.988
2	ENTITIES PASSED	20000.000	.000	20000.000	20000.000
2	MAX QUEUE LENGTH	69.000	.000	69.000	69.000
2	NO. NONZERO WAIT	20055.000	.000	20055.000	20055.000

FINAL STATUS: Q-LENGTH   64 IDLE SERVERS   0

This run establishes that the average queue length does not level off at 20, as suggested by the previous run, but continues to grow, presumably to infinity.

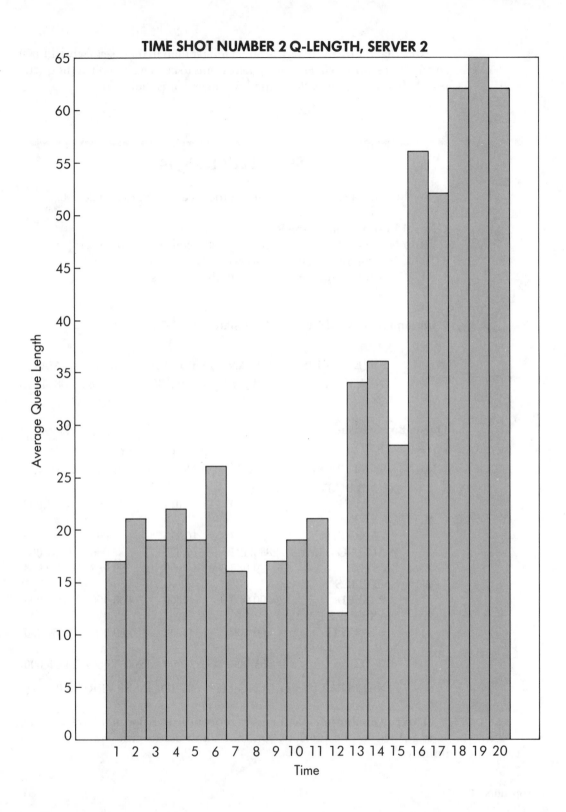

SIMULATION #5

In this run the arrival rate is modified to be uniform on (51,151) to achieve approximately 99 percent utilization of the server. The run is a single pass with 20,000 entities to ensure that the queue length does not continue to grow.

General Information on the Run
Run Name: Service normal, 99% server utilization
This run completed at: 2015489.0000000
The maximum number of entries in the lists was   33

Time and Associated Network Cost Statistics

BOX NUM.	STAT. TYPE	NO. OF OBS.	MEAN	STD. DEV.	MIN.	MAX.
3	INTV	20000	696.145	551.546	52.500	2987.500

Queue Box Statistics

QUE. NUM.	STAT. TYPE	MEAN	STD. DEV.	MIN. OBS.	MAX. OBS.
2	NUMB BUSY SERVER	.993	.084	.000	1.000
2	QUEUE LENGTH	5.916	5.506	.000	29.000
2	WAITING TIME	596.010	551.163	.000	2878.375
2	BUSY %	99.284	.000	99.284	99.284
2	ENTITIES PASSED	20000.000	.000	20000.000	20000.000
2	MAX QUEUE LENGTH	29.000	.000	29.000	29.000
2	NO. NONZERO WAIT	19401.000	.000	19401.000	19401.000

FINAL STATUS: Q-LENGTH   5 IDLE SERVERS   0

Note from the time shot that although the queue does not continue to grow indefinitely, it is subject to large fluctuations.

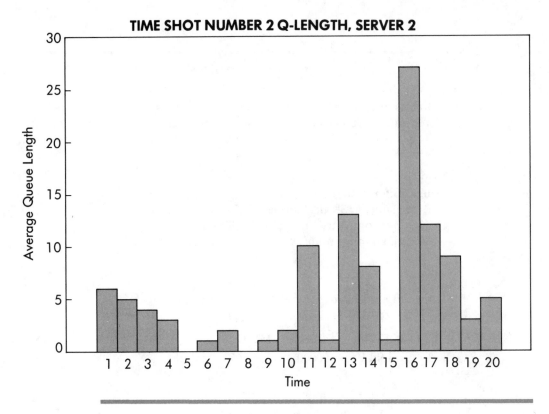

TIME SHOT NUMBER 2 Q-LENGTH, SERVER 2

SIMULATION #6

In this run the arrival rate is set uniform on (52,152) to achieve approximately 98 percent utilization. The simulation has 20,000 entities processed in 1 run.

General Information on the Run
Run Name: Service normal, 98% server utilization
This run completed at: 2035219.0000000
The maximum number of entries in the lists was   24

Time and Associated Network Cost Statistics

BOX NUM.	STAT. TYPE	NO. OF OBS.	MEAN	STD. DEV.	MIN.	MAX.
3	INTV	20000	398.732	331.694	52.500	2039.500

Queue Box Statistics

QUE. NUM.	STAT. TYPE	MEAN	STD. DEV. OBS.	MIN. OBS.	MAX.
2	NUMB BUSY SERVER	.983	.128	.000	1.000

2	QUEUE				
	LENGTH	2.935	3.315	.000	20.000
2	WAITING TIME	298.671	331.229	.000	1930.375
2	BUSY %	98.322	.000	98.322	98.322
2	ENTITIES				
	PASSED	20000.000	.000	20000.000	20000.000
2	MAX QUEUE				
	LENGTH	20.000	.000	20.000	20.000
2	NO. NONZERO				
	WAIT	18563.000	.000	18563.000	18563.000

FINAL STATUS: Q-LENGTH   2 IDLE SERVERS   0

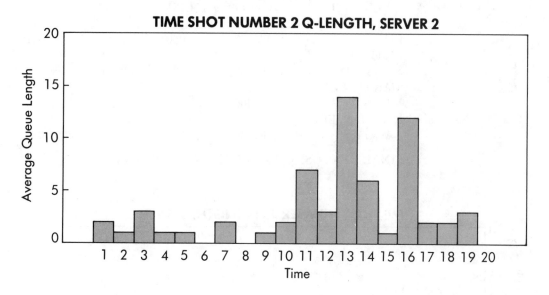

TIME SHOT NUMBER 2 Q-LENGTH, SERVER 2

Note that although average queue length has been cut in half by reducing the utilization from 99 percent to 98 percent, the queue length continues to fluctuate wildly. The maximum length observed by a time shot was 14, but the maximum queue length obtained was 20.

SIMULATION #7

General Information on the Run
    Run Name: Service normal, 95% server utilization
    This run completed at: 2094892.0000000
    The maximum number of entries in the lists was   12

Time and Associated Network Cost Statistics

BOX NUM.	STAT. TYPE	NO. OF OBS.	MEAN	STD. DEV.	MIN.	MAX.
3	INTV	20000	196.150	110.194	52.500	807.500

Queue Box Statistics

QUE. NUM.	STAT. TYPE	MEAN	STD. DEV. OBS.	MIN. OBS.	MAX.
2	NUMB BUSY SERVER	.955	.207	.000	1.000
2	QUEUE LENGTH	.917	1.135	.000	8.000
2	WAITING TIME	96.094	109.137	.000	706.375
2	BUSY %	95.522	.000	95.522	95.522
2	ENTITIES PASSED	20000.000	.000	20000.000	20000.000
2	MAX QUEUE LENGTH	8.000	.000	8.000	8.000
2	NO. NONZERO WAIT	16294.000	.000	16294.000	16294.000

FINAL STATUS: Q-LENGTH　　0　IDLE SERVERS　　0

TIME SHOT NUMBER 2 Q-LENGTH, SERVER 2

It is noteworthy that at 95 percent utilization the queue length seems to be very stable. Very rarely does the number waiting exceed 1.

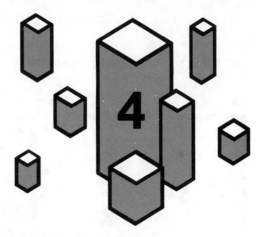

Capacity Requirements Planning

The *APICS Dictionary* (1) defines capacity requirements planning (CRP) as "the function of establishing, measuring, and adjusting limits or levels of capacity. . . . the process of determining how much labor and machine resources are required to accomplish the tasks of production. Open shop orders, and planned orders in the MRP system, are input to CRP, which 'translates' these orders into hours of work by work center by time period."

Often associated with capacity requirements planning is a **closed-loop MRP** system, which not only incorporates planning and execution functions but also provides for feedback from the execution functions so that planning can be kept valid at all times. A closed-loop MRP system is diagrammed in Figure 4.1. Note that the discussion which follows assumes the existence of a closed-loop MRP system.

Capacity requirements planning is a detailed comparison of the material requirements plan (MRP) and orders already in progress with available capacity. CRP verifies that there is sufficient capacity to handle orders due to be released. This action generally constitutes a final acceptance of the master production schedule (MPS). If the MPS is accepted, CRP determines the load that is expected at each work center during each time period. (Chapter 6 discusses a case in which detailed shop simulation is performed prior to MPS acceptance.)

CRP LOGIC

CRP is conceptually very simple. The MPS is exploded via the MRP system. **Planned order** releases are taken from the MRP system and used to per-

FIGURE 4.1   CLOSED-LOOP MRP

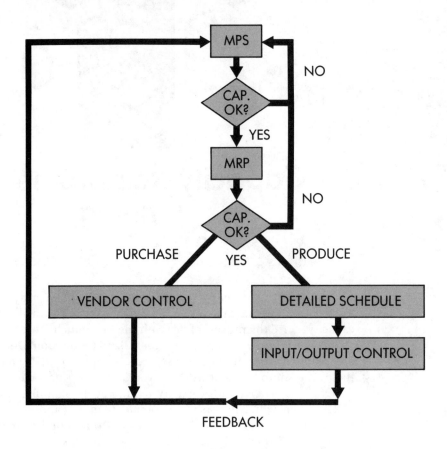

form a deterministic simulation which uses lead-time offsets to determine the time at which each order is processed at each work center. The deterministic simulation continues by including those jobs already released to the shop floor. From this, a machine load report is produced. The machine load report for each work center is compared to capacity available at that center.

The mechanics of CRP become quite tedious even for small shops. An example such as War Eagle Hoists, with a total of about 500 part numbers, is too large to present in detail without obscuring the overall picture. Therefore a hypothetical company using only four parts and three work centers has been created. While this example is quite small, it nevertheless suffices to demonstrate the mechanics of CRP and illustrate how CRP results can have important differences from those obtained through rough-cut capacity planning (RCCP).

EXAMPLE 4.1:
CRP MECHANICS AND RESULTS

Standard Widgets makes one widget from a pair of identical subassemblies, which in turn are made from two sets of components. The bill of material for a widget is shown in Table 4.1. The item master record for each of the four parts is shown in Table 4.2. The routing for each of the four parts is shown in Table 4.3. The work center master files are shown in Table 4.4. The master production schedule for finished widgets is shown in Table 4.5.

Standard Widgets begins its planning process by performing rough-cut capacity planning for all three work centers. The results of these rough-cut calculations are shown in graphical and tabular form in Figure 4.2. The calculations used to derive Figure 4.2 are given in Appendix 4A.

Based on these rough-cut results, Marsha Abrams, production planner for Standard Widgets, decides that the production plan is reasonable and orders the material requirements planning system to be run. Marsha notes that slight overloads exist in some weeks but feels that these will be offset by underloads in other weeks. The MRP system uses the data given in Tables 4.1 through 4.5 to produce the MRP report shown in Table 4.6. The actual material requirements plan contains 12 periods, but only 7 periods are shown in the table.

TABLE 4.1   BILL OF MATERIAL FOR A WIDGET
(effective date 1/1/88)

LEVEL	PART	QTY/PARENT	DESCRIPTION
0	100	1	Finished Widget
1	110	2	Subassembly
2	121	3	Component A
2	122	5	Component B

TABLE 4.2   ITEM MASTER RECORD FILES FOR STANDARD WIDGETS

PART NUMBER	ORDER QUANTITY	ON HAND	ON ORDER	DUE DATE	LEAD TIME (weeks)	ALLOCATED
100	LFL	0	250	7/3	1	0
110	400	500	400	7/10	2	0
121	2,400	1,500	2,400	7/10	3	0
122	6,000	2,500	6,000	7/10	4	0

TABLE 4.3 ROUTING FILES FOR STANDARD WIDGETS

WORK CENTER	SETUP TIME/LOT		RUN TIME/PIECE
		Part 100	
WC1	30		2.5
		Part 110	
WC2	10		0.75
WC1	15		0.5
		Part 121	
WC3	15		0.3
WC1	25		0.25
WC2	15		0.25
		Part 122	
WC2	25		0.75
WC3	30		0.15
WC1	75		0.5
WC3	30		0.35
		Time in minutes	

TABLE 4.4 WORK CENTER MASTER FILES, STANDARD WIDGETS

WORK CENTER	MINUTES AVAILABLE	UTILIZATION	EFFICIENCY	PLANNED QUEUE (days)
WC1	2,400	100%	100%	4
WC2	2,400	100%	100%	4
WC3	2,400	100%	100%	4

TABLE 4.5 MASTER PRODUCTION SCHEDULE FOR FINISHED WIDGETS

	WEEK											
	1	2	3	4	5	6	7	8	9	10	11	12
Quantity	250	200	250	150	200	300	150	250	200	200	250	200

FIGURE 4.2 ROUGH-CUT CAPACITY REQUIREMENTS, STANDARD WIDGETS

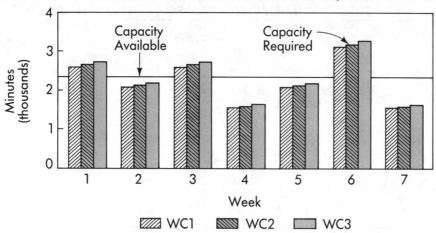

| WORK CENTER | | | | WEEK | | | | AVERAGE |
	1	2	3	4	5	6	7	MINUTES
WC1	2,603	2,083	2,603	1,562	2,083	3,124	1,562	2,231
WC2	2,657	2,126	2,657	1,594	2,126	3,189	1,594	2,278
WC3	2,735	2,188	2,735	1,641	2,188	3,281	1,641	2,344

Capacity required in minutes

The netting logic used in Table 4.6 will now be briefly reviewed.* The Gross Requirements row for part 100 is taken from the MPS, Table 4.5. All other Gross Requirements rows are found by multiplying the Planned Releases of the parent item by the quantity of the component per parent. The Scheduled Receipts row is for orders that have already been released. These data are taken from the item master record, Table 4.2. Projected On Hand in week 0 is the actual On Hand in the item master record. Projected On Hand in all subsequent weeks is found by taking the previous On Hand plus Scheduled Receipts minus Gross Requirements. If the Projected On Hand is below 0, a Net Requirement exists which is equal to the absolute value of the Projected On Hand (the Net Requirement is computed in a different manner if safety stock is greater than 0). Whenever the Net Requirement is greater than 0, a Planned Receipt is created for the order quantity or the Net Requirement, whichever is greater. Revised On Hand is Projected On Hand plus Planned

* Those not familiar with MRP netting logic are referred to Joseph Orlicky, *Material Requirements Planning* (New York: McGraw-Hill Book Co., 1976), ch. 4.

TABLE 4.6 MATERIAL REQUIREMENTS PLAN FOR STANDARD WIDGETS

				PERIOD				
	0	1	2	3	4	5	6	7

PART 100 — Fixed Period Ordering, Periods to Order: 1 — Lead Time: 1

	0	1	2	3	4	5	6	7
Gross Requirements		250	200	250	150	200	300	150
Scheduled Receipts		250						
Projected on Hand	0	0	−200	−250	−150	−200	−300	−150
Net Requirements		0	200	250	150	200	300	150
Planned Receipts		0	200	250	150	200	300	150
Revised On Hand	0	0	0	0	0	0	0	0
Planned Releases		200	250	150	200	300	150	250

PART 110 — Fixed Quantity Ordering, Quantity to Order: 400 — Lead Time: 2

	0	1	2	3	4	5	6	7
Gross Requirements		400	500	300	400	600	300	500
Scheduled Receipts		400						
Projected on Hand	500	100	0	−300	−300	−500	−300	−400
Net Requirements		0	0	300	300	500	300	400
Planned Receipts		0	0	400	400	500	400	400
Revised On Hand	500	100	0	100	100	0	100	0
Planned Releases		400	400	500	400	400	400	400

PART 121 — Fixed Quantity Ordering, Quantity to Order: 2,400 — Lead Time: 3

	0	1	2	3	4	5	6	7
Gross Requirements		1,200	1,200	1,500	1,200	1,200	1,200	1,200
Scheduled Receipts		2,400						
Projected on Hand	1,500	300	1,500	0	−1,200	0	−1,200	0
Net Requirements		0	0	0	1,200	0	1,200	0
Planned Receipts		0	0	0	2,400	0	2,400	0
Revised On Hand	1,500	300	1,500	0	1,200	0	1,200	0
Planned Releases		2,400	0	2,400	0	2,400	2,400	0

PART 122 — Fixed Quantity Ordering, Quantity to Order: 6,000 — Lead Time: 4

	0	1	2	3	4	5	6	7
Gross Requirements		2,000	2,000	2,500	2,000	2,000	2,000	2,000
Scheduled Receipts		6,000						
Projected on Hand	2,500	500	4,500	2,000	0	−2,000	2,000	0
Net Requirements		0	0	0	0	2,000	0	0
Planned Receipts		0	0	0	0	6,000	0	0
Revised On Hand	2,500	500	4,500	2,000	0	4,000	2,000	0
Planned Releases		6,000	0	0	6,000	0	0	0

Receipts. (Most MRP systems do not have a Revised On Hand row. This row exists in Standard Widgets' system because Standard Widgets uses Lotus 1-2-3 to do the MRP netting and the row is required for Lotus 1-2-3 to work properly.) Planned Releases are found by offsetting Planned Receipts by the appropriate lead time.

The set of Planned Releases from MRP is needed to complete CRP. These Planned Releases have been extracted from Table 4.6 and summarized to create Table 4.7.

The effect of batch production is evident in Table 4.7. Note that parts 121 and 122 have an irregular production schedule, with nothing produced in some weeks and a large batch released in other weeks. This "lumpiness" is not considered in the process of rough-cut capacity planning. Note that the MPS, Table 4.5, does not exhibit it. Because of this lumpiness, the actual work load which Standard Widgets is placing on the shop may be much more irregular than that predicted by RCCP in Figure 4.2. Even when RCCP has been properly completed, CRP is needed to determine whether batching orders for components has created an uneven flow of work.

TABLE 4.7   PLANNED ORDER RELEASES, STANDARD WIDGETS

PART	WEEK						
	1	2	3	4	5	6	7
100	200	250	150	200	300	150	250
110	400	400	500	400	400	400	400
121	2,400	0	2,400	0	2,400	2,400	0
122	6,000	0	0	6,000	0	0	0

CRP Computation for Example 4.1

Computation of the capacity requirements plan requires separate calculations of setup time and run time requirements. This section discusses calculation of setup time and then of run time for planned order releases, then the inclusion of orders already on the shop floor, and ends with a presentation of the CRP machine load report. The discussion presented here is a generic discussion of CRP computation principles. It is not intended to represent the algorithm actually used by any commercial CRP system. There may be algorithms which computationally are much more efficient than that presented here. This discussion is intended to present an approach which is both theoretically sound and, it is hoped, easily understood.

Table 4.8 shows setup time matrices for each of the three work centers, created directly from the planned order releases of the MRP system. Each operation has a lead time of one week. Thus, if a job due to be released in week 3 has three operations, setup for operation 1 is shown in week 4, setup for operation 2 is shown in week 5, and setup for operation 3 is shown in week 6.

For a specific example, consider part 122. Table 4.7 shows that an order for 6,000 part 122's is to be released in week 1. From the routing file, Table 4.3, one finds that part 122 is routed to work center 2, then to 3, then to 1, and finally back to 3. Each operation has a one-week planned lead time. In the setup matrix for WC2 one finds a setup in week 1. In the setup matrix for WC3 one finds setups in weeks 2 and 4. In the setup matrix for WC1 one finds a setup in week 3. The setup times at each station agree with the data given in Table 4.3, the routing file. Each planned release in Table 4.7 yields a similar set of setup requirements in Table 4.8.

The run time matrices in Table 4.9 are computed in a similar fashion except that the times are found by multiplying the lot size by the run time per piece shown in Table 4.3.

TABLE 4.8 SETUP TIME MATRICES FOR STANDARD WIDGETS

PART	1	2	3	4	5	6	7
WC1							
100	30	30	30	30	30	30	30
110	0	15	15	15	15	15	15
121	0	25	0	25	0	25	25
122	0	0	75	0	0	75	0
Total	**30**	**70**	**120**	**70**	**45**	**145**	**30**
WC2							
100	0	0	0	0	0	0	0
110	10	10	10	10	10	10	10
121	0	0	15	0	15	0	15
122	25	0	0	25	0	0	0
Total	**35**	**10**	**25**	**35**	**25**	**10**	**25**
WC3							
100	0	0	0	0	0	0	0
110	0	0	0	0	0	0	0
121	15	0	15	0	15	15	0
122	0	30	0	30	30	0	30
Total	**15**	**30**	**15**	**30**	**45**	**15**	**30**

Time in minutes

TABLE 4.9 RUN TIME MATRICES FOR STANDARD WIDGETS

PART	WEEK						
	1	2	3	4	5	6	7
WC1							
100	500	625	375	500	750	375	625
110	0	200	200	250	200	200	200
121	0	600	0	600	0	600	600
122	0	0	3,000	0	0	3,000	0
Total	**500**	**1,425**	**5,000**	**1,350**	**950**	**4,175**	**1,425**
WC2							
100	0	0	0	0	0	0	0
110	300	300	375	300	300	300	300
121	0	0	600	0	600	0	600
122	4,500	0	0	4,500	0	0	0
Total	**4,800**	**300**	**975**	**4,800**	**900**	**300**	**900**
WC3							
100	0	0	0	0	0	0	0
110	0	0	0	0	0	0	0
121	600	0	600	0	600	600	0
122	0	900	0	2,100	900	0	2,100
Total	**600**	**900**	**600**	**2,100**	**1,500**	**600**	**2,100**

Time in minutes

The totals from each setup time and run time matrix can now be extracted and setup time added to run time at each work center to produce capacity required by the planned order releases from the MRP system, Table 4.10.

One must now account for orders released to the shop. According to Table 4.2, four orders have been released to the shop: (1) an order for part 100, quan-

TABLE 4.10 CAPACITY REQUIREMENTS OF PLANNED RELEASES

WORK CENTER	WEEK						
	1	2	3	4	5	6	7
WC1	530	1,495	3,695	1,420	995	4,320	1,495
WC2	4,835	310	1,000	4,835	925	310	925
WC3	615	930	615	2,130	1,545	615	2,130

Capacity required in minutes

tity 250, due week 1; (2) an order for part 110, quantity 400, due week 2; (3) an order for part 121, quantity 2,400, due week 2; and (4) an order for part 122, quantity 6,000, due week 2. These four orders are all on schedule, i.e., the number of operations remaining to be completed is equal to the number of weeks until due. The information on the location of the jobs in the shop has been taken from a shop floor control report which is not shown in any table in this chapter. Such information is always available in a closed-loop MRP system. Part 100 has one operation to be completed, the other three orders have two operations (the final two) to be completed. From this information and information contained in the routing file, Table 4.11 is created.

Table 4.11 illustrates an alternate algorithm for producing capacity requirements, that of determining total operation time by

$$Operation\ time\ =\ \frac{Setup\ time\ per\ lot}{Average\ lot\ size}\ +\ Run\ time\ per\ piece \qquad (4.1)$$

and placing the operation time in the appropriate weekly time bucket. The data from Table 4.11 may now be collected by work center by week to produce Table 4.12.

The capacity required by the planned order releases is now added to the capacity required by orders already released to the shop to produce the capacity requirements plan, portrayed in graphical and tabular form in Figure 4.3.

TABLE 4.11   CAPACITY REQUIRED BY RELEASED ORDERS

PART	WORK CENTER	WEEK	SETUP TIME	RUN TIME CALCULATION	RUN TIME	TOTAL TIME
100	WC1	1	30	250 × 2.5	625	655
110	WC2	1	10	400 × 0.75	300	310
110	WC1	2	15	400 × 0.5	200	215
121	WC1	1	25	2,400 × 0.25	600	625
121	WC2	2	15	2,400 × 0.25	600	615
122	WC1	1	75	6,000 × 0.5	3,000	3,075
122	WC3	2	30	6,000 × 0.35	2,100	2,130

Capacity required in minutes

Multiweek Operation Lead Times

Example 4.1 contains one important simplification which needs to be discussed. All operation lead times in Example 4.1 are one week. How are operations which have a lead time exceeding one week treated? Is all of the load placed in the first week? The last week? Split between weeks? According to the

TABLE 4.12   RELEASED ORDER CAPACITY REQUIREMENTS SUMMARY

WORK CENTER	WEEK 1	2
WC1	4,350	215
WC2	310	615
WC3	0	2,130
	Capacity required in minutes	

FIGURE 4.3   CAPACITY REQUIREMENTS PLAN FOR STANDARD WIDGETS

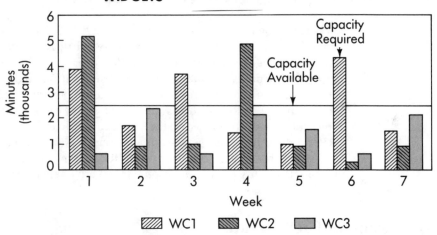

WORK CENTER	WEEK 1	2	3	4	5	6	7
WC1	4,800	1,710	3,695	1,420	995	4,320	1,495
WC2	5,145	925	1,000	4,835	925	310	925
WC3	615	3,060	615	2,130	1,545	615	2,130
	Capacity required in minutes						

IBM system COPICS (3), "Each profile shows the capacity required, based on the assumption that every job is done as late as possible while order due dates are met. The typical profile is highly variable. This type of report shows where and when additional capacity is required to meet the work loads. Furthermore, the cumulative load over all periods can be compared to the cumulative capacity, to determine whether the capacity is adequate on the average." In other words, the capacity is always shown in the last time bucket for a multiple-week lead time. Even though the load for that single week may then be too high, a decision on the validity of the schedule is based on cumulative capacity. The procedure of loading the capacity into the last bucket ensures that cumulative capacity requirements are never exaggerated.

The procedure of placing in the last week all load associated with an order having a multiweek lead time for a single operation is also consistent with the observation that most jobs spend 90 percent of the operation lead time in queue waiting for service and about 10 percent of the lead time in actual service. The move to the next operation usually occurs shortly after the completion of the operation.

Cumulative Capacity Versus Average Capacity

As was shown in the previous section, COPICS discusses the interpretation of CRP in terms of *cumulative capacity*, while RCCP is generally interpreted in terms of average capacity. Why does this difference exist? Very simply, RCCP does not contain sufficient information on the *timing* of order releases for component items to enable accurate portrayal of cumulative capacity required. If RCCP shows sufficient average capacity and the load pattern is not grossly overloaded on the front end, sufficient capacity is presumed. CRP, on the other hand, is based on a deterministic simulation of the shop using exact order release data from the MRP system. If cumulative capacity is inadequate for any period, then some job(s) are likely to be tardy.

Discussion of CRP Results

Examination of Figure 4.3 reveals an interesting pattern. Work centers 1 and 2 are overloaded in week 1. Work center 1 is again overloaded in week 3, work center 2 is overloaded in week 4, and work center 1 is overloaded once more in week 6. These loads as often as not approach 200 percent of the capacity of the work center. Note that there is no single bottleneck at Standard Widgets. Rather, the bottleneck shifts between work center 1 and work center 2, which are alternately overloaded and underloaded. This problem, known as a "floating bottleneck," leads to job tardiness, since jobs wait for much longer than the planned queue time behind the overloaded station.

The problem was not at all evident in RCCP. One might blame failure to discover the problem on a poor choice of RCCP technique and conclude that a better RCCP technique, such as the resource profile approach, would reveal the problem. Let's explore that notion. Figure 4.4 shows in graphical and tabular form a rough-cut machine load report using resource profiles created using the software accompanying the Instructor's Manual. One modification required was that the critical path lead time for Standard Widgets was reduced from 7 weeks to 5 weeks (by overlapping two operations).

The resource profile approach exhibits essentially the same pattern found by the bill of labor approach. An examination of Figure 4.5, in which the resource profile results are converted to cumulative resource requirements and availability, reveals no major capacity shortages. In this figure the first, third, and fifth bars of each set represent the cumulative capacity required at work centers 1, 2, and 3, respectively, while the second, fourth, and sixth bars represent the corresponding capacity available.

FIGURE 4.4   ROUGH-CUT MACHINE LOAD REPORT USING RE-SOURCE PROFILES, STANDARD WIDGETS

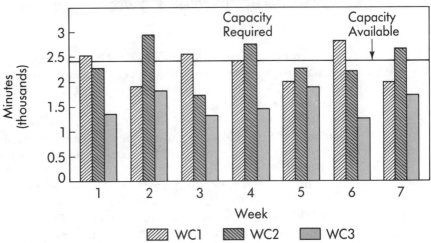

WORK CENTER	WEEKS						
	1	2	3	4	5	6	7
WC1	2,533	1,905	2,538	2,423	1,995	2,810	1,983
WC2	2,276	2,939	1,729	2,744	2,258	2,197	2,647
WC3	1,360	1,820	1,320	1,460	1,880	1,260	1,720
	Capacity required in minutes						

FIGURE 4.5 CUMULATIVE CAPACITY REQUIRED VS. AVAILABLE

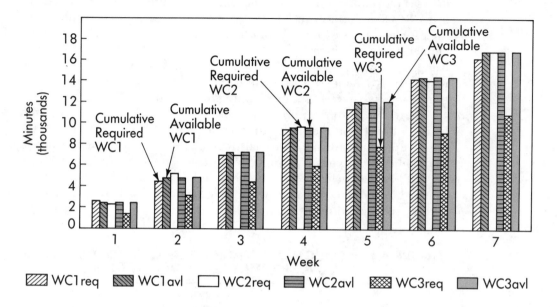

By contrast, Figure 4.6, which uses CRP to make the same comparison of capacity required to cumulative capacity available, clearly exhibits several shortages. These shortages are apparent in work center 1 in weeks 1, 2, 3, 4, 6, and 7 and for work center 2 in weeks 1, 2, 4, and 5. The difference between CRP and RCCP can be explained in part by the inclusion of released orders to CRP but not in RCCP. However, most of the difference is due to lumpiness in the order release schedule which CRP detects but RCCP does not.

Note that the resource profile approach does not detect the lumpiness any more than the bill of labor approach did. This is because the resource profile approach implicitly assumes a lot-for-lot policy of lot sizing, whereas Standard Widgets actually uses a fixed order quantity. The lumpiness is created by the large batch size, not simply by the lead time offset.

A great deal of effort has been expended in creating dispatching rules, i.e., rules to select which job to perform next from a queue awaiting service, in attempts to alleviate the problems illustrated in Figure 4.6. As will be shown in Chapter 7, the problem can be alleviated only slightly by the use of sophisticated dispatching techniques. As Figure 4.6 shows, the problem of floating bottlenecks arises primarily from the lumpy order-release pattern, which in turn arises from processing large batches of orders.

Ironically, the solution to floating bottlenecks was found not by those directly involved with research on shop dispatching but rather by the Japanese, who were working on another problem—lack of cash to fund large batches of inventory. The solution is to reduce the batch size to eliminate the lumpiness.

FIGURE 4.6   CUMULATIVE CAPACITY REQUIRED VS. AVAILABLE BASED ON CRP

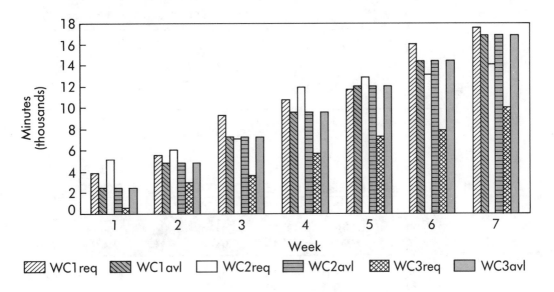

Large batches exist because of long setup times, so smaller batch sizes call for shorter setup times. Both Hall (2) and Schonberger (5) discuss procedures to reduce setup times. Most American companies which have attempted to reduce setup times have discovered that setup times can be reduced by 75 percent without investing money in reconfiguring machines or tools. All that is needed is to do what can be done while the machine is still running and to make sure all tools needed to complete the setup are positioned at the work center before the setup process begins.

EXAMPLE 4.2.: THE EFFECT OF REDUCING BATCH SIZES

This example explores the effect of reducing batch sizes. The example is created by taking Example 4.1 and placing all parts on a lot-for-lot ordering policy. In order to retain approximately the same total setup time, it is assumed that Standard Widgets has reduced all setup times by 50 percent. As previously stated, setup time reductions up to 75 percent have been achieved with little effort in many American companies. The data for Standard Widgets appeared earlier in the chapter. For convenience they are reproduced here, with changes noted, as Tables 4.13 through 4.17. Table 4.18 shows the revised material requirements plan for Standard Widgets.

TABLE 4.13 BILL OF MATERIAL FOR A WIDGET*
(effective date 1/1/88)

LEVEL	PART	QTY/PARENT	DESCRIPTION
0	100	1	Finished Widget
1	110	2	Subassembly
2	121	3	Component A
2	122	5	Component B

*No change from Table 4.1.

TABLE 4.14 ITEM MASTER RECORD FILES FOR STANDARD WIDGETS*

PART NUMBER	ORDER QUANTITY	ON HAND	ON ORDER	DUE DATE	LEAD TIME (weeks)	ALLOCATED
100	LFL	0	250	7/3	1	0
110	LFL	500	400	7/10	2	0
121	LFL	1,500	1,200	7/10	3	0
			1,500	7/17	3	0
122	LFL	2,500	2,000	7/10	4	0
			2,000	7/17	4	0
			1,500	7/24	4	0

*Changed to reflect the lot-for-lot policy. The quantity on order is approximately equal to that shown in Table 4.2.

TABLE 4.15 ROUTING FILES FOR STANDARD WIDGETS*

WORK CENTER	SETUP TIME/LOT	RUN TIME/PIECE
Part 100		
WC1	.15	2.5
Part 110		
WC2	5	0.75
WC1	7.5	0.5
Part 121		
WC3	.7.5	0.3
WC1	.12.5	0.25
WC2	7.5	0.25

```
WC2 ...................... 12.5 ...................... 0.75
WC3 ...................... 15 ...................... 0.15
WC1 ...................... 37.5 ...................... 0.5
WC3 ...................... 15 ...................... 0.75
                                      Time in minutes
```

*Changed from Table 4.3 to reflect the 50 percent reduction in setup time.

TABLE 4.16   WORK CENTER MASTER FILES, STANDARD WIDGETS*

WORK CENTER	MINUTES AVAILABLE	UTILIZATION	EFFICIENCY	PLANNED QUEUE (days)
WC1 2,400	100%	100%	4
WC2 2,400	100%	100%	4
WC3 2,400	100%	100%	4

*No change from Table 4.4.

TABLE 4.17   MASTER PRODUCTION SCHEDULE FOR FINISHED WIDGETS*

	WEEK											
	1	2	3	4	5	6	7	8	9	10	11	12
Quantity	250	200	250	150	200	300	150	250	200	200	250	200

*No change from Table 4.5.

TABLE 4.18   MATERIAL REQUIREMENTS PLAN, STANDARD WIDGETS

	PERIOD							
	0	1	2	3	4	5	6	7
PART 100	Lot-for-Lot Ordering						Lead Time: 1	
Gross Requirements	0	250	200	250	150	200	300	150
Scheduled Receipts		250						
Projected on Hand	0	0	−200	−250	−150	−200	−300	−150
Net Requirements		0	200	250	150	200	300	150
Planned Receipts		0	200	250	150	200	300	150
Revised On Hand	0	0	0	0	0	0	0	0
Planned Releases		200	250	150	200	300	150	250

TABLE 4.18 (CONTINUED)

	PERIOD 0	1	2	3	4	5	6	7
PART 110 Lot-for-Lot Ordering						Lead Time: 2		
Gross Requirements		400	500	300	400	600	300	500
Scheduled Receipts			400					
Projected on Hand	500	100	0	−300	−400	−600	−300	−500
Net Requirements		0	0	300	400	600	300	500
Planned Receipts		0	0	300	400	600	300	500
Revised On Hand	500	100	0	0	0	0	0	0
Planned Releases		300	400	600	300	500	400	400
PART 121 Lot-for-Lot Ordering						Lead Time: 3		
Gross Requirements		900	1,200	1,800	900	1,500	1,200	1,200
Scheduled Receipts			2,400	1,200				
Projected on Hand	1,500	600	600	0	−900	−1,500	−1,200	−1,200
Net Requirements		0	0	0	900	1,500	1,200	1,200
Planned Receipts		0	0	0	900	1,500	1,200	1,200
Revised On Hand	1,500	600	600	0	0	0	0	0
Planned Releases		900	1,500	1,200	1,200	1,500	1,200	0
PART 122 Lot-for-Lot Ordering						Lead Time: 4		
Gross Requirements		1,500	2,000	3,000	1,500	2,500	2,000	2,000
Scheduled Receipts			2,000	2,000	1,500			
Projected on Hand	2,500	1,000	1,000	0	0	−2,500	−2,000	−2,000
Net Requirements		0	0	0	0	2,500	2,000	2,000
Planned Receipts		0	0	0	0	2,500	2,000	2,000
Revised On Hand	2,500	1,000	1,000	0	0	0	0	0
Planned Releases		2,500	2,000	2,000	2,500	2,000	0	0

Table 4.19 lists the planned releases which are data input into the CRP computation. Note that the lumpiness has disappeared. Note also that there are no orders for part 122 in week 6 or 7. This is a result of the end-of-horizon effect; i.e., because the master schedule goes out only 12 weeks and because there is a 7-week cumulative lead time, no orders for component B are generated beyond week 5. The same phenomenon explains the lack of an order for part 121 in week 7. There is a 6-week cumulative lead time from the time the order for part 121 is released until a finished widget is produced. This end-of-

TABLE 4.19   PLANNED ORDER RELEASES FOR STANDARD WIDGETS

PART	1	2	3	WEEK 4	5	6	7
100	200	250	150	200	300	150	250
110	300	400	600	300	500	400	400
121	900	1,500	1,200	1,200	1,500	1,200	0
122	2,500	2,000	2,000	2,500	2,000	0	0

horizon effect is unavoidable and is good reason to have as long a horizon for the MPS as forecast accuracy permits.

Figure 4.7 shows the standard CRP report for Example 4.2—the capacity required by planned orders, by released orders, and their sum (the CRP machine load report). Figure 4.8 shows the cumulative CRP report—cumulative capacity available and cumulative capacity required.

It is evident from Figure 4.7 that the lumpiness problem has been resolved by going from large batches to smaller batches. The entire planning process is made simpler if setup times are reduced to make lot-for-lot ordering economically feasible. Figure 4.8 shows that Standard Widgets seems to have adequate capacity for the long run. There is a slight capacity shortfall in the early weeks for work center 1, but the problem of a floating bottleneck, evidenced in Example 4.1, has disappeared entirely.

SUMMARY OF CRP

The primary mission of CRP is to determine that there is adequate cumulative capacity to perform to schedule, taking into account earliest possible start dates where it is necessary to perform some work early, and overtime and alternative routings where overloads exist. If adequate capacity cannot be established, the master production schedule must be modified.

Let's look again at the definition of CRP that opened this chapter: "the process of determining how much labor and machine resources are required to accomplish the tasks of production. Open shop orders, and planned orders in the MRP system, are input to CRP, which 'translates' these orders into hours of work by work center by time period." In order to complete the capacity requirements plan, one must perform either backward scheduling from the due date or forward scheduling from the release date for every released order in the shop and for every planned release in the MRP system.

FIGURE 4.7 STANDARD CRP REPORT FOR STANDARD WIDGETS (LOT-FOR-LOT ORDERING)

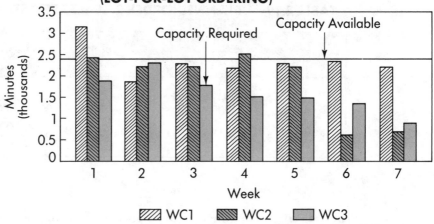

WORK CENTER	1	2	3	4	5	6	7
Capacity Required by Planned Releases							
WC1	515	1,035	2,273	2,173	2,273	2,323	2,198
WC2	2,118	1,818	2,200	2,500	2,200	613	688
WC3	233	773	623	1,513	1,488	1,338	890
Capacity Required by Released Orders							
WC1	2,645	825	0	0	0	0	0
WC2	315	390	0	0	0	0	0
WC3	1,660	1,530	1,155	0	0	0	0
Capacity Requirements Plan							
WC1	3,160	1,860	2,273	2,173	2,273	2,323	2,198
WC2	2,433	2,208	2,200	2,550	2,200	613	688
WC3	1,893	2,303	1,778	1,513	1,488	1,338	890

Capacity required in minutes

Forward and Backward Scheduling

Two terms frequently associated with capacity requirements planning are *forward scheduling* and *backward scheduling*. Forward scheduling, demonstrated but not mentioned in Example 4.1, schedules activities starting at the planned release date and moving forward in time. Backward scheduling schedules activities starting at the planned receipt date (due date) and moving backward in time.

FIGURE 4.8   CUMULATIVE CRP REPORT FOR STANDARD WIDGETS (LOT-FOR-LOT ORDERING)

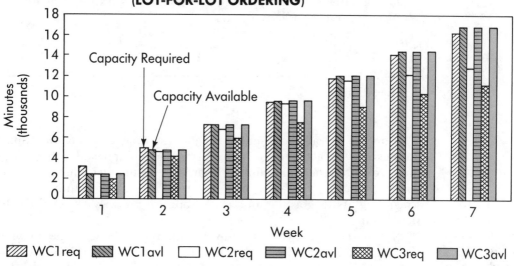

Legend: WC1req, WC1avl, WC2req, WC2avl, WC3req, WC3avl

WORK CENTER	WEEK						
	1	2	3	4	5	6	7
Cumulative Capacity Available							
WC1	2,400	4,800	7,200	9,600	12,000	14,400	16,800
WC2	2,400	4,800	7,200	9,600	12,000	14,400	16,800
WC3	2,400	4,800	7,200	9,600	12,000	14,400	16,800
Cumulative Capacity Required							
WC1	3,160	5,020	7,293	9,465	11,738	14,060	16,258
WC2	2,433	4,640	6,840	9,340	11,540	12,153	12,840
WC3	1,893	4,195	5,973	7,485	8,973	10,310	11,200
Capacity in minutes							

Assume that one lot of 500 part 121's is due in week 3. Then backward scheduling of part 121 would appear as follows:

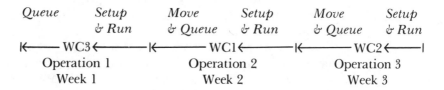

| Queue | Setup & Run | Move & Queue | Setup & Run | Move & Queue | Setup & Run |

WC3 ← | WC1 ← | WC2 ←

Operation 1 — Week 1   Operation 2 — Week 2   Operation 3 — Week 3

Given that part 121 has a three-week lead time, a job due at the end of week 3 would be released at the beginning of week 1. Forward scheduling from the release date would appear as follows:

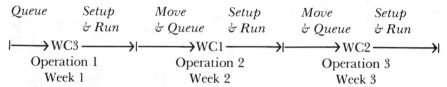

If operation lead times sum to the job lead time, and operation time is assumed to occur at the end of the operation lead time (after all interoperation time), forward scheduling and backward scheduling yield the same result. Some commercial CRP systems use forward scheduling, others backward scheduling. As long as the concepts are applied properly, the choice is not significant.

Note that in both cases the setup and run time is shown at the end of the operation lead time. This procedure is consistent with COPICS (3), which seems to be the standard to which most CRP systems have been designed. This procedure gives the latest date at which a job must start in order to meet its due date. COPICS also recommends the establishment of an earliest start date permissible because of various restrictions (such as material availability). COPICS states further: "It is not known on which day the operation will actually be performed, but it is probable that it will be between these two dates. The actual date will depend on a number of factors, such as completion of the previous operation, tool availability, priority, capacity availability, amount of idle time, etc." (p. 37). Thus, as with rough-cut capacity planning, CRP is developing an estimate of when and how much capacity will be needed.

Finite and Infinite Loading

Capacity requirements planning evolved from two machine loading techniques known as *infinite loading* and *finite loading*.

Infinite loading is really loading to infinite capacity. We have seen infinite loading in action in the creation of Figures 4.4 and 4.7.

Finite loading is not so simple. It also starts with a schedule of work orders. Before finite loading can begin, however, priorities must be established on individual orders. Obviously, the highest-priority orders should get first claim on available capacity in each work center. The next step is to determine limiting capacities in each work center; usually two values, nominal capacity and maximum capacity, are used to define capacity. Maximum capacity includes overtime or an added shift.

The jobs are then loaded into the work centers in priority sequence. As soon as a work center is filled to its limiting capacity, additional jobs are scheduled either earlier or later where unused capacity exists.

Both finite loading and infinite loading techniques have serious drawbacks. It is unrealistic to load work into a plant without regard for its capacity (as infinite loading does) and expect the plant to respond. But if each order is fit into available capacity (finite loading), and nothing is ever done to increase capacity, customer service is likely to be very poor. Further, finite loading masks the need for additional capacity since it does not indicate periods when capacity overloads exist. It simply loads to capacity and carries work forward.

Clearly CRP, which involves the iterative use of infinite loading with modifications to the schedule made as necessary at each iteration, is superior to the use of either finite loading or infinite loading alone.

Estimation of Queue Time

Of all elements of scheduling, as it relates to CRP, the most difficult to do properly is to estimate queue time. A **queue** is a group of elements waiting their turn for processing. In most operations, queue time comprises the largest single element (in some cases 90 percent) of lead time. Queue time is also highly variable, as it is a function of how much work is already at a work center, how urgently the job in question is needed, and how badly the other jobs at the work center are needed. But if CRP is to work, lead time, and hence queue time, must be predictable. As R. L. Lankford (4) so aptly put it, "Lead time must be planned and controlled, meaning that queues must be planned and controlled. . . . The proper queue allowance is the one decided upon as appropriate by production management for the average job under normal operating conditions. Queues must then be maintained at or near planned levels as a routine part of production control, otherwise the execution of the manufacturing plan will bear little resemblance to the expectations of MRP and CRP."

If a shop is arranged in assembly line or group technology fashion so that a gateway operation controls load at a number of work stations, queue control is very achievable. But with a job shop configuration, queue control may be very difficult. Queue control is especially difficult in shops which, like Example 4.1, have extremely lumpy planned order release schedules. Reducing lot sizes, ideally moving to lot-for-lot ordering, helps to produce a more even flow of work to the shop and hence more manageable queues.

SUMMARY

In this chapter a method of creating and evaluating the capacity requirements plan is presented. It is noted that CRP utilizes more information than RCCP, discussed in Chapter 3, but still produces only an estimate of the timing and quantity of capacity needed. CRP is a deterministic technique. To the extent that jobs wait in queue longer than expected, machines break down, supervisors run jobs in a sequence other than planned, and so on, reality deviates from CRP.

Since queue control is such an important aspect of managing capacity within an MRP system, recognizing the random nature of queue lengths is extremely important. In the next chapter we will examine input/output control, a technique designed to control queues.

REFERENCES

1. *APICS Dictionary*. 6th ed. Falls Church, Va.: American Production and Inventory Control Society, 1987.
2. Hall, Robert. *Zero Inventories*. Homewood, Ill.: Dow Jones–Irwin, 1983.
3. International Business Machines Corporation. *Communications Oriented Production Information and Control System* (COPICS). White Plains, N.Y.: IBM Technical Publications Department, 1972.
4. Lankford, R. L. "Short-Term Planning of Manufacturing Capacity." American Production and Inventory Control Society, 21st International Conference, 1978.
5. Schonberger, Richard J. *World Class Manufacturing*. New York: Free Press, 1986.

EXERCISES

1. Describe the capacity requirements planning process for a company operating a material requirements planning system. Discuss why CRP is necessary given that rough-cut capacity planning has been performed properly.
2. Suppose that CRP reveals a capacity shortfall. Discuss the steps that could be taken to correct this shortfall without modifying the material requirements plan. Assume that the capacity shortfall cannot be corrected by these measures; discuss why the master production schedule must be modified rather than directly modifying the material requirements plan. Why not simply ignore the shortfall and let the shop floor deal with the problem?
3. What is meant by a machine load report? Why must the machine load report utilized by CRP include both released orders and planned order releases? Suppose a capacity shortfall exists; since the orders have not yet been released, why can't one simply adjust the timing of planned order releases?

4. Taking the information given in Example 4.1 of this chapter, modify the bill of material quantities as follows: (1) change the quantity of part 110 required by part 100 to 3 per unit; (2) change the quantity of parts 121 and 122 required by part 110 to 4 and 4, respectively; (3) increase the scheduled receipt for part 100 to 750. Retain all other data given for Example 4.1. Develop a CRP report for the first seven weeks of the planning horizon spanned by the master production schedule.

5. Repeat Exercise 4 using data from Example 4.2; i.e., change the data in the bill of material to reflect the quantities given in Example 4.2. Develop the new CRP report reflecting a lot-for-lot policy. Schedule overtime where needed to provide adequate capacity.

6. Compare the results of Exercises 4 and 5 and discuss the effect lumpy planned releases have on this shop.

APPENDIX 4A
Rough-Cut Capacity Planning Calculations for Standard Widgets

In order to create a bill of labor, Sam Johnson took the lot size and routing data from Tables 4.2 and 4.3 (reproduced here as Table 4A.1 and 4A.2) and used them to compute the process time per part shown in Table 4A.3.

In Table 4A.3 column 1 gives the part number, column 2 the lot size (lot size for part 100 is an estimated average), column 3 the setup time per lot, and column 4 the run time per piece. The process time per piece is calculated in column 5 using equation 4A.1:

$$Process\ time/piece = \frac{Setup\ time/lot}{Lot\ size} + Run\ time/piece \qquad (4A.1)$$

A finished widget (part 100) contains 2 subassemblies (part 110) and a total of 6 component A's (part 121) and 10 component B's (part 122). These quantities per end item are reflected in column 6. Column 7 is process time multi-

TABLE 4A.1 ITEM MASTER RECORD FILES FOR STANDARD WIDGETS

PART NUMBER	ORDER QUANTITY	ON HAND	ON ORDER	DUE DATE	LEAD TIME (weeks)	ALLOCATED
100	LFL	0	250	7/3	1	0
110	400	500	400	7/10	2	0
121	2,400	1,500	2,400	7/10	3	0
122	6,000	2,500	6,000	7/10	4	0

TABLE 4A.2 ROUTING FILES FOR STANDARD WIDGETS

WORK CENTER	SETUP TIME/LOT	RUN TIME/PIECE
Part 100		
WC1	30	2.5
Part 110		
WC2	10	0.75
WC1	15	0.5
Part 121		
WC3	15	0.3
WC1	25	0.25
WC2	15	0.25
Part 122		
WC2	25	0.75
WC3	30	0.15
WC1	75	0.5
WC3	30	0.75

Time in minutes

TABLE 4A.3 PROCESS TIME COMPUTATION

1 PART	2 LOT SIZE	3 SETUP	4 RUN	5 PROCESS	6 QUANTITY	7 TOTAL	8 WC
100	200	30	2.50	2.650	1	2.650	WC1
110	400	10	0.75	0.775	2	1.550	WC2
110	400	15	0.50	0.538	2	1.075	WC1
121	2,400	15	0.30	0.306	6	1.838	WC3
121	2,400	25	0.25	0.260	6	1.563	WC1
121	2,400	15	0.25	0.256	6	1.538	WC2
122	6,000	25	0.75	0.754	10	7.542	WC2
122	6,000	30	0.15	0.155	10	1.550	WC3
122	6,000	75	0.50	0.513	10	5.125	WC1
122	6,000	30	0.75	0.755	10	7.550	WC3

Time in minutes

plied by quantity per finished widget, yielding the total time spent on the operation for a finished widget. Column 8 shows the work center at which the operation is performed. In Table 4A.4, the data from Table 4A.3 have been sorted by work center in order to obtain total time in each work center. The rightmost column of Table 4A.4 is a bill of labor which has been extracted to form Table 4A.5.

TABLE 4A.4   BILL OF LABOR COMPUTATION

PART	LOT SIZE	SETUP	RUN	PROCESS	QUANTITY	TOTAL	WC	WC/ TOTAL
110	400	15	0.5	0.538	2	1.075	1	
122	6,000	75	0.5	0.513	10	5.125	1	
121	2,400	25	0.25	0.260	6	1.563	1	
100	200	30	2.5	2.650	1	2.650	1	10.413
121	2,400	15	0.25	0.256	6	1.538	2	
110	400	10	0.75	0.775	2	1.550	2	
122	6,000	25	0.75	0.754	10	7.542	2	10.629
122	6,000	30	0.15	0.155	10	1.550	3	
122	6,000	30	0.75	0.755	10	7.550	3	
121	2,400	15	0.3	0.306	6	1.838	3	10.938

Time in minutes

TABLE 4A.5   BILL OF LABOR FOR STANDARD WIDGETS

WORK CENTER	MINUTES/WIDGET
WC1	10.413
WC2	10.629
WC3	10.938

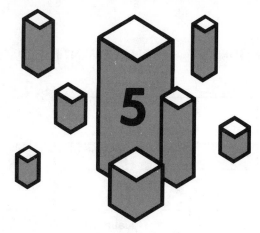

Input/Output Control

Chapter 4 noted that queue control is the key to production planning and control in a job shop. Very often 90 percent of lead time is spent in queue. If queues are out of control, actual lead times in no way resemble planned lead times. If actual lead times exceed planned lead times, due dates are missed and orders are delivered late, causing customer dissatisfaction. The importance of queue control, and hence lead time control, cannot be overemphasized.

Plossl and Wight (2) point out that there are two handles through which a queue can be controlled, the input stream and the output stream. If input exceeds output, the queue awaiting processing grows. If output exceeds input, the queue awaiting processing diminishes. It's really not quite that simple, but the statement is nevertheless useful in creating a mental image of the shop.

It is useful to visualize the queue in front of a work center as a water trough with two spigots, one an input spigot controlling order releases and the other an output spigot which is the work center capacity, as shown in Figure 5.1.

Figure 5.1 is useful for several reasons. First, it reminds us that capacity is a *rate of output per time unit*. Second, it illustrates that management does have the capability to control queues. If the amount of work awaiting processing at a station is too great, management may correct this by reducing the input, increasing the output, or both. Work awaiting processing is also called work in process (WIP), or load. When the load on one or more work centers becomes excessive, jobs start to be delivered late because actual queue times are excessive, as illustrated in Figure 5.2.

PRIORITY CONTROL

When due dates start to be missed, management often acts in a myopic fashion. One typical response is to concentrate on priority control rather than

FIGURE 5.1   MANAGEMENT HANDLES ON LEAD TIME

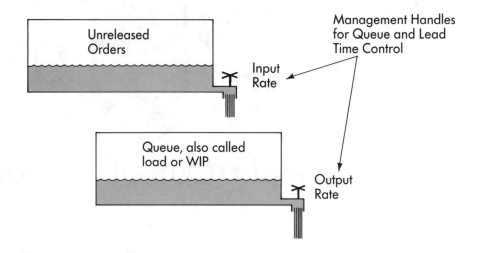

capacity control. **Priority** refers to the relative importance of jobs—i.e., the sequence in which jobs should be processed. By focusing on priority control, management can cause any single job which is behind schedule to be finished on time, but such actions are short-sighted because they adversely affect on-time delivery of other jobs and/or overall capacity availability. Let's look at some specific examples.

Reducing Interoperation Time

If all work is performed first come, first served (usually called first in, first out, or FIFO), the amount of interoperation time a job experiences is to some extent a function of chance. Since management may choose which job to perform next (if FIFO is not used), interoperation time may be reduced on any single job by giving it a high priority. But, recalling Figure 5.1, changing the priority of a job changes neither the rate of input to nor the rate of output from the station. The *load*, and hence the *average* queue or wait time, is unchanged. If some jobs wait for shorter periods, other jobs must wait for longer periods (specifically, they must wait while the high-priority jobs are processed).

Giving special priority to a particular job may mean that some seemingly insignificant component waits in queue for a long time, later delaying the assembly of an extremely important job (for want of a nail the shoe was lost, etc.). If a shop is not completing enough jobs (i.e., does not have enough

FIGURE 5.2   ANATOMY OF A LATE ORDER

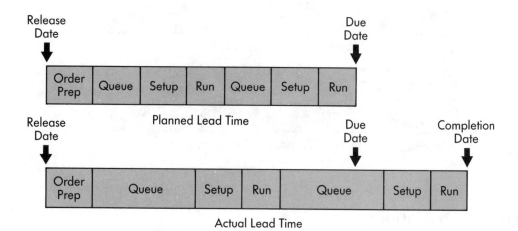

capacity) it cannot possibly always finish the right jobs on time. In the long run, the most effective way to reduce interoperation time and, more important, lead time is to reduce queue lengths.

Lot Splitting

Another way to reduce the lead time of a particular job is to run it on more than one machine in a given department, as illustrated in Figure 5.3. This practice is known as *lot splitting*; it represents a deviation from the standard practice of running each job on a single machine.

Lot splitting is also a myopic solution to insufficient capacity because it actually leads to a reduction of capacity. Suppose that when one machine is used, as illustrated in Figure 5.3, the setup time is 3 hours and the run time is 7 hours. Then setup time is 30 percent of total operation time. When the job is run on two machines they each must be set up, requiring 3 hours each. Since each machine does half the work, run time is 3.5 hours on each machine. Setup time becomes 46 percent of total operation time. The department has effectively lost 3 hours of output because of the second setup. Thus for a work center which is already overloaded, lot splitting is a poor strategy.

Lot splitting may be used effectively to expedite orders when excess capacity exists in the work center. Even when excess capacity exists, however, lot splitting should be used with discretion since it will cause a delay for jobs which otherwise would have been run on the second machine. The overall benefit of lot splitting is to reduce the lead time on one order.

FIGURE 5.3 REDUCING LEAD TIME BY LOT SPLITTING

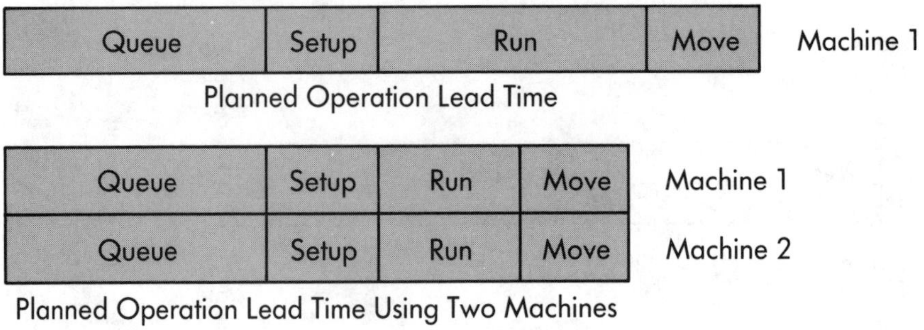

Queue	Setup	Run	Move	Machine 1

Planned Operation Lead Time

Queue	Setup	Run	Move	Machine 1
Queue	Setup	Run	Move	Machine 2

Planned Operation Lead Time Using Two Machines

Operation Overlapping

The greatest reduction in lead time is achieved when multiple departments work on a job at the same time, in assembly line fashion, as illustrated in Figure 5.4. This procedure is known as *operation overlapping*.

Operation overlapping obviously achieves a tremendous lead time reduction. In the most extreme case, operation overlapping can convert a shop with job-shop–like flows to one with assembly-line–like flows. But there are costs involved. First, move costs increase. Someone must shuttle parts between the work centers, which may be at opposite ends of the plant. A student of the author's once spent a summer hand-carrying one part at a time from one work center to a second to help a company deliver a job on time (the contract had an extremely high late penalty). When materials-handling personnel are heavily used in one area, move times elsewhere may grow, adding to lead times. Also, as Figure 5.4 shows, the jobs which would otherwise have run on machines 2 and 3 are delayed. As in the case of changing priorities, operation overlapping does not increase capacity. The only way to get all jobs out on time is to have sufficient capacity. Any approach that changes the priorities of jobs to be run at a particular work center creates the risk of causing other customer orders to be late.

Alternate Routing

Another way to expedite a single job is to seek an alternate routing. A primary routing is chosen for one of two reasons: either the work center produces the parts better than other work centers or it produces them more cheaply. If using an alternate work center will lead to significant quality problems, then the original work center must be used. When a work center is over-

FIGURE 5.4 REDUCING LEAD TIME BY OPERATION OVERLAPPING

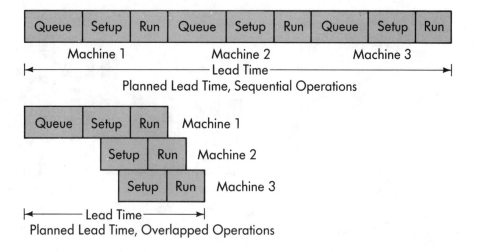

Planned Lead Time, Sequential Operations

Planned Lead Time, Overlapped Operations

loaded, however, there are often some jobs that can be performed elsewhere with no loss of quality. Even when the manufacturing data base indicates that the primary station should be chosen because it produces the part more cheaply, alternate routing should be strongly considered if the primary station is overloaded and the secondary station is underloaded.

EXAMPLE 5.1: THE IMPACT OF ALTERNATE ROUTING

Consider the situation that exists at Standard Widgets, Example 4.2, after the completion of CRP. This cumulative CRP report, originally shown in Chapter 4 as Figure 4.8, is reproduced in this chapter as Figure 5.5.

Now suppose that operation 1 for part 100 can be performed at work center 3 rather than work center 1. Recall from Table 4.3 that part 100 requires 2.5 minutes per unit at work center 1. Suppose that at work center 3, part 100 will require half again as much time, i.e., 3.75 minutes per unit. Since work center 3 has some idle time, it is possible that an alternate routing is a good solution to the problem of having work center 1 overloaded in the early weeks of the planning period. The CRP report which would result from this change is shown in Figure 5.6.

Note that the revised schedule requires 1,085 minutes of overtime in work center 3 (17,885 − 16,800), while the original schedule, shown in Figure 5.5, requires some overtime in work center 1 in the early weeks. The shop is no

FIGURE 5.5   CUMULATIVE CRP REPORT FOR STANDARD WIDGETS FROM EXAMPLE 4.2

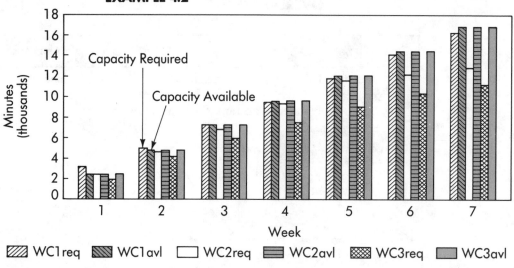

WORK CENTER	WEEK						
	1	2	3	4	5	6	7
Cumulative Capacity Available							
WC1	2,400	4,800	7,200	9,600	12,000	14,400	16,800
WC2	2,400	4,800	7,200	9,600	12,000	14,400	16,800
WC3	2,400	4,800	7,200	9,600	12,000	14,400	16,800
Cumulative Capacity Required							
WC1	3,160	5,020	7,293	9,465	11,738	14,060	16,258
WC2	2,433	4,640	6,840	9,340	11,540	12,153	12,840
WC3	1,893	4,195	5,973	7,485	8,973	10,310	11,200
Capacity in minutes							

better off by moving all orders for part 100 to work center 3. A possible solution would be to occasionally move a lot to work center 3 or to split the lot, performing half at work center 1 and half at work center 3. Unfortunately, the accounting system is likely to be a barrier to implementation of the alternate routing. Not recognizing that the worker would otherwise have been idle, the accounting system will note that the direct labor charged to part 100 is 50 percent larger than allowed and will report a labor variance. More than likely the manager will be asked to explain why these parts were built at a cost so much greater than standard cost. The "waste" found by the accounting system

FIGURE 5.6   CRP FOR STANDARD WIDGETS FROM EXAMPLE 5.1

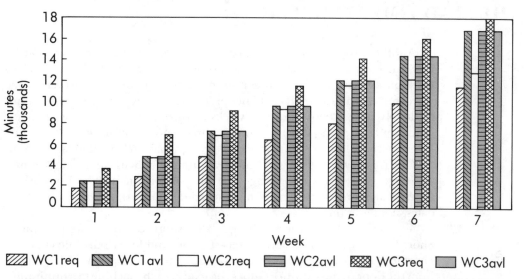

WORK CENTER	1	2	3	WEEK 4	5	6	7
Capacity Requirements Plan							
WC1	1,690	1,220	1,883	1,658	1,508	1,933	1,558
WC2	2,433	2,280	2,200	2,500	2,200	613	688
WC3	3,613	3,255	2,355	2,278	2,628	1,915	1,843
Cumulative Capacity Available							
WC1	2,400	4,800	7,200	9,600	12,000	14,400	16,800
WC2	2,400	4,800	7,200	9,600	12,000	14,400	16,800
WC3	2,400	4,800	7,200	9,600	12,000	14,400	16,800
Cumulative Capacity Required							
WC1	1,690	2,910	4,793	6,450	7,958	9,890	11,448
WC2	2,433	4,640	6,840	9,340	11,540	12,153	12,840
WC3	3,613	6,868	9,223	11,500	14,128	16,043	17,885

Capacity in minutes

does not exist if the operator who works on part 100 at WC3 would otherwise be idle. The overtime saved at work center 1 is quite real.

Alternate routings to take advantage of temporary excess capacity in the shop represent one of the better ways to offload work from bottleneck workstations (temporary or permanent). Accounting systems need to be changed to reflect real savings and not to find purely fictional wastes.

THE LEAD TIME SYNDROME

Another myopic management policy is to increase lead times arbitrarily. The rationale behind increasing lead times is that if one had more time to work on jobs one could get them out on time more often. However, if one increases lead times for all customer orders by, say, two weeks, one must immediately release two additional weeks of work to the shop floor. This increases queue times so that the extra lead time is no longer *extra*. With production slowed by longer queue waits, one is right back where one started from.

One is really worse off with long lead times than with short ones because the longer the lead time, the longer the forecast horizon must be. Longer lead times mean more forecast errors, more schedule changes, and *more* missed due dates, not fewer ones.

To do a good job of meeting due dates, short lead times are preferable. Short lead times involve fewer forecast errors and fewer schedule changes. Short lead times are achievable by good queue management. Withhold work from the floor (reduce input), reduce the load at each machine to a minimum, and lead times diminish. Thus, within limits, management can reduce lead time simply by deciding to do so.

Why Queues Exist

Queues exist because both input to and output from a work center are erratic. A machine may break down, causing output to cease while input continues. A new worker, still learning his or her skills, may cause output to fall below the planned level while input continues as planned. A large, high-priority job may come in ("If we get this one big job out on time we'll have a valuable new customer," says marketing), causing input to exceed planned input while output continues as normal. All these things cause queues to form. Thus, a better picture of load on a shop than Figure 5.1 is Figure 5.7.

Figure 5.1 would depict reality if machines never broke down, if strikes never occurred, and if workers were never absent. Unfortunately, all of these things do happen—so a plug has been added to the diagram to depict times when nothing is output. Queues would not grow during work outages if management could completely shut off input into the work center. But salespeople continue to take orders. A backlog of unreleased orders builds. Further, not all work centers are *gateways*, i.e., first on the list of operations to be performed. Jobs already released to the floor will have preceding operations completed and will move to the work center in question to be worked on. This process is depicted as a funnel having an outlet but no cut-off mechanism.

FIGURE 5.7   A MORE ACCURATE REPRESENTATION OF CAPACITY

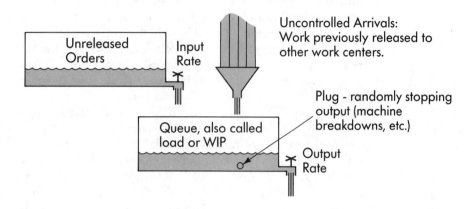

How Long Should Queues Be?

At one time the pat answer to the question of optimal queue length was: "Just long enough to prevent the work center from running out of work." This answer will be explained in some detail and then a discussion of why it may no longer be valid will be given.

Consider WC1 from Figure 5.6, which has idle time in every week. Traditional thought indicates that the queue preceding WC1 is not long enough. One could eliminate some of these idle periods by placing additional work in WC1 or by reducing the number of hours worked per week, thereby increasing the "efficiency" of the work center as the industrial engineers and accountants measure it. Let's explore the ramifications of each of these approaches. First, we'll explore doing more work, then working fewer hours.

The shop could do more work by releasing jobs early in order to keep WC1 busy all the time. The shop apparently has gained something, since it is no longer paying workers to be idle. But what has it really gained?

Assume that the master production schedule represents a set of actual orders. Customers insist on delivery when specified and no sooner. By working ahead, the shop has created no additional sales and no additional revenue. It has perhaps even reduced revenue slightly by causing materials to be purchased early to support the early build schedule. Had it held to the original build schedule it could at least have earned additional daily interest on its cash. Thus, there seems to be no point in working ahead merely to avoid an idle period. The purported savings just go into excess inventory. Further, releasing jobs early immediately creates a backlog of work, so that all jobs which pass through WC1 wait longer than necessary. Such action may increase the number of tardy jobs, incurring more cost. Clearly, releasing work early just to keep a worker busy causes a real increase in cost and no real savings.

What about working fewer hours? Since no one would argue that scheduling unneeded overtime is a good idea, this discussion really centers on the question of making a full-time worker into a part-time worker. It is likely that the worker in question is valuable to the enterprise, or otherwise the job would in all likelihood already be staffed part time rather than full time. By reducing the hours paid, one risks losing the employee. Nor is the possibility of losing a valuable worker the only cost; one must also consider increased tardiness cost due to the higher utilization of the station.

In Chapter 3 it was shown that there is a direct relationship between server utilization and queue length. In fact, as server utilization approaches 100 percent, the queue grows in an exponential fashion. A corollary to this principle is that as utilization approaches 100 percent, tardiness increases because more jobs have to wait in queue for a longer time than was allowed in scheduling. Before reducing the number of hours worked one must therefore consider how much customer goodwill and how many future sales are likely to be lost, and how much time is likely to be spent answering queries about the status of late orders.

No one really knows what "optimal" work center utilization is because no one has collected the proper data relative to the trade-offs between utilization, lead time, customer service levels, and work-in-process inventory. Such data cannot be collected from actual systems because one cannot perform controlled, scientific experiments in a shop setting. Good simulation models could provide such data, but at this point no company has, to the author's knowledge, even asked the question.

As the trade-off between capacity utilization, lead time, lot sizing, and customer service becomes more widely understood, companies will begin to simulate their own environments in order to collect data concerning the "optimal" queue length at various work centers. A strategy of keeping direct labor busy 100 percent of the time is no longer appropriate in a world in which direct labor cost has been reduced to 5 to 10 percent of total product cost while cost of materials has increased to about 50 percent.

THE INPUT/OUTPUT CONTROL TECHNIQUE

Input/output control is a method of monitoring the two handles of queue control depicted in Figure 5.1. It is a form of management by exception. One monitors actual input versus planned input and takes action if the cumulative deviation exceeds some threshold. Similarly, one compares actual output with planned output to determine whether cumulative deviation is within tolerance.

Input/output control is a short-term control technique, commonly performed using daily, rather than weekly, time buckets. The planned input and output data can be taken from the same data used to perform CRP. Consider the hypothetical example shown in Table 5.1. There exists a work center, called work center 2, for which data concerning planned and actual input have been collected. At the start of day 232, WC2 has an 11-hour backlog. This information can be determined by taking the jobs awaiting service and multiplying each by its standard processing time. Planned input into the station comes from the CRP report directly (although one may have to alter the CRP report presented in Chapter 4, Figure 4.7, to get daily, rather than weekly, information).

TABLE 5.1   INPUT CONTROL CHART FOR WC2: PLANNED VERSUS ACTUAL INPUT

	DAY 232	233	234	235	236	237	238	239	240	241
Planned	0	7.2	0	27.8	5.2	21.2	0	0	15.1	5.2
Actual	7.2	12	5.5	10.3	16.2	10.2	10	5.1	0	5.2
Deviation	7.2	4.8	5.5	−17.5	11	−11	10	5.1	−15.1	0
Cum. Deviation	7.2	12	17.5	0	11	0	10	15.1	0	0

Input in hours

The actual input deviates from the plan, but by the end of the planning horizon, cumulative deviation from the plan is 0. In using an input report to determine whether jobs are being released to work centers properly, it is important to use cumulative deviations rather than individual deviations. Sometimes one must work ahead of schedule. However, the student should realize by now that a problem exists if the input report indicates a sustained tendency to release work early (i.e., if the cumulative deviation continues to grow). Such a condition would indicate adoption of a strategy of keeping the work center 100 percent utilized whether the work is needed or not, a strategy shown in the previous section to be ill advised.

Input/output control is a form of management by exception because no action is taken unless the cumulative deviation exceeds some threshold. Whenever the threshold is exceeded, the computer creates a high-priority action message to be sent to the production manager, or whoever supervises order releasing. The threshold should be high enough to permit helpful deviations, as depicted in Table 5.1.

Turning to the output side, after day 241 the output report might look like Table 5.2.

TABLE 5.2   OUTPUT CONTROL CHART FOR WC2: PLANNED VERSUS ACTUAL INPUT

	DAY									
	232	233	234	235	236	237	238	239	240	241
Planned	9.3	9.3	9.3	9.3	9.3	9.3	9.3	9.3	9.3	9.3
Actual	0	18.2	12	6.5	10.3	12.4	14	0	10.5	5.2
Deviation	−9.3	8.9	2.7	−2.8	1	3.1	4.7	−9.3	1.2	−4.1
Cum. Deviation	−9.3	−0.4	2.1	−0.5	0.5	3.6	8.3	−1.0	0.2	−3.9

Output in hours

Planned output is shown as a constant amount, found by dividing the output from the CRP report into equal daily buckets. Of course, if overtime is planned for certain days, so that an uneven number of hours are worked, the planned output might be prorated on the basis of the number of hours worked. Actual output may be quite lumpy, since total labor hours on a job are usually credited to the day the job is completed. The lumpiness created by reporting labor only when a job is completed should not be a concern, however, since one is interested in cumulative deviations from the plan, not average deviations. Cumulative deviation from the plan in Table 5.2 is never great enough to cause much concern.

Controlling Queues via Input/Output Control

To illustrate how the input/output report may be used as a vehicle for queue control, consider the following example. Assume one desires to maintain a planned queue of about 11 hours at a particular work center. Suppose also that at the end of day 250 one finds a backlog of 45 standard hours of output, 34 over plan. Recalling that input control and output control are the only alternatives, one realizes that either input must be reduced or output increased. One may consider both alternatives. If input were to be reduced, one might arrive at the situation depicted in Table 5.3.

The projected backlog at the end of the reporting period is found by the formula

$$B_E = B_B - O + I \qquad (5.1)$$

where

B_E is projected backlog, end of planning period
B_B is actual backlog, beginning of planning period

TABLE 5.3   PLANNED INPUT REDUCTION TO REDUCE BACKLOG

	DAY									
	232	233	234	235	236	237	238	239	240	241
Planned Input	6.3	6.3	6.3	6.3	6.3	6.3	6.3	6.3	6.3	6.3
Planned Output	9.3	9.3	9.3	9.3	9.3	9.3	9.3	9.3	9.3	9.3

Beginning Backlog: 45 hours   Ending Backlog: 15 hours

O is planned output
I is planned input

In this case one would obtain

$$B_E = 45 - 93 + 63$$
$$= 15$$

projecting a return to a near normal queue length.

Let us further suppose that the CRP for the 10-day period in question projects 88 hours of input, rather than the 63 indicated as planned input. What does the planner do with the additional 25 standard hours of work?

The first option the planner should consider is de-expediting, i.e., moving a due date further out into the future. In most companies **expediting**—moving work up to be performed sooner—is frequently performed, but de-expediting is considered low priority. Nevertheless, jobs frequently are not needed as early as originally scheduled. Since failure to de-expedite is a common cause of queue buildup, appropriate rescheduling should be the first option considered in reducing queues. De-expediting can be performed by using the pegging capabilities built into the MRP system. Through pegging, a planner can trace a particular job to the order which created it. He or she can then check to see if the end item is still desired on the original date. If a later delivery date is acceptable, then the end item may be rescheduled and a net change MRP run to determine the new required date of the component under consideration.

If the planner cannot achieve the necessary reduction in input via de-expediting, other options are alternate routing (use of another machine within the same department or shop) and subcontracting (sending work out of the shop).

Suppose that in this instance none of the input reduction tactics is helpful and that the work center must have 88 hours of input. In this case the planner must seek additional capacity. It may be, for instance, that on the second shift there is an operator skilled in the use of this machine who can be moved part time from other duties. Assume that such an operator is found and scheduled to perform an additional 25 hours of work over the next 10 days. Then planned output may be raised from 93 hours to 118 hours, or 11.8 hours per day. The input/output report would appear as shown in Table 5.4.

As a result of the planner's efforts, backlog is projected to be reduced from 45 hours to 15 hours.

TABLE 5.4   PLANNED OUTPUT INCREASE TO REDUCE BACKLOG

	232	233	234	235	236	237	238	239	240	241
Planned Input	8.8	8.8	8.8	8.8	8.8	8.8	8.8	8.8	8.8	8.8
Planned Output	11.8	11.8	11.8	11.8	11.8	11.8	11.8	11.8	11.8	11.8

Beginning Backlog: 45 hours   Ending Backlog: 15 hours

Basic Principle of Input/Output Control

In an excellent article, Wight stated the basic principle of input/output control: "Never put into a manufacturing facility or to a vendor's facility more than you believe that he can produce" (2). If this rule is invariably followed, queues will closely resemble their planned lengths, wait times for individual jobs will be about as expected, and due dates should almost always be met.

Note that the use of the input/output control chart is as applicable to vendor control as it is to internal work center control. Vendor capacity planning is discussed in Carter and Ho (1).

SUMMARY

In this chapter the importance of input/output control to the overall functioning of an MRP system is demonstrated and the input/output technique is explained. The input/output control technique is important because it is used to maintain actual queue lengths near planned queue lengths. Since queue time represents most of the time a typical job spends in a shop, queue control is tantamount to lead time control. It is reasonable to say that MRP will work properly only if lead times are met by a technique such as input/output control. The technique monitors planned versus actual input and output into a work center. It is a management-by-exception technique, drawing attention to those work centers whose actual input and/or output deviates from the plan by more than some tolerance.

Queues exist in a shop having a process layout because it is not possible to completely control input to machines in such an environment. It is necessary to have some queue of work to avoid excessive idle time during periods in which no work is coming into a department. Early approaches to maintaining an "optimal" queue length assumed that all work centers should attempt 100 percent utilization. Such an approach overestimates the length of queue needed in front of non-bottleneck work centers. It is important to determine how heavily a station must be utilized before attempting to calculate an optimal queue length.

REFERENCES

1. Carter, Phillip L., and Chrwan-Jyh Ho. "Vendor Capacity Planning: An Approach to Vendor Scheduling." *Production and Inventory Management* (Fourth Quarter 1984): 63–73.
2. Plossl, George W., and Oliver W. Wight. "Capacity Planning and Control." *APICS Capacity Planning and Control Reprints*. Falls Church, Va.: American Production and Inventory Control Society, 1975. Pp. 50–86.
3. Wight, Oliver. "Input/Output Control: A Real Handle on Lead Time." *APICS Capacity Management Reprints*. Falls Church, Va.: American Production and Inventory Control Society, 1984. Pp. 107–129.

EXERCISES

1. Discuss the relationship between queue time and lead time. Discuss how lead time may be compressed by lot splitting and operation overlapping. Discuss the impact of lot splitting on work center capacity. Discuss the relationship between input/output control and customer service (meeting due dates).
2. Work center 46 employs two workers on one 40-hour shift. Historical utilization and efficiency figures for work center 46 are 93 percent and 112 percent, respectively. Work center 46 has a planned queue of 15 hours. At present, the actual queue is 35 hours. In the coming 5 weeks the standard hours of work scheduled to arrive at work center 46 are 70, 86, 72, 74, and 84, respectively.
    a. Each worker may work up to 10 hours overtime per week. Schedule work center 46 in order to reduce the actual queue by 4 hours each week so that at the end of 5 weeks the actual queue is 15 hours.
    b. Schedule work center 46 so that the actual queue is returned to 15 hours as quickly as possible, i.e., using the full overtime allowable as long as is necessary to return the queue to 15 hours.

c. Assume an alternate station has been identified which will accept 4 standard hours of work from work center 46 each week. Without using overtime, schedule work center 46 in a way that will reduce the backlog to 15 hours by the end of the 5th week.

3. Using the data from Exercise 2, assume that work center 46 currently has no work. Schedule the next 5 weeks so that at the end of the period 15 standard hours of backlog exist and so that no overtime is worked during the period. Discuss why such a deliberate buildup of work is desirable.

4. Discuss the statement "Capacity control must precede priority control."

5. The following queue exists at work center 17 on day 152:

Job	Setup Hours	Run Hours	Due Date
1	0.5	10	156
2	3.0	12	154
3	1.5	8	157
4	1.0	9	153

Work center 17 works 8 hours per day and has efficiency and utilization of 100 percent. Make a Gantt chart showing the completion time of the four jobs using (a) FIFO and (b) earliest job due date first. Determine the number of tardy jobs and average days tardy for each approach. A job is not tardy if it is completed at any time on or before its due date. Each day or fraction of a day beyond the due date counts as a day tardy.

6. The following problem involves both lot splitting and operation overlapping. Today is day 232. An order for 100 green widgets has two operations remaining, one each at work centers 27 and 42. The current queues at the two work centers are as follows:

Work Center 27

Job	Setup Hours	Run Hours	Due Date
Brown Widgets	5	22	234
Red Widgets	2	16	235
Blue Widgets	7	30	236
Green Widgets	6	24	237

Work Center 42

Job	Setup Hours	Run Hours	Due Date
Orange Widgets	1	42	240

Work center 27 has two machines which each operate 8 hours per day. Work center 42 has one machine which operates 8 hours per day. At present, all three machines are being set up, taking jobs in earliest due date sequence. Both work centers have 100 percent utilization and efficiency. Widge Williams, company president, decrees that setups are to cease and, instead, the green widgets are to be run on both machines in work center 27, overlapped onto the machine at work center 42. Transfer from work center 27 to 42 is to occur in batches of 10 units. Setup and process time for green widgets at work center 42 are 3 hours and 10 hours, respectively.

a. When will the order for 100 green widgets be completed? Use a Gantt chart to demonstrate.

b. When would the order for 100 green widgets have been finished without intervention?

c. What are the costs of expediting? Be specific, showing which jobs are late which otherwise would not have been.

APPENDIX 5A
Instructions for Creating an Input/Output Control Chart Using Lotus 1-2-3

Creating an input/output control chart in Lotus 1-2-3 is so simple that anyone having a fair knowledge of 1-2-3 can easily implement it without assistance. For the novice, this application is a good place to get started using 1-2-3.

After booting 1-2-3, looking at a blank spreadsheet with the cursor in cell A1, issue the following command sequence to set the spreadsheet to a useful size:

1. / Worksheet Global Column_width 7 {return}
2. / Worksheet Column_width Set 15 {return} (Version 2: / Worksheet Column Set_width)
3. / Worksheet Global Format Fixed 0 {return}

These instructions (1) change the global column width from 9 to 7, (2) change the width of column A to 15 to accommodate label size, and (3) change the display format to 0 decimal places. If you'd like to have decimal hours, repeat instruction 3 setting the format to 1 instead of 0.

4. Place the cursor in cell C1. Type 'Input/Output Control Chart' {return}. Do not type the quotes in this or other instructions.
5. Place the cursor in cell E3. Type 'Week' {return}.
6. Place the cursor in cell B5. Issue the command sequence

/ Data Fill B5...I5 {start} 1 {step} 1 {stop} 8 {return}

This should cause the numbers 1 to 8 to appear in cells B5 and I5.

7. Type the following labels into the cells indicated:

Cell	Label
A6	Planned Input
A7	Actual Input
A8	Deviation
A9	Cum. Deviation
A11	Planned Output
A12	Actual Output
A13	Deviation
A14	Cum. Deviation

8. Place the cursor in cell B8. Type '+B7−B6'. The number 0 should appear in the cell.

9. Place the cursor in cell B9. Type '@sum($B8.B8)'. The number 0 should appear.

10. Place the cursor in cell B8. Issue the command sequence

/ Copy B8.B9 {return} B8.I8 {return}

The number 0 should appear in rows 8 and 9, columns B through I.

After setting up the margins of the chart, we told Lotus to define the deviation by subtracting planned from actual. The instruction in cell B9, when copied, results in a cumulative sum of row 8.

11. Place the cursor in cell B13. Type '+B12−B11' {return}.

12. Place the cursor in cell B14. Type '@sum($B13.B13)'.

13. Place the cursor in cell B13. Issue the command sequence

/ Copy B13.B14 {return} B13.I13 {return}.

A set of 0's should appear in rows 13 and 14, columns B through I.

The worksheet should look like the one shown below:

Input/Output Control Chart

	Week							
	1	2	3	4	5	6	7	8
Planned Input								
Actual Input								
Deviation	0	0	0	0	0	0	0	0
Cum. Deviation	0	0	0	0	0	0	0	0

Planned Output								
Actual Output								
Deviation	0	0	0	0	0	0	0	0
Cum. Deviation	0	0	0	0	0	0	0	0

To verify that this spreadsheet is performing as it should, enter any set of numbers into the planned input and actual input rows and calculate the proper values manually.

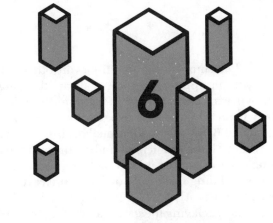

Operations Scheduling

To illustrate the complexity of scheduling even a single work center, suppose one has a set of 10 jobs to be scheduled through WC2. For each job one knows the approximate operation time and the due date. One desires to schedule the jobs in order to minimize average tardiness, where tardiness is defined to be 0 if the job is early and the time late if the job is late. Baker (1) states that for the tardiness minimization problem no simple **heuristic**, such as earliest due date first, will always produce the best solution. To guarantee the optimal solution, one must consider all possible alternatives. How many different ways can one sequence 10 jobs through one work center?

Any of the 10 jobs may be scheduled first. Given that one job is chosen, any of the 9 remaining may be scheduled second, and so on. Thus there are $10 \times 9 \times 8 \times 7 \times 6 \times 5 \times 4 \times 3 \times 2 \times 1$ possible sequences. This number is expressed 10! (read 10 factorial). The total is 3,628,800. One cannot afford the computer time required to list and evaluate all possible combinations of sequences. Fortunately, there are techniques available for finding the best solution short of explicit enumeration. Suppose, for example, that scheduling the jobs by due date, with the earliest due date first, yields a total tardiness of 20 time periods, that there are a total of 200 time periods of work, and that job 1 is due in period 24. If job 1 is instead performed last, it will be completed at time 200 (the sum of all job times). The tardiness of job 1 alone would be $200 - 24 = 176$, which exceeds the total tardiness achieved by earliest-due-date sequencing. Thus, all 9! sequences which are possible if job 1 is performed last may be eliminated from consideration since they all have at least 176 time units of tardiness. A technique which takes advantage of such properties is known as an implicit enumeration technique because it attempts to consider all options by eliminating as many as possible in the manner just shown.

135

Implicit enumeration techniques are often computationally efficient. but in any single application there is always the danger that the computational time will exceed what can be afforded since one does not know in advance how many sequences will have to be explicitly evaluated. The interested reader is referred to Baker (1) for additional details.

Although the problem of finding the optimal average tardiness in scheduling one work center is large, at least it is finite. Consider that in actual job shop scheduling one would of course prefer that jobs be completed on time, that is, neither early nor late. It is quite possible that the best sequence involves deliberately delaying the start of a job at some non-bottleneck work center. To optimize this choice one must decide how much idle time, if any, to place between jobs while they are being sequenced. Since time is infinitely divisible, one finds there are now an infinite number of possible solutions. The possibility of finding an exact answer to minimizing the deviation from the due date is thus very remote, although a line of research recently started by Fry et al. (2) holds promise. Furthermore, a real job shop has not one work center but many, with mutually dependent schedules. It is not surprising, then, that most shops use ad hoc scheduling procedures.

ESTABLISHING DUE DATES

Before considering the problem of sequencing jobs to meet due dates, one must first verify that the due dates themselves are valid. Plossl and Wight (4) list four different categories of shops from the point of view of maintaining due-date validity:

1. One piece, make-to-order shop. Here it is easy to keep track of priority; it is given by the order promise date. Although the date itself may change, it is always known.
2. Assembled product, make-to-order shop. When components are assembled to make the end item, component priorities are dependent upon the due date of the end item and on the availability of other components (it is foolish to give component A a high priority because the order due date is close if component B is out of stock and unavailable for several weeks).
3. One piece, make-to-stock shop. The real due date of an item to be stocked is the date on which the existing stock will be exhausted. Since demand during the fabrication period is a random variable, the date of actual need is likely to change while the order is on the shop floor. Note that the need date is subject to forecast error and is not known with certainty.
4. Assembled product, make-to-stock shop. This situation combines the problems of forecast error and random demand with the problems of deriving component due dates and of having all components simultaneously available. This situation is obviously the most difficult one in which to maintain valid due dates.

As Plossl and Wight point out, "The inability of most formal priority planning systems to keep priorities (due dates) properly updated has been one of the most significant causes of machine load reports (CRP and planned input reports) that simply aren't credible to shop people" (4, p. 58). In turn, lack of belief in system output is one of the most frequent causes of MRP system failure. Thus, maintaining valid due dates is a prerequisite for MRP system success.

LIMITATIONS OF CRP AND INPUT/OUTPUT CONTROL

As necessary as CRP and input/output control are, neither one attempts to deal with detailed operations sequencing to verify that components will be completed when needed. Few formal capacity planning systems schedule special resources such as setup teams and tooling, for example. If such resources are needed, it is usually left to the individual supervisor to obtain them and to determine the exact sequence in which jobs are to be run, often with very little in the way of guidance. There are few tools available to help the supervisor see the consequences of running jobs out of due-date sequence. Almost all sequencing research has ignored the dependent-demand, dependent-routing, sequence-dependent setup time situation found in real job shops.

AN ADDED TECHNIQUE: OPERATIONS SEQUENCING

A case reported in 1984 by Lankford and Moore (3) presents an effort to formalize the operations sequencing procedure. After an examination of the case, the technique utilized will then be applied to Example 5.1, the illustration of the impact of alternate routing in Chapter 5. Chapter 7 will discuss recent research which may help in developing formal operations scheduling procedures.

A CASE STUDY
Remmele Engineering, Inc.

Remmele Engineering, Inc., is a classic job shop with three types of business: (1) fabrication, (2) contract machining, and (3) designing and building special machines. At the time of the study the company had established two primary business objectives:

1. To improve the ability to set accurate delivery dates.
2. Once these delivery dates are set, to improve on-time delivery performance.

As Moore describes Remmele's problem:

> What was needed was the ability to simulate the manufacturing process on each of the jobs to give a realistic delivery estimate. This simulation needed to deal with the complexities of the routings and the diversity of the work centers. It also needed to recognize the finite capacity that existed in all the work centers. [3, p. 63]

Remmele realized that a CRP load profile by itself would be of limited usefulness in such a simulation, because it regards capacity as static. The "capacity" field of a CRP is simply *planned* output, based on demonstrated capability from actual output tracking in the recent past. Another problem is the unpredictability of *required* output. As Lankford explains it:

> The required output in any period will, in fact, be required *only* if the jobs comprising it arrive in time to be worked on during that period. That will occur only if these jobs wait in queues in various preceding work centers. If queues are longer or shorter than planned, the timing of required capacity may be quite different from that shown in CRP.

Needed in addition to a CRP load profile, therefore, was a detailed load report—a list of all the jobs comprising the load in each period. With the information on this list, "jobs may be routed to alternate work centers, shifted to other time periods, or pegged to end items which are to be rescheduled in the master schedule" (3, p. 65).

Finding that commercial software packages lacked the capability to do the type of simulation desired, Remmele therefore developed their program in house. CRP was put in place in July 1981, and operations sequencing (simulation) in August 1981. Lankford describes how the Remmele system works:

> We have a file of all current and future jobs with their priorities expressed by their required dates. We also know from production labor reporting those jobs currently working in the plan, with their status of completion. . . .
>
> What operations sequencing does is to produce a manufacturing job schedule which shows for each job the following information:
>
> 1. Required date—from MRP or MPS.
> 2. Planned start and finish date—the standard lead time using planned move and queue times.
> 3. Scheduled start and finish dates—the probable actual load time, recognizing available capacity and the job's relative priority.

Thus, the planner can see the jobs which will probably be late. From detailed operations dating, bottleneck operations are evident. Using this information the planner can go to work solving the problem.

Simulation is needed in step 3 to determine likely start and finish dates. Two approaches are possible: *deterministic simulation*, in which all operation times are considered to be constant and the times when machines are available for service are known, and *stochastic simulation*, in which operation times are assumed to be random variables (having a known probability distribution) and machines are allowed to break down at intervals mimicking conditions found in the actual shop. Deterministic simulation, also known as Gantt charting, is well defined, and probably grossly underutilized. (Remmele actually extended the Gantt charting process somewhat to produce the reports described.)

THE MECHANICS OF DETERMIN-ISTIC SIMULATION

The approach Remmele Engineering follows is so sensible and useful that it should be a standard part of capacity management software. This procedure will be described in detail, using Example 5.1 data, in the hope that the description will be useful to those developing software. A *stochastic simulator* such as one built in GEMS or SLAM, although more expensive to operate and generally less applicable, may also be useful. An obvious limitation of a deterministic simulation is that it misses the long queues which occur with near-100 percent capacity utilization.

Tables 6.1 through 6.6 give the pertinent details for preparing a **Gantt chart.** These figures have been taken from data supporting Example 5.1. Recall that in an attempt to achieve a more balanced shop, an alternate route was selected for part 100, using work station 3 rather than work center 1 for the only operation needed. (The attempt failed in that work center 3 ended up being more overloaded than work center 1 had been.) This version of the data uses lot-for-lot ordering throughout.

TABLE 6.1 BILL OF MATERIAL FOR A WIDGET
(effective date 1/1/88)

LEVEL	PART	QTY/PARENT	DESCRIPTION
0	100	1	Finished Widget
1	110	2	Subassembly
2	121	3	Component A
2	122	5	Component B

TABLE 6.2 ITEM MASTER RECORD FILES FOR STANDARD WIDGETS

PART NUMBER	ORDER QUANTITY	ON HAND	ON ORDER	DUE DATE	LEAD TIME (weeks)	ALLOCATED
100	LFL	0	250	7/3	1	0
110	LFL	500	400	7/10	2	0
121	LFL	1,500	1,200	7/10	3	0
			1,500	7/17	3	0
122	LFL	2,500	2,000	7/10	4	0
			2,000	7/17	4	0
			1,500	7/24	4	0

TABLE 6.3 ROUTING FILES FOR STANDARD WIDGETS

WORK CENTER	OPN. NO.	SETUP TIME/LOT	RUN TIME/PIECE
Part 100			
WC1	1	30	2.5
Part 110			
WC2	1	10	0.75
WC1	2	15	0.5
Part 121			
WC3	1	15	0.3
WC1	2	25	0.25
WC2	3	15	0.25
Part 122			
WC2	1	25	0.75
WC3	2	30	0.15
WC1	3	75	0.5
WC3	4	30	0.75

Time in minutes

TABLE 6.4 WORK CENTER MASTER FILES, STANDARD WIDGETS

WORK CENTER	MINUTES AVAILABLE	UTILIZATION	EFFICIENCY	PLANNED QUEUE (days)
WC1	2,400	100%	100%	4
WC2	2,400	100%	100%	4
WC3	2,400	100%	100%	4

TABLE 6.5   MASTER PRODUCTION SCHEDULE FOR FINISHED WIDGETS

	WEEK											
	1	**2**	**3**	**4**	**5**	**6**	**7**	**8**	**9**	**10**	**11**	**12**
Quantity	250	200	250	150	200	300	150	250	200	200	250	200

TABLE 6.6   PLANNED ORDER RELEASES FOR STANDARD WIDGETS

	WEEK						
PART	**1**	**2**	**3**	**4**	**5**	**6**	**7**
100	200	250	150	200	300	150	250
110	300	400	600	300	500	400	400
121	900	1,500	1,200	1,200	1,500	1,200	0
122	2,500	2,000	2,000	2,500	2,000	0	0

DEVELOPMENT OF A GANTT CHART

Figure 6.1 is a Gantt chart for Example 5.1. The interpretation of this chart will be discussed first, followed by a few comments on the creation of the chart. Full details concerning chart creation are contained in Appendix 6A.

In performing a deterministic simulation one must have the following data:

1. A list of released orders and their present locations
2. A list of planned order releases from the MRP system
3. A list of tentative capacities available
4. Time standards from routing data
5. A list of events, called the *event list*, whose times are known (such as time of planned order release)
6. A list of future events whose times are not at present known (such as start time for a job in queue awaiting the completion of a previous job). This list is called the *waiting list* and is organized by work center.
7. A way of representing what has occurred in the simulation
8. A simulation clock

Using these data one determines the total processing time for each job as it goes into service, placing jobs in service from among those queued using the shop's dispatching technique (earliest operation due date first, breaking ties by first in, first out in this case). One can determine the ending time of each job

FIGURE 6.1   GANTT CHART FOR EXAMPLE 5.1

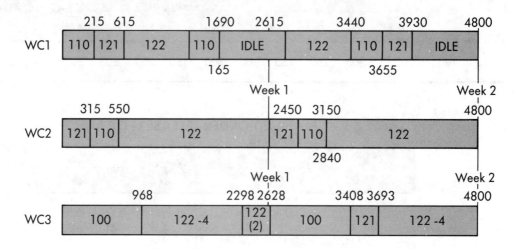

and the beginning time of the next provided no machines break down, no material shortages occur, and all process times precisely equal their respective standard times. Full details concerning the creation of Figure 6.1 are provided in Appendix 6A.

It is now possible to compare Figure 6.1 to the CRP report for Example 5.1, which is reproduced here as Figure 6.2.

Note from Figure 6.2 that WC1 is projected to have idle time in both weeks 1 and 2, that WC2 has almost precisely two weeks' work, and that WC3 is overloaded in both weeks. The Gantt chart for WC1, WC2, and WC3 is as expected, i.e., WC1 has some idle periods during the two weeks while WC2 and WC3 have none. The Gantt chart contains added information which may be used to anticipate and correct potential problems.

WC1 is in fine shape. Note that two batches of part 110 are processed in week 1. Only one batch is due in week 1, but WC2 finished the batch at time 550 and, having nothing else to work on at time 1690, WC1 processed the part. Thus, WC1 simply works slightly ahead of schedule and goes idle again at the end of week 2, when there is no more work available for the center. Working ahead in this fashion is permissible. The work was released at the time indicated by the MRP system. MRP lead times are estimates, so even in ideal conditions some jobs will be completed slightly ahead of schedule and some behind.

WC1 will be idle for the period 3930 to 4800. At time 4800 planned order releases for week 3 will arrive for work. In calendar days, if one assumes the 40-hour workweek is eight to five, Monday through Friday (with one hour daily for lunch and breaks), WC1 becomes idle about 9:30 a.m. Thursday and remains idle the rest of the week.

FIGURE 6.2 **CRP REPORT FOR EXAMPLE 5.1**

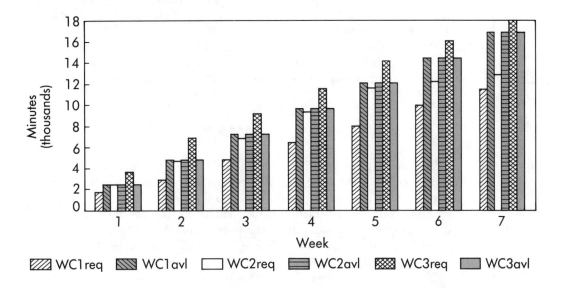

Work due to be released the third week should not be released early to WC1 in order to occupy the worker Thursday and Friday. It is very tempting to release work. Intuitively, it seems that having a worker idle is a waste. But having the worker work ahead in this situation would be a bigger waste. The work is not needed. The CRP report indicates there are no future periods of capacity shortfall anticipated. Any work released early will simply move to the most heavily loaded center (WC2 in this case) and wait. Nothing has really been gained by occupying the worker. But since early releases may cause early purchases and since the extra jobs tend to clog the floor, early releases have real costs. It would be better to have the worker assist someone else, perform preventive maintenance on his or her machine, or cross-train for another task. If none of these alternatives is feasible it would be better to have the worker do nothing than to work ahead.

Gantt charts are more informative than CRP reports concerning the timing of idle periods and also the total number of hours of production expected at various stations. The overload problem arises from the decision to move part 100 from WC1 to WC3. Since WC1 now shows idle time, some or all of the lots might be processed through WC1. The Gantt chart can be used to do some "what if" analysis. Perhaps the best approach to scheduling part 100 is to use the Gantt chart to decide whether the primary or alternate route should be used. This will depend on whether WC1 or WC3 has the smaller queue at the time of release. The Gantt chart shows that the order for part 100's released during week 2 is not processed during week 2. That order could therefore be sent to WC1, eliminating some of its idle time.

Companies often do Gantt charting manually, using Velcro boards and strips of cloth cut to predetermined length (to indicate time) and color coded to indicate part number. Replanning is easily performed if a machine breakdown or other unplanned event disrupts the schedule. Good microcomputer software in this area would be valuable. Although software is available for developing project management Gantt charts, unfortunately none is available for developing manufacturing Gantt charts.

SUMMARY

In this chapter operations scheduling, using a deterministic simulation approach, is shown to be a useful approach for determining the short-run timing of the need for capacity. It is also noted that stochastic simulation, which captures the interaction between all of the sources of variation in the shop (scrap, rework, machine breakdowns, missing components, etc.), can greatly assist in the understanding of why queues tend to fluctuate and due dates are missed.

Finally, it should be noted that for the deterministic simulation to be an effective management tool one must work to eliminate variation. To the extent that machine breakdowns and other sources of variation cause the schedule to be modified, deterministic simulation is inaccurate.

REFERENCES

1. Baker, Kenneth R. *Introduction to Sequencing and Scheduling.* New York: John Wiley & Sons, 1974.
2. Fry, Timothy D., Ronald Armstrong, and John H. Blackstone, Jr. "A Solution Procedure for Minimal Deviation Single Machine Scheduling." *IIE Transactions* 19, no. 4 (1987): 445–449.
3. Lankford, Ray, and Tom Moore. "Job Shop Scheduling: A Case Study." *APICS Capacity Management Reprints.* Falls Church, Va.: American Production and Inventory Control Society, 1984.
4. Plossl, George, and Oliver Wight. "Capacity Planning and Control." *APICS Capacity Planning and Control Reprints.* Falls Church, Va.: American Production and Inventory Control Society, 1984.

EXERCISES

1. How many ways can four jobs be sequenced at one work center? List all sequences. Using a computer, is it feasible to examine all possible se-

quences if there are 5 jobs waiting to be sequenced at a work center? 10 jobs? Is it necessary to consider all possible sequences?

2. An MRP system has the capability of assigning operation due dates to every operation. Most shop floor control systems utilize this information to create dispatch lists, i.e., lists of jobs awaiting processing and the sequence in which the jobs should be produced. Discuss reasons a supervisor may choose to deviate from this schedule and, for each reason, discuss whether the deviation is appropriate from the point of view of the entire organization.

3. Due dates are usually assigned in one of two ways. One method is to allow a fixed lead time, such as one week, for each operation. A second method is to use a variable lead time per operation, in which case a multiple of the processing time is often used. Which of these methods is more likely to yield good customer service performance? Neither method recognizes whether an operation is to be performed at a bottleneck or nonbottleneck work center. Describe a method of setting due dates which would consider whether or not a center is a bottleneck. Describe a method of setting due dates which would recognize historical utilization at every work center. Discuss the advantages and disadvantages for the entire MRP process of the two suggested methods of setting due dates.

4. Discuss the Remmele Engineering case. Why is CRP inadequate? What information would be added by a deterministic simulation? Would a stochastic simulation add still more information? Would it be worth the effort?

5. Develop a Gantt chart of the first two weeks of Example 4.1.

6. Develop a Gantt chart of the first two weeks of Example 4.2.

7. Based on results of Exercises 5 and 6, discuss the impact of reducing lot size on job tardiness.

8. *Advanced.* Use GEMS, SLAM, SIMAN, or GPSS to develop a simulation model of Example 4.2. Run it for 10 replications of 8 weeks.

APPENDIX 6A
Gantt Chart
Development

Data required for Gantt chart development (Figure 6.1) are reproduced in Tables 6A.1 through 6A.6.

Using the information in the item master records, the shop files, and the routing files, one can develop the following information regarding jobs already on the shop floor:

Part	Opn. No.	Quantity	Location	Process Time	Next
100	1	250	WC3	968	Stock
110	2	400	WC1	215	Stock
121	3	1,200	WC2	315	Stock
122	4	2,000	WC3	1,330	Stock
121	2	1,500	WC1	400	WC2
122	3	2,000	WC1	1,075	WC3
122	2	1,500	WC3	330	WC1

These jobs are joined by the following jobs released at the start of week 1 (time 0):

Part	Opn. No.	Quantity	Location	Process Time	Next
100	1	200	WC3	780	Stock
110	1	300	WC2	235	WC1
121	1	900	WC3	285	WC1
122	1	2,500	WC2	1,900	WC3

TABLE 6A.1   **BILL OF MATERIAL FOR A WIDGET**
(effective date 1/1/88)

LEVEL	PART	QTY/PARENT	DESCRIPTION
0	100	1	Finished Widget
1	110	2	Subassembly
2	121	3	Component A
2	122	5	Component B

TABLE 6A.2   **ITEM MASTER RECORD FILES FOR STANDARD WIDGETS**

PART NUMBER	ORDER QUANTITY	ON HAND	ON ORDER	OPN NO.*	LEAD TIME (weeks)	ALLOCATED
100	LFL	0	250	1	1	0
110	LFL	500	400	2	2	0
121	LFL	1,500	1,200	3	3	0
			1,500	2	3	0
122	LFL	2,500	2,000	4	4	0
			2,000	3	4	0
			1,500	2	4	0

*Numbers in this column reflect the current position of the order. In developing the Gantt chart it was assumed that no work has been completed and that each work center is idle and available.

TABLE 6A.3   **ROUTING FILES FOR STANDARD WIDGETS**

WORK CENTER	OPN. NO.	SETUP TIME/LOT	RUN TIME/PIECE
		Part 100	
WC1	1	 30	2.5
		Part 110	
WC2	1	 10	0.75
WC1	2	 15	0.5
		Part 121	
WC3	1	 15	0.3
WC1	2	 25	0.25
WC2	3	 15	0.25
		Part 122	
WC2	1	 25	0.75
WC3	2	 30	0.15
WC1	3	 75	0.5
WC3	4	 30	0.75

Time in minutes

TABLE 6A.4 WORK CENTER MASTER FILES, STANDARD WIDGETS

WORK CENTER	MINUTES AVAILABLE	UTILIZATION	EFFICIENCY	PLANNED QUEUE (days)
WC1	2,400	100%	100%	4
WC2	2,400	100%	100%	4
WC3	2,400	100%	100%	4

TABLE 6A.5 MASTER PRODUCTION SCHEDULE FOR FINISHED WIDGETS

	WEEK											
	1	2	3	4	5	6	7	8	9	10	11	12
Quantity	250	200	250	150	200	300	150	250	200	200	250	200

TABLE 6A.6 PLANNED ORDER RELEASES FOR STANDARD WIDGETS

PART	WEEK						
	1	2	3	4	5	6	7
100	200	250	150	200	300	150	250
110	300	400	600	300	500	400	400
121	900	1,500	1,200	1,200	1,500	1,200	0
122	2,500	2,000	2,000	2,500	2,000	0	0

At time 2400 another week's planned orders will be released:

Part	Opn. No.	Quantity	Location	Process Time	Next
100	1	250	WC3	968	Stock
110	1	400	WC2	310	WC1
121	1	1,500	WC3	465	WC1
122	1	2,000	WC2	1,525	WC3

Organizing this information by work center, one finds that after the first week's set of planned orders have been released, the queues at the three work centers are as shown in Table 6A.7

Table 6A.8 gives part number, operation number, arrival time, operation process time, operation finish time, and next station for each job. As each job

TABLE 6A.7 FIRST OPERATIONS, JOBS IN QUEUE AT TIME 0

PART-OPN.	QUANTITY	ARRIVAL	PROCESS TIME	FINISH TIME	NEXT STATION
		WC1			
110–2	400	0	215	215	Stock
121–2	1,500	0	400	615	WC2
122–3	2,000	0	1,075	1690	WC3
		WC2			
121–3	1,200	0	315	315	Stock
110–1	300	0	235	550	WC1
122–1	2,500	0	1,900	2450	WC3
		WC3			
100–1	250	0	968	968	Stock
122–4	2,000	0	1,330	2298	Stock
122–2	1,500	0	330	2628	WC1
100–1	200	0	780	3408	Stock
121–1	900	0	285	3693	WC1

Process time in minutes

TABLE 6A.8 FINISH TIMES BY WORK CENTER

PART-OPN.	QUANTITY	ARRIVAL	PROCESS TIME	FINISH TIME	NEXT STATION
		WC1			
110–2	400	0	215	215	Stock
121–2	1,500	0	400	615	WC2
122–3	2,000	0	1,075	1690	WC3
110–2	300	550	165	1855	Stock
122–3	1,500	2615	825	3440	WC3
110–2	400	3150	215	3655	Stock
121–2	900	3680	250	3930	WC2
		WC2			
121–3	1,200	0	315	315	Stock
110–1	300	0	235	550	WC1
122–1	2,500	0	1,900	2450	WC3
121–3	1,500	615	390	2840	Stock
110–1	400	2400	310	3150	WC1
122–1	2,000	2400	1,900	5050	
		WC3			
100–1	250	0	968	968	Stock
122–4	2,000	0	1,330	2298	Stock
122–2	1,500	0	330	2628	WC1

TABLE 6A.8 (CONTINUED)

PART-OPN.	QUANTITY	ARRIVAL	PROCESS TIME	FINISH TIME	NEXT STATION
			WC3		
100–1	200	0	780	3408	Stock
121–1	900	0	285	3693	WC1
122–4	1,500	1690	1,155	4848	Stock
100–1	250	2400	955	5803	Stock
121–1	1,500	2400	465	6248	WC1
122–2	2,500	2450	405	6653	WC1
122–4	1,500	3440	1,155	7808	Stock
		Process time in minutes			

finishes it moves to the next station. Thus, at time 215, part 110 finishes WC1 and is placed in stock. At time 315 part 121 finishes WC2 and is placed in stock. At time 550 part 110 finishes WC2 and joins the queue at WC1. Each job is processed in the sequence completed. At time 2400, the set of jobs shown in Table 6A.7 join the queue. Continuing to process jobs not in queue at time 0 yields Table 6A.8.

The Gantt chart is created by portraying graphically the information given in the Part-Opn. column and the Finish Time column.

Dispatching

Whenever a worker finishes a job, someone, usually his or her supervisor, must decide which job is to be performed next (provided more than one choice exists). The term **dispatching** refers to deciding which job to do next. The term **sequencing** refers to the process of determining the order in which several jobs should be performed. Thus, sequencing involves a larger problem than dispatching. Although most dispatching rules can be used to sequence an entire queue, it is important to remember that the dispatching decision is always made one job at a time. In manufacturing, it is more important to make dispatching decisions than sequencing decisions since by the time the next job has been completed the set of choices may have changed (or their priorities may have changed).

A major goal of capacity management is to get the right jobs out at the right time (perform to schedule). Since the type of dispatching used to assign jobs to work centers can have an important influence on ability to perform to schedule, this chapter examines some of the more important dispatching techniques and their impact on due-date performance within an MRP-planned shop. As this topic usually is considered a part of shop floor control, no attempt to provide a complete review of the subject is made here. Melnyk, Carter, Dilts, and Lyth (19) provide an excellent review of dispatching rules in their text *Shop Floor Control*. Baker (1) provides the most comprehensive examination of sequencing procedures in his text *Introduction to Sequencing and Scheduling*.

A discussion of the influence of sequence-dependent setups on the dispatching decision is presented next. Although setup times are treated in almost all capacity management literature as unrelated to the sequence in which jobs are performed, in fact setup times are frequently sequence dependent. Consider a paint shop which is currently processing a set of black widgets.

The remaining set of widgets are to be painted white, green, red, and black, with the other set of black widgets due to be processed fourth. The paint shop supervisor will immediately recognize that a major setup cost can be avoided by processing the second set of black widgets first instead of fourth because the paint lines have to be cleaned very thoroughly before each change of color to avoid contamination of the next color used. This type of situation occurs frequently. The practice of running a job early to save setup time is frequently called "cherry picking." Some people feel a supervisor should be encouraged to cherry pick; other feel it costs more in late costs by delaying important jobs than it saves in labor costs.

Finally, the use of heuristics to modify dispatching decisions will be examined. Dispatching heuristics attempt to account for conditions at other work centers, whereas dispatching rules tend to focus only on the current work center. Since all work centers in the shop are interrelated, perhaps dispatching heuristics can improve upon the performance of dispatching rules. Research is under way to incorporate some dispatching heuristics into expert systems (computer programs which mimic the decision making of human experts). A speculative discussion of the future of artificial intelligence within capacity management concludes the chapter.

THE MAJOR DISPATCHING RULES

The dispatching rules to be discussed are as follows: **first-in, first-out (FIFO), earliest job due date (EDD), earliest operation due date (ODD), least slack per operation (OPS), critical ratio (CRR), cost over time (COVERT), shortest processing time (SPT), highest-value job first (HVF),** and **modified operation due date (MOD).** Each of the rules will be defined formally, including a discussion of alternative definitions in use. Then a review of recent research relating to the performance of such rules in an MRP environment is presented.

First In, First Out (FIFO)

Perhaps the most commonly used dispatching rule is simply first in, first out. As the name implies, jobs are performed in the sequence in which they arrive at the work center. Bank tellers and movie ticket sellers operate in this fashion.

Earliest Job Due Date (EDD)

The job processed first will be the one with the earliest due date for the job. In Example 4.1, part 110 has a two-week lead time, consisting of two operations each having a one-week lead time. Using EDD dispatching, the priority of a lot of part 110 is based on the due date of the final (second) operation.

Earliest Operation Due Date (ODD)

The job processed first will be the one with the earliest operation due date. Thus, if a lot of part 110 is released, the priority of that lot at each operation is based on the date the operation is due, not on the date the final operation is due.

Least Slack per Operation (OPS)

Slack is defined as the time from today until the due date minus remaining processing time. Formally:

$$S_i = d_i - t - \sum_{j=m}^{n} p_{ij} \qquad (7.1)$$

where

S_i is the slack available for job
d_i is the due date for job i
t is today's date
m is the sequence number of the current operation
n is the total number of operations
p_{ij} is processing time, job i, station j

There are two ways to define slack. Static slack defines slack once, at the time a job enters the queue. Dynamic slack redefines slack each time a dispatching decision has to be made. In this chapter slack will always mean dynamic slack. A number of studies found dynamic slack to be a reasonable dispatching technique and static slack to be a poor one.

Slack per operation is, as it sounds, total slack divided by the number of operations remaining. The concept behind this rule is that slack measures the amount of time a job can spend in queue and still be finished on time. Slack per operation then attempts to allocate remaining slack among the various operations.

Critical Ratio (CRR)

Critical ratio is defined as the time remaining until the due date divided by the time required to complete all remaining operations plus the planned interoperation time:

$$CR_i = \frac{(d_i - t)}{\sum\limits_{j=m}^{n} (p_{ij} + q_{ij})} \qquad (7.2)$$

where CR_i is the critical ratio of job i and q_{ij} is the planned queue time of job i, operation j. All other terms are as in equation 7.1.

The concept behind critical ratio is that it will indicate whether a job is on time, early, or late. If

$Critical\ ratio$ = 1, the job is on time.
              > 1, the job is early.
              < 1, the job is late.

The job chosen to be performed next is the one having the smallest critical ratio.

Cost over Time (COVERT)

COVERT is an attempt to recognize that all jobs are not equally profitable to the company. COVERT sets priorities by finding the total cost of the job and dividing that by the time remaining until due date. COVERT recognizes that it is more important to finish high-value jobs on time.

Shortest Processing Time (SPT)

Shortest processing time dispatching selects to be performed next the operation that will require the least amount of time to complete at this station. It can be shown that for a single processor, SPT maximizes throughput. This principle is the reason express checkout lines are so popular in supermarkets. Unfortunately, a very negative property of SPT dispatching is that long jobs (which COVERT would expedite) tend to be very late.

Highest-Value Job First (HVF)

The concept of performing the highest-value job first has a lot of intuitive appeal to managers, since high-value jobs tend to also be high-margin jobs. Managers are also quite aware of the costs associated with delivering very large jobs late. Shops that perform a lot of expediting tend to operate as though highest-value job first dispatching were being performed. Given that virtually all accounting systems value the job in direct proportion to the labor content, highest-value job first is essentially the same thing as longest job first. A negative aspect of this approach is that, just as SPT maximizes throughput, longest processing time first dispatching minimizes throughput. One may anticipate that this dispatching rule is likely to increase shop congestion by reducing the number of jobs which are completed in a given time period.

Biggs (3) studied two variations of this rule, which he called the dollar unit rule (DUR) and the dollar cost rule (DCR). The dollar unit rule is: "Process that component first that is a component or subassembly of the final product with the highest unit cost." The dollar cost rule is: "Process that component first that has the largest unit cost." The DCR is a single-level implementation of the highest-value-first concept, while DUR is a multiple-level implementation of the concept.

Modified Operation Due Date (MOD)

Modified operation due date is a dispatching rule recently introduced by Baker and Kanet (2). The modified operation due date rule defines the operation due date to be the operation's original due date or the operation's early finish time, whichever comes later. Early finish time is defined as today's date plus remaining processing time, assuming no queue time but also no lot splitting or operation overlapping. Jobs are chosen for processing by smallest operation due date.

MEASURES OF DISPATCHING RULE PERFORMANCE

There are a number of ways to evaluate the performance of dispatching rules relative to a schedule. Some good performance measures are (a) number of tardy jobs, (b) average tardiness, (c) average absolute deviation from due date, (d) dollar days late, (e) weighted earliness and tardiness penalties, and (f) total profit maximization.

Evaluating the impact of delivering a job late is very difficult. There is perhaps some absolute level of cost incurred simply from having any job late at all. This fixed cost arises from the fact that there is likely to be an inquiry from the customer about the status of the job. Someone will have to respond to the customer, having first determined the status of the job and the likely delivery date. Further, some action may have to be taken to ensure that the customer is not too upset by the experience. In all likelihood there is also a variable late cost which is a function of the degree of lateness, the value of the job, and the value of the customer. Many contracts contain specific provision for late penalties which are variable penalties.

Measuring the number of tardy jobs is appropriate if most of the late cost is fixed. If there is a high variable cost, however, average tardiness, absolute deviation from due date, and dollar days late would be more appropriate measures.

Tardiness is defined to be 0 if a job is early and the time late if the job is late. Average tardiness is the simple average of individual job tardiness. Average absolute deviation from due date is just what it sounds like, the average of the absolute value of the difference between the due date and the date delivered. Dollar days late is defined as the sum of the number of days late times the dollar value of the job, days late being 0 if the job is early.

Weighted earliness and tardiness penalties permit one to place a value on the customer in addition to the value of the job itself. Total profitability measures allow one to factor other costs, such as inventory and overtime costs, into the equation.

STUDIES OF DISPATCHING RULE PERFORMANCE

All studies of dispatching rule performance which have relevance to a shop planned by an MRP system have been simulation studies rather than analytical studies. Analytical modeling would be useful only if the shop could be decomposed into a set of independent queues. Jackson (16) proved that such decomposition could be performed only if

1. The interarrival times for jobs arriving from outside the system are exponentially distributed.
2. The processing times at each machine are exponentially distributed. Each machine is preceded by a queue having infinite capacity.
3. The jobs are routed to a machine by a fixed probability transition matrix.
4. The dispatching rule is first in, first out.

In an MRP-planned shop, none of these four conditions is likely to hold. First, interarrival times are not exponentially distributed. The exponential distribution exhibits a large number of short, near 0, intervals and a few exceptionally long intervals. If one is attempting to smooth production, and is using input/output analysis, the times between releases of jobs to the shop floor will not be distributed exponentially. Second, processing times at machines have been found to be lognormally distributed, as a general rule. Even if machine times were exponentially distributed, queues at machines are not infinite, particularly if good input/output control is maintaining the actual queue near the planned length. Third, the mix of jobs in the shop tends to shift over time, also shifting the frequency with which various machines are needed. It is not correct to represent this process as a fixed probability transition matrix (although it would be appropriate if product mix were constant). Finally, although many shops use first in, first out dispatching, many use earliest due date, least slack, critical ratio, and other rules. Even those using first in, first out often override the ordinary dispatching because of presidential decrees or to save setup time in a sequence-dependent setup situation.

It was clear in 1967 (and suspected earlier) that analytical models would be of no use in analyzing queues in a real job shop. Efforts to use simulation models began about 1960. One of the most useful early studies was performed by Conway, Johnson, and Maxwell (7). This is a very helpful study for the beginning analyst because the authors have carefully reported all their mistakes as well as their final achievements. It is very easy to bias unintentionally the results of a comparison of dispatching rules, as Conway, Johnson, and Maxwell discovered. Anyone interested in studying such rules for application in his or her own shop would do well to begin by reading this study.

Early efforts to study a job shop via simulation modeled what is known as an "open" job shop. That is, rather than using fixed routing data as in Example 4.1, the modeler would, at the completion of each operation, draw a random number to determine whether the job is to exit the shop or, if not, which machine it is to go to next. This approach was dictated by the limited storage capacity of 1960s-era computers and the general inability to process a large data base such as that required by MRP. (For that matter, MRP did not come into common usage until the 1970s.) Unfortunately, modeling a shop in this fashion fails to capture the dependent-material, dependent-sequencing, dependent-routing relationships which exist in a shop in which components are eventually brought together to be assembled.

Some of the early efforts which make worthwhile reading include Conway (5,6), Deane and Moodie (9), Elvers (10), Gere (14), and Hershauer and Ebert (15). Three good survey articles are Day and Hottenstein (8), Panwalker and Iskander (22), and Blackstone, Phillips, and Hogg (4).

Results of Early Dispatching Studies

Some results of early studies which appear likely to hold up in MRP-planned environments are as follows:

1. First in, first out performs poorly, having a tardiness performance comparable to that achieved by random selection. Rules which explicitly recognize due dates, such as EDD, ODD, OPS, and CRR, generally do much better.
2. Longest processing time does much worse than FIFO and should generally be avoided. Anyone wishing to factor job importance into the dispatching decision would do much better using COVERT.
3. Shortest processing time does fairly well on number of tardy jobs, but much worse on average tardiness and dollar days late because a few large jobs tend to be very late.
4. It is difficult to establish that there is a statistically significant difference between the good rules based on due date, such as EDD, ODD, OPS, and CRR. All seem to be preferable to FIFO, HVF, and SPT.
5. The performance of all rules is sensitive to the manner in which due dates are set. If rules are set in an arbitrary manner, rather than relying on expected operation and interoperation time, then rules based on due date are often outperformed by SPT.

6. The performance of all rules seems to be sensitive to overall capacity utilization. It seems that as the shop gets very congested the SPT rule does better, perhaps because by maximizing throughput it helps to eliminate some of the congestion. This finding suggests that during periods of shop overload a useful strategy might be to use some form of SPT at the bottlenecks and a rule based on due date at non-bottlenecks.

7. A number of variations of the SPT rule have been studied in an effort to find one that maintains throughput maximization without causing excessive delays on large jobs. These rules are known collectively as truncated SPT rules. All involve switching from SPT dispatching to some other rule when one or more jobs have been waiting in queue for a long time. A recent study by Fry, Philipoom, and Blackstone (12) compared the performance of various truncated SPT rules in an open job shop under conditions of severe shop congestion.

Recent Studies of Dispatching Rule Performance

Studies have recently been made of dispatching rules in MRP-planned assembly shops, i.e., shops in which some parts are components or subassemblies of other parts. Using a factory described by Kriebel (17) having 3 departments, 8 purchased items, and 32 manufactured items, Biggs (3) studied SPT, CRR, the two previously defined high-value-first rules (DUR and DCR), and two additional rules, the dollar volume rule (DVR) and the unit volume rule (UVR). The DVR rule processes first the components of end items having the highest dollar volume. The UVR rule processes first the component having the most successor (parent) items. The results of Biggs's experiment, ranking these rules against four performance criteria, are summarized in Table 7.1.

Since no single rule dominated all performance criteria, Biggs then used several weighting schemes to rank the criteria. The results of this weighting procedure are summarized in Table 7.2.

TABLE 7.1   RANKING OF SEQUENCING RULES WITH UNWEIGHTED PERFORMANCE CRITERIA ($p < 0.05$)

RANK	NUMBER STOCKOUTS	UNITS STOCKOUT	SETUPS	DOLLARS INVENTORY
1	DUR(100)	UVR(100)	SPT(100)	DUR(100)
2	CRR(92)	CRR(86)	DCR(76)	SPT(97)
3	UVR(88)	DVR(84)	CRR(76)	CRR(83)
4	SPT(85)	SPT(62)	DUR(74)	DCR(82)
5	DCR(57)	DUR(60)	UVR(64)	DVR(80)
6	DVR(55)	DCR(60)	DVR(63)	UVR(70)

TABLE 7.2   RANKING OF SEQUENCING RULES WITH UNWEIGHTED PERFORMANCE CRITERIA ($p < 0.05$)

	NUMBER STOCKOUTS	UNITS STOCKOUT	SETUPS	DOLLARS INVENTORY	NUMBER STOCKOUTS	UNITS STOCKOUT	SETUPS	DOLLARS INVENTORY	NUMBER STOCKOUTS	UNITS STOCKOUT	SETUPS	DOLLARS INVENTORY
WEIGHTS	1/8	1/8	1/4	1/2	1/8	1/8	1/2	1/4	1/6	1/6	1/3	1/3
		SPT(100)				SPT(100)				SPT(100)		
		DUR(57)				CRR(66)				DUR(62)		
		DCR(57)				DCR(66)				CRR(56)		
		CRR(55)				DUR(64)				DCR(56)		
		DVR(42)				DVR(50)				DVR(42)		
		UVR(41)				UVR(49)				UVR(42)		
WEIGHTS	1/5	1/5	1/5	2/5	1/4	1/4	1/4	1/4	1/3	1/3	1/6	1/6
		SPT(100)				SPT(100)				CRR(100)		
		DUR(60)				CRR(69)				SPT(95)		
		DCR(60)				DUR(58)				DVR(69)		
		CRR(54)				DCR(54)				DUR(57)		
		DVR(43)				DVR(45)				UVR(53)		
		UVR(42)				UVR(44)				DCR(53)		

It is somewhat surprising to find SPT yielding generally the best performance. Earliest due date and least slack per operation were not included in Biggs's study, but critical ratio was. One suspects, based on results of earlier studies, that in Biggs's study either (1) capacity utilization was quite high or (2) due dates were not a function of planned operation plus interoperation time.

The most thorough study of dispatching rule performance to date was performed by Gardiner (13) in his dissertation research. Gardiner used a 15-department, 150-part factory, setting cost relationships on the same basis as that used in Biggs's study. All published studies prior to Gardiner's used the MRP system on the front end of the simulation, creating an unchanging set of orders to be released. Gardiner simulated MPS nervousness by allowing 10 percent of the orders to have their due dates changed each month (order quantities were not changed). Changes in due date were limited to plus or minus 3 weeks, with each of the six possible changes ($-3, -2, \ldots, +3$) being equally likely. The MRP system was then rerun within the simulation and the schedule of orders to be released was updated, as were the due dates of orders already released. Gardiner studied eight dispatching rules—EDD, ODD, MOD, CRR, FIFO, COVERT, OPS, and a modified SPT—in conjunction with several different lot-sizing rules. The SPT modification was that SPT was used only at two bottleneck work centers (out of 15 total), while EDD was used elsewhere. Further, SPT was truncated and FIFO used if any job had missed its operation due date. He also tested a hypothesis that there is no interaction between lot-sizing rules and dispatching rules within an MRP environment. The lot-sizing rules tested included **economic order quantity, period order quantity, least total cost**, the **Silver-Meal algorithm**, and a modified, multistage version of the Silver-Meal algorithm.

Gardiner used several performance measures, including value of work in process, percentage of jobs tardy, and total operating profit. In measuring total profit, sales were offset by a weekly operating expense plus purchases. The remaining cash was assumed to be invested, paying 6 percent per annum for each day held as cash. A finished item was not sold until its due date (a make-to-order environment was used).

A number of Gardiner's results are extremely interesting. First, Silver-Meal was found to be hypersensitive to nervousness. This finding is significant since Silver-Meal was found to have the best performance in a number of studies which did not involve nervousness, including Melnyk and Piper (18). As Table 7.3 shows, single-stage Silver-Meal finished last, by a wide margin, in operating profit and percentage of jobs tardy.

The difference between Silver-Meal and the other techniques in both percentage of jobs tardy and total operating profit was found to be statistically significant. The differences between the remaining techniques were not sig-

TABLE 7.3 PERFORMANCE MEASURES OF VARIOUS LOT-SIZING TECHNIQUES

	PERFORMANCE MEASURE		
LOT-SIZING TECHNIQUE*	OPERATING PROFIT	AVERAGE WIP	PERCENT TARDY
GCK	$373,236	$128,078	6.9
EOQ	$370,962	$188,446	9.5
LTC	$369,661	$152,947	9.7
POQ	$368,254	$148,523	10.8
SML	$301,637	$122,535	18.8

*GCK Multistage Silver-Meal
EOQ Economic Order Quantity
LTC Least Total Cost
POQ Period Order Quantity
SML Single-Stage Silver-Meal

nificant. Since the degree of nervousness included in this study is very small, it appears that Silver-Meal should not be used in an environment with any MPS instability. One hesitates to generalize from one study of one specific environment, but in this instance the differences are so great that one should assume that Silver-Meal will perform poorly in any environment having MPS instability unless some later study contradicts Gardiner's findings in a specific environment.

Silver-Meal did obtain the minimum average WIP, but this cost savings did not translate into improved operating profits. Another interesting result is that the multistage version of Silver-Meal had the best performance. The multistage algorithm involved a multiplier, k, multiplied by the single-stage setup cost to obtain multistage setup cost. The multiplier is a function of the number of components at all levels of the bill of material. It recognizes that an additional setup in a parent item is likely to cause further additional setups throughout the component items. Although Gardiner studied only one multistage lot-sizing procedure, the dramatic improvement created by that one procedure suggests that many multistage lot-sizing procedures should be studied. This finding is similar to that of Biggs, who found that the dollar unit rule, which focused on the value of multiple levels, did about as well as critical ratio, long considered perhaps the best of all single-level rules, while single-level high-value-first rules did poorly.

Gardiner studied the effectiveness of a 4-week to 8-week time fence (i.e., a prohibition on MPS changes in the first 4 weeks of the planning horizon) in controlling nervousness. He also looked at the use of safety stock at all levels of the bill of material as a nervousness-reduction technique. As Table 7.4 indicates, both the time fence and safety stock helped the dismal performance of Silver-Meal but not the performance of any of the other lot-sizing techniques. These findings strongly suggest that capacity management can be greatly improved by the creation of lot-sizing rules which recognize the dependent-demand, dependent-routing environment actually found in manufacturing.

TABLE 7.4   CHANGE IN OPERATING PROFIT DUE TO TIME FENCE AND SAFETY STOCK

| | MEAN INCREASE* | |
LOT-SIZING TECHNIQUE	WITH 4-WEEK TIME FENCE	WITH USE OF SAFETY STOCK
SML	$20,588	$48,345
EOQ	0	0
POQ	0	0
LTC	0	0
EOQ	0	0

*An increase of zero means that actual results were not significantly different from zero.

Like many previous studies, Gardiner's study found no significant differences among the better dispatching rules. In studying how dispatching rules performed, Gardiner eliminated results found using the Silver-Meal lot-sizing approach because the major differences created by Silver-Meal made it impossible to judge the significance of the minor differences created by dispatching. Using the simulation results from 480 runs involving the four other lot-sizing techniques, Gardiner found that first in, first out, modified operation due date, and least slack per operation performed worst on operating profit and total WIP. The due date, critical ratio, and COVERT rules did better, with no significant differences between them. The modified SPT rule was also found to perform with the better rules.

The modified operation due date rule did perform best on the performance measure it was designed to optimize (percentage of jobs tardy). However, MOD had mediocre performance on average tardiness and poor performance on maximum tardiness. These results are summarized in Table 7.5.

TABLE 7.5   RANKING OF DISPATCHING RULES ON FIVE PERFORMANCE MEASURES

	PERFORMANCE MEASURE				
RANK	OPERATING PROFIT	AVERAGE WIP	PERCENT TARDY	AVERAGE DAYS TARDY PER JOB	MAXIMUM DAYS TARDY PER JOB
1..........	EDD*	CRR*	MOD	CRR*	EDD*
2..........	CRR*	SPT*	SPT	SPT*	SPT*
3..........	SPT*	EDD*	CRR	EDD*	CRR*
4..........	ODD*	ODD*	EDD	COVERT*	ODD*
5..........	COVERT*	COVERT*	ODD	ODD*	COVERT*
6..........	OPS*	OPS	COVERT	MOD*	OPS*
7..........	MOD	MOD	OPS	OPS	MOD
8..........	FIFO	FIFO	FIFO	FIFO	FIFO

*No statistically significant difference from best rule, $\alpha = 0.05$.

These studies indicate that the choice of dispatching technique within an MRP system has limited impact on system performance. One can harm system performance by choosing a poor technique, such as FIFO, but one cannot improve performance by using a sophisticated technique such as critical ratio or COVERT. The easiest dispatching technique to implement in an MRP environment is earliest operation due date. This technique is also the most logical, since it attempts to keep all jobs on the schedule used for planning. Until a clearly superior technique is created, ODD is a logical choice for all MRP environments.

The Effect of Bottlenecks

In recent months a number of researchers have begun to accept the notion originated by Goldratt in the OPT (optimized production technology) software that bottleneck work centers must be treated differently from non-bottlenecks. Goldratt's procedure schedules the bottleneck work centers first and then schedules non-bottlenecks to be consistent with bottlenecks. A detailed description of the OPT software and philosophy is contained in Chapter 9. Goldratt advocates dispatching by operation due date to conform to schedules determined by the OPT software. An interesting area for future research is to determine how dispatching within an environment planned by MRP rather than OPT should respond to the presence of bottlenecks. Should there be one dispatching procedure for bottlenecks and another for non-bottlenecks? It seems probable that there should be two procedures, but what those two procedures should be remains to be determined.

SEQUENCE-DEPENDENT SETUPS

Consider the following situation. A supervisor must choose between three jobs in queue at a work center. The documentation accompanying the jobs indicates the following:

Job	Setup Time	Processing Time	Due Date
1	4 hours	8 hours	Today
2	7 hours	12 hours	Tomorrow
3	10 hours	9 hours	Day after tomorrow

The supervisor knows, however, that the job just completed on the machine is very similar to job 3 and thinks that since the setup would be less complicated, it could be completed within 2 hours. The shop works 16 hours per day. (Assume utilization and efficiency are 100 percent.) Should job 3 be run first?

The supervisor really lacks enough information to make this decision. Processing job 3 first will cause jobs 1 and 2 to be late, but there is no way to know whether the lost time can be made up at other work centers. Nor does the supervisor know how important it is to finish either job on time or whether the due date of either job is still valid. Nevertheless a decision must be made. Unless someone is pressing for immediate completion of job 1 or 2, the supervisor will run job 3 first. The reason for this is that the supervisor is judged on the basis of efficiency, defined as standard hours completed per hour worked. By saving 8 hours of setup (nonproductive) time, the supervisor will be credited with 19 hours of output (based on setup plus processing-time standards) with only 11 hours of actual labor.

Until very recently, letting the supervisor make such decisions without decision aids was not only the practical way to do it, it was the *only* way. Consider, however, the tools available today. Given a CRT which can access an MRP system having operations-scheduling capabilities such as those described in the Remmele Engineering case in Chapter 6, the supervisor should be able to ask for and quickly receive a revised schedule for all work centers which would be affected by the three jobs in question (which the computer would determine from the routings of each part). With detailed information about which jobs are projected to miss their due dates if the plan is followed or if it is modified, and with a summary of the implications of the change, the supervisor is then in a position to discuss the implications of this decision with planners and with marketing. The supervisor would still have to make the decision, and take responsibility for it, but the decision would be based on additional, perhaps extremely valuable, information.

Making additional information available to supervisors will not change their behavior, however, if the performance measure used to evaluate supervisors continues to be work-center efficiency. It will be necessary to include as a performance measure some factor which measures performance to schedule and places a higher value on performance to schedule than on efficiency.

At this point, it appears that most shops are not taking advantage of all the capacity information available to them when dispatching decisions are made. There appears to be a great need for academic studies of the sequence-dependent setup phenomenon in order to formulate rules of thumb on when the firm should take advantage of a setup savings.

DISPATCHING HEURISTICS

Gere (14) investigates a number of forward-looking heuristics, all of which are feasible given today's information systems. One is a simple look ahead to see if any critical jobs are due to arrive in the queue in a short period. If a critical job is due, the station starts setup for the anticipated job instead of starting work on a less critical job which will be preempted.

Another simple heuristic is to look downstream at the next work center on each job's routing to see whether the center is crowded. With this information one might decide to de-expedite a job which would go to an already overcrowded work center and/or expedite a job which would go to a center about to run out of work.

Gere found that the heuristics worked very well, but his research was not conducted using an MRP-planned shop. Although it is likely that Gere's findings have application to MRP-planned systems, this research really should be repeated to find out whether they do and to attempt to establish rules of thumb about when resequencing the queue based on downstream considerations is useful.

It also seems likely that dispatching based on the status of related components might be useful. It seems foolish to expedite an order of component A because the due date is approaching if component A must wait for component B, which is unavoidably delayed and will not be available for several days. Such expediting is not only possible but likely in all single-center dispatching rules discussed in this chapter.

DEVELOPMENT OF EXPERT SYSTEMS

Artificial intelligence (AI) techniques attempt to have a computer perform the same type of reasoning, and come to the same conclusion, that a human expert would. To truly be an AI technique, the computer program must be able to show the logic by which the conclusion was reached. There are two possible implementations of AI technology. An *expert system* not only makes a decision, it acts on it. Expert systems are likely to be very useful in scheduling flexible manufacturing systems (FMS), as will be explained later. A *decision support system* simply recommends a course of action; the human must make the decision. Decision support systems are widely used as a diagnostic aid in medicine. Decision support systems might be quite useful in capacity management, giving the novice scheduler access to the advice of an expert.

Flexible manufacturing systems need expert systems to schedule them. Work is under way to develop such systems, since at present FMS's do not operate at full capacity because of the need for human intervention to manage capacity. An FMS is a set of fully automated machines connected by automatic guided vehicles which transfer parts between machines. The typical automated machine has perhaps 50 tools and is controlled by a microprocessor which in turn is controlled by a central computer. When a part is delivered to the automatic machine, the central computer downloads to the machine's microprocessor instructions for one or more tasks. When the tasks are completed, more instructions are downloaded until processing on the part is completed. Then the automated guided vehicle is called to bring a new part and to take the old part to the next machine to process it.

The concept behind an FMS is that it should enable low-volume job shops to achieve efficiencies comparable to those in high-volume flow shops by going to near-total automation. Unfortunately, machining times are random variables for machines as well as for people, because of factors such as tool wear and uneven hardness of materials. The first algorithms used to schedule FMS's assumed that machining times were constants. These algorithms allow backlogs to build as machine activation approaches 100 percent. A backlog may cause machine A to be blocked, since the part cannot be removed until machine B is ready to receive it. Creating good expert systems to run an FMS is thus a high priority. Since the systems cost several million dollars, capacity utilization must be very high for them to be cost effective. A by-product of such research is likely to be good decision support systems for job shops.

Researchers at Carnegie-Mellon have begun a study of the application of artificial intelligence techniques to the job shop scheduling problem (20, 21, 23). Overall progress on the system, which they call OPIS, is quite impressive. What is most impressive is that the researchers are taking full advantage of the information available to the computer in managing capacity. For example, current practice is to treat alternative routing as a last resort. OPIS considers alternative routing first. When an order is received, the capacity already committed on the primary route is compared with that on the secondary. If the primary routing is likely to be unable to meet the customer's desired delivery date, then the trade-off between late cost, efficiency, and quality is considered and the system decides whether to use a primary or alternate route.

After routings have been settled, OPIS then identifies bottlenecks, i.e., the most heavily utilized resources. The bottlenecks are scheduled with the objective of minimizing tardiness costs. Non-bottlenecks are scheduled using forward scheduling from completion on bottleneck to stock and backward scheduling from start at bottleneck to release.

Those familiar with OPT (discussed in Chapter 9) will see some obvious parallels. The Carnegie-Mellon group developed OPIS after extensively interviewing personnel at a company (Westinghouse) which uses OPT in some plants. It is not apparent from published articles whether the researchers were familiar with OPT itself.

The research reported to date on expert system development for capacity management is most promising. The major drawback seems to be that computer processing times are quite long. However, computing continues to become less expensive as time passes. With the introduction of 80386-based microcomputers in 1987, microcomputers became fast enough to run fairly large artificial intelligence programs. A challenge to capacity management professionals is to begin to utilize this technology effectively.

The present MRP approach to planning does not recognize the existence of capacity constraints or sequence-dependent setups in timing orders. Expediting, in the form of lot splitting or operation overlapping, is not part of formal MRP logic, nor is the possibility of alternate routing for a particular job. The advantage of an artificial intelligence approach is that, in theory, all these factors can be considered at planning time. The difficulty in implementing a more sophisticated capacity planning approach lies in the fact that manufacturing is a very dynamic environment. If a computer program requires a great deal of time to execute, uncontrollable factors such as machine breakdowns and changes to orders by customers are likely to have changed the problem while the computer is still working on a solution to the original problem. Faster computers are not the sole answer. Reducing unplanned variation, for example, by using preventive maintenance to reduce the occurrence of unplanned repairs, makes the capacity management task simpler whether planning is performed manually or automatically.

SUMMARY

This chapter examines several dispatching rules which focus on information pertinent to one work center, including least slack per operation, earliest job and operation due date, critical ratio, cost over time, and others. Based on currently available information, which is admittedly incomplete, it seems that earliest operation due date is the most logical choice among such rules for an MRP system. The existence of heuristics that take into account congestion at the next work center in the part's routing or the status of related component orders is noted. Research performed in non-MRP environments indicates that such techniques have merit; this research needs to be brought up to date by testing in a variety of MRP-planned environments. Finally, the emergence of artificial intelligence programs to control completely automated factories and to advise managers in other factories is discussed. Artificial intelligence techniques may eventually replace MRP logic with a system which recognizes constraints in a more efficient manner than the current MRP approach of master schedule to rough-cut to MRP to CRP to replanning.

REFERENCES

1. Baker, K. R. *Introduction to Sequencing and Scheduling.* New York: John Wiley & Sons, 1974.
2. Baker, K. R., and J. J. Kanet. "Job Shop Scheduling with Modified Due Dates." *Journal of Operations Management* 4 (1983): 11–22.
3. Biggs, J. R. "Priority Rules for Shop Floor Control in a Material Requirements Planning System Under Various Levels of Capacity." *International Journal of Production Research* 23 (1985): 33–46.
4. Blackstone, J. H., Jr., D. T. Phillips, and G. L. Hogg. "A State-of-Art Survey of Job Shop Dispatching Rules." *International Journal of Production Research* 20 (1982).
5. Conway, R. W. "Priority Dispatching and Job Lateness in a Job Shop." *Journal of Industrial Engineering* 16 (1965).
6. Conway, R. W. "Priority Dispatching and Work-in-Process Inventory in a Job Shop." *Journal of Industrial Engineering* 16 (1965).
7. Conway, R. W., B. M. Johnson, and W. L. Maxwell. "An Experimental Investigation of Priority Dispatching." *Journal of Industrial Engineering* 11 (1960): 221.
8. Day, J. E., and M. P. Hottenstein. "Review of Sequencing Research." *Naval Research Logistics Quarterly* 17 (1970).
9. Deane, R. H., and C. L. Moodie. "A Dispatching Methodology for Balancing Workload Assignments in a Job Shop Production Facility." *A.I.E.E. Transactions* 4 (1972).

10. Elvers, D. A. "Job Shop Dispatching Rules Using Various Delivery Date Setting Criteria." *Production and Inventory Management* 14 (1973).

11. Fox, M. S., and S. F. Smith. "The Role of Intelligent Reactive Processing in Production Management." *Proceedings*, CAM-I 13th Annual Meeting and Technical Conference, Clearwater Beach, Fla., November 1984.

12. Fry, T. D., P. R. Philipoom, and J. H. Blackstone, Jr. "A Simulation Study of Processing Time Dispatching Rules." *Journal of Operations Management*, forthcoming, 1988.

13. Gardiner, S. C. "A Simulation Study of Lot Sizing and Dispatching Techniques in a Material Requirements Planning Environment with Master Production Schedule Instability." Ph.D. dissertation, University of Georgia, 1987.

14. Gere, W. S., Jr. "Heuristics in Job Shop Scheduling." *Management Science* 21 (1974).

15. Hershauer, J. C., and J. Ebert. "Search and Simulation Selection of a Job Shop Scheduling Rule." *Management Science* 21 (1974).

16. Jackson, J. R. "Networks of Waiting Lines." *Operations Research* 5 (August 1967): 518.

17. Kriebel, C. H. "A Production Management Operating System Simulation: Factory 2." Management Sciences Research Report No. 232, Carnegie-Mellon University, 1971.

18. Melnyk, S. A., and C. J. Piper. "Leadtime Errors in MRP: The Lot-Sizing Effect." *International Journal of Production Research* 23 (1985).

19. Melnyk, S. A., P. L. Carter, D. M. Dilts, and D. M. Lyth. *Shop Floor Control.* Homewood, Ill.: Dow Jones–Irwin, 1985.

20. Ow, P. S., and S. F. Smith. "Viewing Scheduling as an Opportunistic Problem Solving Process." Working Paper, Carnegie-Mellon University, May 1986.

21. Ow, P. S., and S. F. Smith. "Two Design Principles for Knowledge-based Systems." *Decision Sciences* 18 (1987): 430–447.

22. Panwalker, S. S., and W. Iskander. "A Survey of Scheduling Rules." *Operations Research* 25 (1977).

23. Smith, S. F., M. S. Fox, and P. S. Ow. "Constructing and Maintaining Detailed Production Plans: Investigations into the Development of Knowledge-based Factory Scheduling Systems." *AI Magazine* (Fall 1986).

EXERCISES

1. Distinguish between the terms *sequencing* and *dispatching*. When a work center goes idle and several options exist for what is to be processed

next, both dispatching and sequencing techniques can solve the problem. Discuss the advantages and disadvantages of each.

2. Discuss why setup times are often sequence dependent, i.e., are a function of the job just completed. A supervisor can often realize a considerable savings of setup time over a set of jobs by sequencing them to minimize setup time. Since minimizing setup times maximizes the efficiency of a work center, shouldn't a supervisor be encouraged to use sequence-dependent setups as the primary factor in making dispatching decisions? Why or why not?

3. What is the difference between earliest job due date and earliest operation due date? Which is more consistent with an MRP system?

4. What is the difference between slack per operation and critical ratio? Why might either rule be preferable to earliest due date?

5. What is meant by COVERT? What factor does this rule consider which is not considered by earliest due date? Discuss the advantages and disadvantages of COVERT compared to earliest due date.

6. Describe the shortest processing time rule. Why is this rule seldom used by manufacturers? Why is the rule often used by computer centers?

7. How should the performance of a dispatching rule be measured? Should one consider inventory cost, tardiness cost, or other factors? Should one consider profit performance? How can the performance be compared in actual practice? In a simulation study? Is study of dispatching rule performance worthwhile?

8. Why did Gardiner obtain results which differ from those of earlier studies? Which set of results are most meaningful for a situation in which the master production schedule will never be modified? Discuss the advantages and disadvantages of freezing the master production schedule for one month, two months, and six months.

9. Discuss how the dispatching heuristics studied by Gere differ from simple dispatching rules such as earliest operation due date. Are dispatching heuristics likely to improve overall MRP system performance?

10. Discuss the advantages and disadvantages of artificial intelligence as a tool for managing dispatching decisions.

11. Create a Gantt chart for Example 4.1 using shortest processing time dispatching.

12. Create a Gantt chart for Example 4.1 using earliest operation due date processing.

13. Given the following data:

Job	Processing Time	Due Date	Job Value
1	12	25	$500
2	18	45	$800
3	9	15	$400
4	15	60	$650
5	10	35	$450

Sequence the jobs using (1) shortest processing time (2) earliest operation due date (3) least slack (4) highest value first (5) cost over time remaining. For each sequence determine (1) number of tardy jobs (2) average tardiness among all jobs (3) total dollar days tardy. Discuss which tardiness measure is most appropriate and which sequence seems to work best.

14. *Advanced.* Modify the simulation model created in Exercise 8, Chapter 6, so that dispatching is done by SPT instead of EDD. Compare the results of the two simulations.

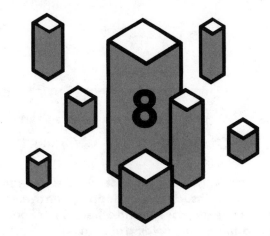

Capacity Planning for Adjunct Resources

Capacity management includes not only the scheduling of parts, people, and machines directly involved in production but also the scheduling of other needed items such as setup crews, equipment maintenance, and consumable and nonconsumable tooling. The set of resources required to make parts, people, and machines productive will be called *adjunct resources*. A setup crew is a team of workers who remove a tool or die used in the previous operation and replace it with one for the next operation. Since setup often involves precise calibration of the machine to operate with the new tool or die, setup sometimes takes hours. Maintenance of machines and of tooling is necessary periodically. If a machine is to be out for maintenance for several days, it may be necessary to stockpile the items that the machine builds before taking it out for maintenance. Consumable tools are tools such as drill bits, grinding wheels, and cutters which wear out regularly and must be replaced. Good capacity management requires planning the acquisition of such tools as well as of the material going directly into the product. A case study which typifies the problem of performing capacity planning for adjunct resources was recently published by Finch and Cox (1). After the case study is presented briefly, the management of consumable and nonconsumable tools will be discussed.

A CASE STUDY
Company P

Company P is a producer for the pharmaceutical industry of rubber components such as vial stoppers, intravenous unit rubber components, rubber needle covers, and other rubber items. It produces these items by the compression molding of both natural and synthetic rubbers. The basic steps in the manufacturing process are compounding the formula, molding the product, and trimming to remove bits of scrap.

The molding process can be accomplished by several different compression molding machines, each of which can handle a variety of different molds. In the molding process, rubber is forced into the mold cavities under pressure and cured at a predetermined temperature for a given time, resulting in a sheet of products which must later be separated. Defective units cannot be recycled; they are removed from the sheet and destroyed. Because of the occurrence of defects, the exact number of units produced is not known until trimming and packing have been completed.

The company is about 25 percent make-to-stock and 75 percent make-to-order. Most orders are for large quantities (100,000 or more), but the plant does accommodate smaller orders. The company produces approximately 750 end items out of 150 raw materials. The typical bill of materials has three levels. Since the end items include several products that differ in formulation or color but not in shape, Company P uses about 100 different molds to produce the 750 end items. Average manufacturing lead time is two weeks. Average lead time to the customer is six weeks. Most of the additional lead time is due to stringent quality control checks required because the products are used in the pharmaceutical industry.

Setup time to change a mold has a significant impact on machine efficiencies. The molding department is the bottleneck. Because it is difficult to stabilize the molding process, setup is lengthy, requiring an average of four hours. Once a mold is in place the company would prefer to make fairly long production runs.

Tool availability constrains the capacity of the department at times. Molds are very expensive, often costing more than $100,000 each. Because of the high cost, few duplicate molds are kept. Periodic cleaning of the molds is necessary and may take several days.

Company P typifies the need for planning adjunct capacity, tooling, setup, and maintenance. The company's planning and control system is built around a heavily modified commercial MRP system. Customer orders are keyed into the system, which creates manufacturing orders with suggested completion dates. Completion date feasibility is confirmed or amended at the plant, using rough-cut capacity planning to identify capacity problems in molding. As orders are scheduled, the plant scheduler assigns them to one or another of the molding machines manually, using a spreadsheet. Once a molding machine is scheduled, the scheduler forward-schedules the trimming operation to determine the completion date and backward-schedules mixing of materials to determine when the materials are required.

MRP is run weekly, driven by the MPS which is composed of customer orders and forecasts. The output of the MRP run is not used to create production orders. However, MRP data are used to manually create purchase orders for raw material. Because of the shallow bills of material, little WIP inventory, and short routings, scheduling of production is performed manually. The most critical factor in scheduling orders on molding machines is to keep similar-colored items from being run consecutively. The pharmaceutical companies that are customers of Company P use different-colored stoppers to identify the contents of the containers before they are labeled. Mixing of the colors by Company P can result in improperly labeling a drug. By not scheduling similar colors on adjacent runs, Company P minimizes the incidence of such contamination.

The most critical capacity constraint for Company P is the molding area. There are two potential capacity problems in this area. The first occurs if no molding machine is available; the second occurs if the required mold is not available. The latter is the more frequent problem. A mold may be unavailable for one of two reasons. First, the mold may be in use to complete other orders. Second, molds are cleaned periodically, each cleaning taking the mold out of service from 4 to 8 hours. Company P is unable to schedule cleaning in advance. Cleaning is done as necessary, several times a year.

Because of the small number of machines, on-site schedulers track capacity and set promise dates for customers. Detailed capacity planning is not part of the computerized planning and control system, with the result that Company P cannot compare planned activity to actual activity within shop floor control. Company P hopes to add detailed capacity planning and shop floor control to its computerized system in the near future.

Another difficulty in planning capacity at Company P is the fact that yield is uncertain. Accurate piece counts cannot be obtained until after the trimming operation has been completed. Occasionally, yield will be considerably lower than normal, resulting in insufficient pieces to fill an order. When this happens, the part must be rerun (and the high setup cost incurred a second time). Company P is initiating a company-wide statistical process control program to identify and eliminate causes of yield variation.

In summary, Company P has a manual capacity management system which interfaces with the MRP system. Because of the small amount of WIP and short routings, manual planning works well for Company P. Further, the scheduler is familiar with the compatibility of molds to various machines. Company P has a very effective system.

DETAILED SCHEDULING OF TOOLS

The case of Company P has a number of parallels to the case of Remmele Engineering, examined in Chapter 6. Like Remmele, Company P would like to have a computerized system but found that no formal system could simultaneously consider machine availability and tool availability in creating the detailed schedule. They are currently in the process of developing a computer system in house.

Consider operations scheduling as a decision aid for Company P. In addition to providing a Gantt chart of the use of the molding machines themselves, such a program could easily produce a Gantt chart of activity scheduled on each mold. The program could then immediately identify situations in which the mold is scheduled to be on two machines simultaneously, permitting the scheduler to make schedule adjustments. Further, it should be possible to use this system to schedule cleaning of the molds. It should not be too difficult to determine how many hours of operation are usually performed between cleanings. The computer could easily track accumulated hours of use for each mold, determine approximate times when cleaning would be necessary, and suggest windows of time during which the mold is not scheduled for use and would be available for cleaning. This system could be used to schedule the cleaning facility itself. It is likely that a good deal of replanning would have to be done, but it would appear that the use of such a program would increase the efficiency of the molding department.

It is surprising that a program to perform detailed scheduling of tools, maintenance, and setup crews is not already available. The problem is not limited to compression molding of rubber products. The same problems occur in injection molding of plastic products and in the use of dies in metal fabrication industries. Like the molds that Company P uses, dies are also quite expensive and are rarely duplicated. Dies ordinarily can be used on a variety of presses. They also have to be cleaned periodically.

TOOLING: THE FRONTIER OF CAPACITY MANAGEMENT

The growing awareness of the need to treat tooling as capacity to be managed is exemplified by a recent paper by Kupferberg (2) entitled "Tooling: The Frontier of Capacity Management." Kupferberg differentiates between consumable and nonconsumable tools. He equates a consumable tool to a production component and a nonconsumable tool to a work center.

Consumable tools have long been treated as production components. The APICS *MRP Training Aid* (3) points out that consumable tools can be listed on the bill of materials. For example, a bill of materials for a widget could include 0.001 drill bits having a particular stock number. This entry means that for every 1,000 widgets one drill bit is consumed. One can then create a time-phased record of drill-bit utilization, derived as dependent demand, and use this to manage inventory. Consumable tools have long been managed within MRP systems, but little has been written about nonconsumable tools, which is perhaps surprising since most companies have a far larger investment in nonconsumable tools than in consumable ones.

Kupferberg suggests that nonconsumable tools be treated as work centers:

> For example, a plastics molding tool center may consist of all molds capable of making the same parts. Each of the tools may have a different capacity since each may have a different number of cavities. If tools within the tool center have different capacities it is usually necessary to select the capacity of a standard tool. This provides a consistent basis for operation that is recorded in the parent item's routing. Stating tool center capacity can then be readily done in terms of the number of "standard" tools and the scheduled production hours. For example, a tool center has two molds, one with six cavities and the other with twelve. If the twelve-cavity mold is the standard, the number of standard tools would be 1.5. The availability of tool center capacity as it changes over time needs to reflect the number of available standard tools and hours per workday.
>
> The tool center load concept is very similar to a machine work center load. Performing a manufacturing operation generates a certain number of standard hours per piece of load on the machine center where it is made. The same standard hours of load is created for the tool center in which the part is made. The relationship between an item and the tool center that makes it is represented by an operation on the item's routing. This may be done by physically adding tooling operations to the routing or logically associating the required tool center with the routing operation (i.e., operation 10 uses tool centers T50, T55). The tooling operation should be fully overlapped with its associated operation to provide for the accurate time phasing of load on the tool center and to avoid distortion of the operation start and end dates of the machine operation. . . .
>
> The display of tool center load information and the comparison to available capacity is readily accomplished using the format of a CRP time-phased-report. [2, p. 187]

The example Kupferberg uses is an interesting one. In the case of Company P, a CRP time-phased report would be inadequate. Since Company P has only one mold for each of the different shapes required, it really needs to do detailed operations scheduling, since otherwise conflicts will arise in which two molding machines request the same mold for the same period.

However, for a company with multiple molds or dies which are interchangeable, the CRP time-phased-report format could well be more useful than attempting to create a detailed schedule for each mold or die.

SUMMARY

This chapter explores the use of capacity planning for consumable and nonconsumable tools. A case is presented in which lack of capacity planning for molds to be used on injection molding machines frequently frustrated an otherwise good effort to schedule the machines. Consumable tools have long been added to bills of material and planned automatically through MRP's netting logic. An article by Kupferberg explores how nonconsumable tools can also be planned. Most firms can, and should, plan tooling capacity with little or no modification of existing software.

EXERCISES

1. ChildeArte, Inc., manufactures a number of art tools for children. A child's drawing easel has four legs, each of which has four predrilled holes. ChildeArte requires that a drill bit be replaced after every 10,000 holes. ChildeArte plans to build 2,500 easels per month for the coming 12 months. How many drill bits will be consumed during that period?
2. Using the data from Exercise 1, show how ChildeArte can use MRP to calculate the number of drill bits which will be consumed. Discuss the creation of a policy which will cause replacement orders for drill bits to be placed automatically.
3. Acme Tables, Inc., manufactures an oak breakfast table which has a single-piece top. This top must be sanded twice before it is varnished, using first a coarse sandpaper and then a fine paper. The bill of materials for the oak breakfast table top includes the following:

Table Top
0.25 sheets, coarse sandpaper
0.20 sheets, fine sandpaper

Acme manufactures 100 table tops per week. At present there are 150 sheets of coarse sandpaper and 100 sheets of fine sandpaper on hand. Since a single supplier furnishes both types of paper, a single order is placed for both items. Lead time for sandpaper is two weeks. Set up a time-phased plan showing the quantity of each type of paper projected to be on hand at the end of each week and use this to determine in what week the next order for sandpaper must be placed.

4. Roy's Toys makes red, green, and blue water pistols as well as black and red plastic darts and dart guns using injection molding. Roy's has two injection molding machines and one die each for water pistols, darts, and dart guns. Color must be added to the plastic compound before it is injected into the die. The mold for water pistols has 8 cavities (i.e., it makes 8 pistols simultaneously). The mold for darts has 20 cavities. The mold for dart guns has 6 cavities. Roy's works one 40-hour shift each week. Roy's must deliver to a wholesaler 1,000 red, 500 green, and 800 blue water pistols each week. Dart guns are delivered in packages containing one gun and three darts. Roy's delivers 250 (150 black, 100 red) sets of dart guns/darts each week. To make one batch of 8 water pistols requires 10 minutes. To make one batch of 20 darts requires 5 minutes. To make one batch of 6 dart guns requires 6 minutes. For all three dies, when a color change occurs, the die must be cleaned for 30 minutes. Cleaning does not occupy the molding machine, but only one mold can be cleaned at a time. Both of the molding machines accept all three dies with equal facility. Assume molding machine efficiency is 100 percent and there is no lost time due to breakdown or operator absenteeism. Changing dies requires 30 minutes setup. The die must be available at the start of setup.
   a. Use a rough-cut capacity planning approach to determine the weekly capacity required for each molding machine and each mold.
   b. Use the Gantt chart technique to schedule the molding machines, keeping track of which mold is in use and when molds are cleaned.

REFERENCES

1. Finch, B. J., and J. F. Cox. *Planning and Control System Design: Principles and Cases for Process Manufacturers.* Falls Church, Va.: American Production and Inventory Control Society, 1987.
2. Kupferberg, M. "Tooling: The Frontier of Capacity Management." *Proceedings of the 29th International APICS Conference*, St. Louis, October 1986.
3. *Material Requirements Planning Training Aid.* Falls Church, Va.: American Production and Inventory Control Society.

Synchronized Production

Chapters 3 through 8 focus on the traditional material requirements planning approach to managing shops. This approach has two key features. First, material is processed in batches or lots. Much of the information system for shop floor management involves paperwork authorizing batches to be processed or moved. Many systems include daily dispatch lists which specify the order in which such batches are to be processed. Almost always such batches are kept together. Batches are separated only when expediting is necessary. Lot splitting separates a batch so that it can be processed on multiple machines in one work center. Operation overlapping separates a batch so that it can be processed in two or more work centers simultaneously. Both lot splitting and operation overlapping are considered to be unusual modes of operation within an MRP framework.

The second feature of the MRP approach is that capacity planning occurs sequentially. First a master schedule is formulated. Then rough-cut capacity planning is performed. If capacity shortfalls are revealed, the master schedule must be revised and rough-cut performed again. The sequence may be repeated at the CRP stage. Figure 9.1 illustrates the sequential nature of the process.

In the early 1980s another approach to capacity management appeared. This approach has been controversial for two reasons. First, the approach is embodied in an algorithm available only with the purchase of expensive software. Second, the basic approach violates both the batch and the sequential features of MRP. The software, called **OPT** (for **optimized production technology**), uses an approach that simultaneously (rather than sequentially) schedules critical (bottleneck) resources by means of the undisclosed algorithm. Further, the solutions often involve intentional lot splitting and operation overlapping at non-bottleneck work centers (i.e., splitting and recollect-

FIGURE 9.1   SEQUENTIAL PRODUCTION PLANNING IN MRP

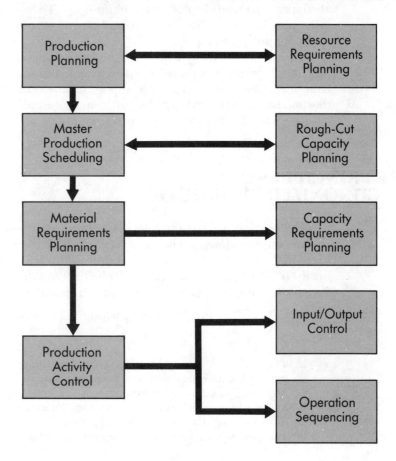

ing batches while they are on the shop floor). A number of firms have purchased and are using the software and are reporting success. Results of a survey of OPT software users are reported in Chapter 11.

By 1986 the creator of OPT, Eliyahu Goldratt, stated that many of the benefits of his approach to capacity management are achievable without the software. He advocates an approach he calls the *synchronized production philosophy*. Goldratt's method of teaching is Socratic, i.e., rather than providing answers he asks questions which he feels will eventually lead the student to the correct answer. This approach is illustrated in *The Goal* (6), a novel about a plant manager who discovers through a friend's questions the basics of synchronized production. *The Goal* is very interesting reading for any serious student of capacity management. Because of Goldratt's use of the Socratic approach, the book does not provide much straightforward information about the synchronized production philosophy. There exists a set of general principles, but no methodology for applying these rules to manage capacity (short of purchasing OPT).

There is merit to the synchronized production approach. For that reason I provide a description of the rules and my interpretation of how these rules can be applied. The principles are then applied to develop a detailed schedule for the shop presented in Chapter 2 and to compare the synchronized production schedule with the schedule that results from MRP.

THE PRINCIPLES OF SYNCHRONIZED PRODUCTION

In this section the ten principles of synchronized production are presented and an example is used to clarify each principle. These principles have been stated in somewhat different form over time. The wording used in the following list is taken from a 1982 article by Robert E. Fox (2), then vice-president of Creative Output, Inc., the company that markets OPT.

The Principles of Synchronized Production

Scheduling

1. The utilization of a non-bottleneck resource is not determined by its own potential, but by some other constraint in the system.
2. Activating a resource is not synonymous with utilizing a resource.
3. An hour lost at a bottleneck is an hour lost for the total system.
4. An hour saved at a non-bottleneck is a mirage.
5. The transfer batch may not and many times should not be equal to the process batch.
6. The process batch size should be variable and not fixed.
7. Capacity and priority need to be considered simultaneously and not sequentially.
8. Murphy is not an unknown and his damage can be isolated and minimized.

Cost Accounting—Performance Measurement

9. Plant capacity should not be balanced.
10. The sum of local optimums is not equal to the optimum of the whole.

It is evident from this list that the synchronized production philosophy treats resources differently depending on whether or not the resource is a bottleneck. What is a bottleneck? A bottleneck is any resource which constrains **throughput**, defined as the rate at which a company produces revenue through sales. Throughput, as Goldratt defines it, is a measure of capacity for the entire company.

Examples to Illustrate the Meaning of the Principles

To illustrate what is meant by each of the ten principles, JB's Bikes, a hypothetical bicycle factory, is introduced. JB's Bikes produces 20″ and 26″ bicycles in a variety of styles and colors. JB's Bikes is presented purely to illustrate the synchronized production principles. Some aspects of the example are unrealistic; the processes and process times were created primarily to create bottlenecks and non-bottlenecks, rather than to give an entirely accurate picture of bicycle production. Forecasted sales for the coming year are 40,000 units. Unfortunately, production is limited to 36,500 units because of a bottleneck at the handlebar machine, which produces exactly 100 handlebars each day working 3 shifts 7 days a week. JB's handlebars are unique and cannot be obtained from another source. The next most constrained machine is a wheel assembler, a robot with a capacity of 250 wheels per day (i.e., enough wheels for 125 bicycles) working 3 shifts.

Principle 1: The utilization of a non-bottleneck resource is not determined by its own potential, but by some other constraint in the system. The utilization of the wheel assembler, a non-bottleneck resource, is determined by some other constraint in the system—in this case the handlebar machine, which can produce only 100 handlebars in the time it takes to produce enough wheels for 125 bicycles. Thus, the utilization of the wheel assembler is 80 percent (i.e., 100/125). If the wheel assembler chooses to make more than 100 sets of wheels per day, inventory simply accumulates. The only way to increase the utilization of the wheel assembler is to find an outside market for wheels.

Principle 2: Activating a resource is not synonymous with utilizing a resource. Activation of the wheel assembler would be 100 percent if it produced 125 pairs of wheels per day. After four weeks, 700 extra pairs of wheels would have accumulated (25 × 28 = 700). Thus, although the wheel assembler was activated, it was not utilized in the sense that it produced a useful product. At some point the wheel assembler will be forced to go idle and wait for the handlebar machine to catch up.

Principle 3: An hour lost at a bottleneck is an hour lost for the total system. If the handlebar machine breaks down and is out of service for one full day, 100 bicycles will not be shipped. Production for the year will be reduced from 36,500 to 36,400. If lost production is not lost forever, the machine is not a true bottleneck. Many plants have no true bottleneck. For a plant which can produce more than can be sold, the market is the bottleneck.

Principle 4: An hour saved at a non-bottleneck is a mirage. Failing to understand principle 1, Otto Engineer reprograms the wheel assembler robot to give it a capacity of 260 wheels per day. His reprogramming time has been wasted, since the wheel assembler still can only usefully produce 200 wheels per day and there is no other task the wheel assembler can usefully perform.

Otto should spend his time devising a way to get more than 100 handlebars a day out of the handlebar machine.

Principle 5: The transfer batch may not and many times should not be equal to the process batch. Handlebars are produced in two styles, regular and racer. To save setups, each style is produced for two weeks and then the handlebar machine is switched to the other style. Handlebars are taken to the bicycle assembly area in lots of 10. The transfer batch in this example is 10 units, the process batch is 1,400 units (14 days' production of bicycles).

The principle that the process batch need not equal the transfer batch is one of the revolutionary concepts of the synchronized production philosophy. Note that MRP planning assumes that the transfer batch is different from the process batch only when a lot is expedited (lot splitting and operation overlapping, both considered expediting techniques by MRP, are what create unequal transfer and process batch sizes). All lot-sizing techniques used by MRP assume equal transfer and process batch sizes. Unfortunately, Dr. Goldratt has chosen not to make public how OPT determines transfer and process batch sizes.

Principle 6: The process batch should be variable and not fixed. Handlebars are moved to the assembly line where they become part of a fully assembled bike. On a particular day JB plans to assemble 100 20″ boys' bicycles, all with racer handlebars. For this assembly, 200 plastic handlebar grips are needed. Handlebar grips are molded using a plastic injection-molding process. The injection-molding machine makes a number of plastic parts. Because of the time required to stabilize the molding process, the batch size for handlebar grips is 2,000. Handlebar grips are then moved to a trim area for removal of excess plastic. The trim area processes the grips in batches of 200, i.e., one day's production. Each day the set of handlebar grips to be assembled that day is moved to the appropriate station on the assembly line. Note that the process batch size of handlebar grips at injection molding is 2,000, while the process batch size at the trim area is 200. There is no inherent reason why these two batch sizes must be the same, although in an MRP-planned system they almost certainly would be.

Principle 7: Capacity and priority need to be considered simultaneously and not sequentially. The most efficient use of the handlebar machine at JB's Bikes would be to run only racer handlebars for six months and then only regular handlebars for six months, thereby minimizing downtime due to setup. It is, however, unlikely that the buying public can be trained to demand only bikes having regular handlebars for six months and only bikes having racer handlebars for the other six. From the standpoint of meeting demand, the ideal situation would be to produce each day the number of racer and regular handlebars sold the day before, but unfortunately the setup time required to make a daily changeover would reduce overall plant output. Note that capacity and priority considerations conflict. Considering both capacity and priority needs, a two-week cycle is established as a compromise.

Principle 8: Murphy is not an unknown and his damage can be isolated and minimized. One version of Murphy's law is: "If anything can go wrong, it will—usually at the worst possible time." A popular sign among production control people reads: "Murphy was an optimist!" Good quality-control procedures can limit the impact of problems while the problems are being corrected. Until recently JB's Bikes was experiencing a major quality problem with handlebars. On inspection of finished handlebars, 20 percent were found defective and had to be scrapped, limiting output from the plant to 80 handlebars (and bicycles) per day. The handlebar machine operator felt the problem was poor incoming materials. After reading *The Goal*, JB's management realized that inspections should occur before, rather than after, a bottleneck operation so that the time of the bottleneck is not wasted on an already defective product. Handlebar blanks are now 100 percent inspected before going on the handlebar machine. Production is back to 100 units per day. An inquiry is in progress to identify and correct the causes of defective blanks.

Principle 9: Plant capacity should not be balanced. Principle 9 should be expanded to read "Plant capacity should not be balanced *when variation in operation times is significant.*" If no variation in operating times exists, the handlebar machine can be fed by a machine which also produces 100 units per day, i.e., the plant can be balanced. The following scenario illustrates the problem which arises when a plant is balanced and significant variation exists. The handlebar machine produces 100 units per day without variation. Suppose it is preceded by a machine which has variation in output, producing between 80 and 120 handlebar blanks per day, uniformly distributed. Note that the configuration is balanced, since both the handlebar machine and the feeding machine have average capacities of 100 units per day. Suppose further that there is a queue of 30 units in front of the handlebar machine. How much production will the handlebar machine average? On the surface it would seem that the handlebar machine should average 100 units with the queue in front of it fluctuating somewhat. I used Lotus 1-2-3 to simulate this situation for 100 days and found an average output of 99.36 units. Output from the feeding station was then raised, to between 85 and 125 units, uniformly distributed. The shop is now unbalanced, since the feeding unit averages 105 units of output. I also assumed that a maximum queue of 60 units is permitted in front of the handlebar machine (otherwise the queue would grow indefinitely). Under this scenario the handlebar machine averages 100 units per day. But the same result should be achievable by limiting variation and balancing the shop. I tested a third scenario in which the feeding machine produced 95 to 105 units, uniformly distributed, and the handlebar machine initially had a queue of 30 units, as before. In this scenario the handlebar machine averaged 100 units of output. All three simulations are shown in Appendix 9A.

The synchronized production philosophy centers on careful control of a few bottleneck stations, perhaps only one. For this situation to exist, the other stations must by definition have more capacity, creating an unbalanced plant.

The just-in-time philosophy, presented in the next chapter, focuses on reducing variation by attacking its causes (such as machine breakdown, poor incoming quality, etc.). As is demonstrated by the three simulations, both approaches can increase output. There is no reason the two approaches cannot be used in tandem.

Principle 10: The sum of local optimums is not equal to the optimum of the whole. That the sum of local optima is not a global optimum is well known to management scientists. The principle even has a name, the principle of suboptimization. Unfortunately, local optima are easier to find than global optima. It is extremely difficult to formulate the problem of finding the handlebar blank lot size that will maximize company profit. One can, however, formulate and solve the problem of finding the handlebar blank lot size which minimizes the sum of setup and holding costs associated with handlebar blanks. The latter procedure is the traditional economic order quantity (EOQ) approach. Traditional thought is to accept the local optimum as better than nothing and therefore to produce in economic order quantity batches (or to use some other lot-sizing technique such as least total cost (LTC) or the Wagner-Whitin dynamic programming approach, both of which attempt to minimize the sum of setup and holding costs). The synchronized production philosophy sizes production and transfer batches to maximize throughput ignoring some setup and holding costs, attempting a global rather than a local solution.

A corollary of principle 10 is that the optimal global solution, if known, would appear to be suboptimal by local performance measures. The first APICS teams to visit Japanese just-in-time plants were astonished to find that the Japanese arbitrarily pick lot sizes and were often unfamiliar with the EOQ formula. The Americans came to realize that they were viewing the problem too narrowly and that the Japanese had a better global solution to the inventory problem. Despite this, Americans are reluctant to abandon local optima, such as EOQ and departmental efficiency, in favor of a global approach. This reluctance appears to be diminishing as American successes with the synchronized production philosophy and just-in-time continue to grow.

IMPLICATIONS OF THE SYNCHRONIZED PRODUCTION PRINCIPLES

As stated previously, it is possible that for some companies the only constraint on throughput is the market, i.e., the company can produce more than it can sell in any period. For this company, MRP should work exceedingly well. MRP assumes that capacity is infinite. If the market is the bottleneck, capacity is essentially infinite. There should be few problems. The manufacturer should, however, reduce lot sizes and lead times to become more competitive.

More commonly, however, there are certain expensive and/or hard-to-replace resources (highly skilled workers, for example) which limit the throughput of the company. For such a company the lot-sizing procedure built into MRP has a fundamental flaw. All lot-sizing procedures are based on the trade-off between the cost of setting up a resource and the cost of holding inventory. All assume that no constraint on the number of setups exists. In defining setup costs, one typically includes the time of the setup crew or machine operator as the major setup cost. Goldratt points out that for a bottleneck this cost estimate is too low and for a non-bottleneck it is too high. For a bottleneck station, the cost of an hour of setup should include the value of the lost throughput. By definition, an hour of setup at a bottleneck involves loss of throughput. Thus, setup time at a bottleneck may be very expensive. On the other hand, the marginal cost of setup at a non-bottleneck may be zero if it is performed by the machine operator using time which would otherwise be idle. A non-bottleneck station does not limit throughput but may limit lead time. It must have some idle time. The synchronized production approach is based on the concept that non-bottlenecks should be used to feed bottlenecks. Such feeding involves frequent setups and small lots to minimize lead time and keep a bottleneck always working.

EXAMPLE 9.1:
MANAGEMENT OF BOTTLENECKS

Consider the following. Resources A and B are bottlenecks. Resource C is not. Resources A and B each have just run out of work. Resource C has two jobs to be processed. One will go next to A, the other to B. Each job requires a 30-minute setup. Each consists of 1,200 units requiring 1 minute per piece at resource C (i.e., the run time for the 1,200 units totals 20 hours). Resource C has no other jobs due within the next 80 working hours. Resources A and B have no more work due to arrive for two working days. Resources A and B each require one hour to set up for the part in question, and 4 minutes per piece to process it. If the standard approach is used, that is, if resource C processes all of one job and then switches to the other, either A or B must be idle for 20 hours, as even the use of operation overlapping would permit only one station to be fed parts.

There is, however, a simple solution to the problem, which should be obvious to anyone familiar with the synchronized production philosophy. The key is that resource C is not a bottleneck and there is no reason not to incur additional setups. Resource C can set up for part 1 (30 minutes), produce 30 units (30 minutes), set up for part 2 (30 minutes), produce 30 units (30 minutes), and repeat this cycle 40 times until all parts are finished. The cycle lasts 80 hours. Each two-hour cycle sends 30 parts (two hours of work) to both A and B, keeping each in continuous production. This solution avoids the loss of 20 hours' output to the plant. It is likely to improve the overall profitability of the plant by hundreds, perhaps thousands, of dollars.

The irony of this situation is that on the basis of traditional performance measurement techniques, the supervisor of resource C would be judged to have made a serious mistake in choosing this solution. Remember, supervisors are judged by efficiency, standard hours produced divided by hours worked. In this case, the supervisor had 41 hours of work—two thirty-minute setups and two twenty-hour runs. Performing 80 thirty-minute setups followed by 80 thirty-minute runs took 80 hours. The efficiency of the supervisor is thus only 51 percent (41/80), and direct labor cost has almost doubled. The fact that the overall throughput of the plant has been increased, using time which would otherwise have been nonproductive, isn't factored into the supervisor's performance evaluation. It is unlikely that a plant which is not using the synchronized production philosophy would utilize resource C in the proper manner to keep A and B fed, not because the plant could not find the solution, but because the supervisor of resource C would refuse to implement it. If the synchronized production philosophy is to be attempted, the performance measurement system must first be changed to eliminate departmental efficiency measures at non-bottleneck stations, where the measures have little if any meaning.

Good bottleneck management also calls for a reexamination of routings. There may be jobs which could be produced using non-bottleneck machinery. Often the bottleneck machine is chosen because it is more efficient and, using local optimization again, is considered to be cheaper. However, a longer processing time at a non-bottleneck station may actually be cheaper than a shorter processing time at the bottleneck when one views the problem from a global perspective. The researchers at Carnegie-Mellon (9) who are working on an expert system for scheduling are certainly aware of this. Their expert system looks at all feasible routings and attempts to choose a routing which will result in low labor costs but which also considers the relative workloads already on various stations.

Principle 7, which calls for all bottlenecks to be scheduled simultaneously, is the most difficult of the OPT principles to implement in multi-bottleneck plants. Many plants, however, have only one bottleneck. Traditional optimization techniques, such as dynamic programming, can be used to solve the multi-bottleneck scheduling problem, but they are difficult to set up and slow to execute, even for small examples. Goldratt has stated (5) that OPT uses an approach derived from the many-body problem of physics, i.e., the problem of determining the motion of a body which is simultaneously subjected to the gravitational pull of many other bodies. The value of the OPT software is that it may be used to obtain a quick solution to the problem of simultaneously scheduling a number of bottlenecks. Goldratt insists that anyone who follows the synchronized production philosophy can achieve 90 percent of its benefits by applying the principles without the software. Though this claim remains to be substantiated, it seems plausible since one should be able to use a technique as simple as Gantt charting to arrive at a good schedule for bottleneck work centers.

COMMENTS ON OPT FROM T. E. VOLLMANN

During 1986 OPT's marketing company, Creative Output, held three workshops to acquaint academicians with details of the OPT philosophy. An attendee at one of the workshops was T. E. Vollmann, one of the leading academicians in operations management and co-author of *Master Production Scheduling: Principles and Practice*. The paper he published after the workshop (10) is one of the few articles on OPT not written by Creative Output. Here is some of what Vollmann has to say:

> When we first studied OPT, . . . the conclusion was that OPT . . . was a sophisticated shop floor control system based on finite loading procedures. It seemed to be an improvement over CAPOSS in that it concentrated on a subset of work centers (the bottlenecks) . . . to produce better results faster.

> This is in fact a shortsighted view of OPT which does not recognize its fundamental contributions. OPT begins its process by combining the data in the bill of material file with those in the routing file. The result is a network or extended tree diagram where each part in the network can be enhanced to include alternate routing data, different work center definitions such as manpower constraints, and other additional data used in typical finite loading models. . . . The average loads are sorted in descending order, and the most heavily loaded are studied. . . . Not only is bottleneck capacity utilized more intensively by finite loading of this small subset of work centers. Identifying these bottlenecks allows one to reduce the variability by specially targeted efforts in quality as well as in scheduling. It is in the bottlenecks that better utilization will pay the greatest dividends for the firm. . . .

> [In non-bottlenecks] OPT operates almost like classic MRP. The difference is that OPT in this case will change batch sizes (reducing them) to the point where some resources almost become bottlenecks. The result is less WIP, reduced lead time, and a move toward "zero inventory" manufacturing. OPT does much of this by overlapping schedules using unequal batch sizes for transferring and processing. . . .

> In practice, the small/large lot size issue has two major implications. The first is that lead times should be shorter: smaller batches will move faster through non-bottleneck work centers. The second implication is less felicitous: procedures have to be developed to split/join batches as they go through production. . . .

The net result is a need for education throughout the company, a change in mores for many firms, and a top management commitment to the basic concept, the philosophy, and the resultant actions required (e.g., let non-bottleneck people do some non-direct production work or even be idle).

OPT presents several difficulties in implementation. . . . Some of these relate directly to the philosophy. . . . The cost accounting tenets of OPT have just not been accepted. A related issue is the secret algorithm used for scheduling the plant. Many of us were brought up on a belief in "system transparency." OPT is anything BUT transparent. It is truly difficult to understand, and it is even more difficult to understand why some schedules have been produced. . . . OPT requires sophisticated managers who are committed. . . . The solutions produced by OPT are not optimal. The procedures used for finite loading are "heuristics": They produce "good" but not optimal answers. . . .

OPT also makes an important contribution as a master production scheduling procedure. This comes from a feedback from the finite loading of the bottleneck resources to the MPS. . . . Another contribution made by OPT is in the at least partial resolution of the conflicting priorities produced by finite loading procedures and MRP. By only forward finite loading those work centers or resources that are bottlenecks, inconsistent due date priority problems will be greatly reduced.

The final set of arguments made in this paper is that it makes sense to integrate OPT approaches into existing MRP II software. Accomplishing this objective will foster understanding of OPT and its integration into the mainstream of manufacturing planning/control. When this occurs, a whole new dialogue should result. As this dialogue is disseminated to practitioners, we will see still more evolution. This all sounds interesting. One of the greatest things about our field is how it continually changes.

APPLYING THE PRINCIPLES OF SYNCHRONIZED PRODUCTION

Product Mix

The first item a plant should look at is what is to be produced, i.e., what combination of goods. In a talk given to the 1985 APICS International Conference Goldratt (4) suggested that a good rule of thumb was that the product-mix ratio should be based on the ratio of margin to time required at the bottleneck(s). By Goldratt's definition, margin is selling price minus the cost of purchased materials. Goldratt treats both direct and indirect labor as fixed overhead and does not use them in production decision making. He insists that including these expenses leads to suboptimal decisions.

The traditional approach to product-mix decisions views labor costs at bottleneck and non-bottleneck resources as variable costs to be minimized. It seems likely that reviewing the product-mix decision from the synchronized production point of view may lead to a change in the master schedule.

Goldratt also suggests that the manager try to identify any items which involve no time whatever on bottleneck resources and market these items aggressively. Since labor for these items is coming from time which would otherwise be idle, one could sell the item for a small margin over the cost of components and still make a good profit. Of course the cost accountants will argue that the item is selling at a loss and insist that the practice stop. The reason for this difference of opinion is that accountants use average cost, while actual profitability of an item is a function of marginal cost. Marginal cost, however, is extremely difficult to identify. On balance, it would seem that the approach of aggressively pricing items which do not require bottleneck resources is a good one and should be pursued until a point is reached where another bottleneck is created.

Lot Sizing and Scheduling

After the product-mix decision has been made, one has information concerning the number and type of units to be built over the planning horizon. One also knows what the bottlenecks are, and how much time is available at the bottlenecks. Time at the bottlenecks would be minimized if each bottleneck were set up only once for each item passing through it. One can determine the minimum time requirement by adding total run time requirements to setup time required assuming only one setup of each product. If the time available at a bottleneck is less than minimum time required, there is no feasible schedule and the aggregate production plan must be reduced.

Ideally, there will be more time available at bottlenecks than the minimum time required, permitting some products to be produced more than once during the planning period. Smaller lots mean smaller inventory costs. Often, smaller lots mean quicker identification and correction of quality problems as well. How does one allocate among setups the time remaining at the bottleneck? As this procedure is part of the undisclosed algorithm, Creative Output has been understandably silent on this matter. The discussion which follows is therefore substantially speculation. Apparently the first step is to see if lot-for-lot is feasible. Lot-for-lot treats each individual order as a separate lot. If lot-for-lot is capacity feasible at the bottleneck, OPT will apparently choose this strategy automatically. Usually, however, this approach requires too many setups.

One must also consider the definition of available capacity. If both output and input are subject to fluctuations, one cannot aim for 100 percent capacity activation. This principle was demonstrated in Appendix 1A. One must decide what the planned queue will be and set available capacity using this definition. One may overcome this difficulty, and obtain 100 percent bottleneck utilization, by having the bottleneck pace all other operations, including release of new jobs to the floor. Input thus is synchronized with output. Both still vary, but not independently. Goldratt calls the bottleneck a "drum" (beating time) and the signaling mechanism to the order-releasing function a "rope."

The next criterion is fairly obvious: one must have multiple orders for the item. If only one shipment is to be made, it makes no sense to produce the shipment in two batches. One may first cull items having only one order. Among items having multiple orders, one would like to choose those having short setup times and large material costs for multiple batches. One chooses items having short setup times in order to preserve as much of the bottleneck resource as possible. One chooses items having large material costs since it is the material cost which is being reduced by reducing the lot size. A secondary consideration might be to choose items which go into very few end items, preferably one. Parts used in a number of items will have to be produced or purchased in volume. Adding one setup may not affect the timing of the purchase of raw materials. True cost reductions occur when the time the material spends in the system is reduced.

Recall that, using the synchronized production philosophy, holding cost is a function only of the cost of purchased items. No cost roll-up is performed to find the inventory value at each stage of production. The performance measure which Goldratt uses for inventory is dollar days, that is, dollars of value times days in inventory. Perhaps a useful rule of thumb would be to define *dollar days of inventory saved*, using the time between the first order and the second order multiplied by the volume of orders from the second order to the end of the horizon. This would measure the potential reduction in dollar days by producing a second lot. Consider the ratio of dollar days saved to setup time. Items with high dollar days savings and low setup would have a very high ratio using this formula. The ratio in fact measures dollar days of inventory saved per hour of setup utilized.

EXAMPLE 9.2:
ALLOCATION OF AN ADDITIONAL SETUP

This example will illustrate a case in which there is time for one additional setup. We must choose whether to allocate this setup to part X or part Y.

Suppose that the following orders exist for parts X and Y in periods 1 through 8:

Part	1	2	3	4	5	6	7	8
X	0	100	00	200	0	50	0	300
Y	100	100	200	100	0	100	200	300

Suppose further that the length of each period is 1 day and that the purchased cost of components for part X is $3 and for part Y is $2. Part X requires a 6-hour setup, part Y requires a 7-hour setup. Table 9.1 shows a calculation of dollar days savings for each part, in each case assuming (1) an order in the first period having positive demand for the entire horizon, and then (2) two orders, the second in period 6.

The calculations in Table 9.1 assume beginning period consumption, that is, carrying cost is assessed for the period based on quantity on hand at the end

TABLE 9.1 CALCULATION OF DOLLAR DAYS SAVINGS PER SETUP HOUR

	PERIOD							
	1	2	3	4	5	6	7	8
Part X								
Demand	0	100	0	200	0	50	0	300
Order (1)		650						
On Hand		550	550	350	350	300	300	0
$ Days	0	1,650	1,650	1,050	1,050	900	900	0
Cum. $ Days	0	1,650	3,300	4,350	5,400	6,300	7,200	7,200
Orders (2)		300				350		
On Hand		200	200	0	0	300	300	0
$ Days		600	600	0	0	900	900	0
Cum. $ Days	0	600	1,200	1,200	1,200	2,300	3,200	3,200
Savings in Dollar Days: 4,000 (7,200−3,200)						Dollar Days Savings per Hours of Setup: 667 (4,000/6)		
Part Y								
Demand	100	100	200	100	0	100	200	300
Order (1)	1,100							
On Hand	1,000	900	700	600	600	500	300	0
$ Days	2,000	1,800	1,400	1,200	1,200	1,000	600	0
Cum. $ Days	2,000	3,800	5,200	6,400	7,600	8,600	9,200	9,200
Orders (2)	500					600		
On Hand	400	300	100	0	0	500	300	0
$ Days	800	600	200	0	0	1,000	600	0
Cum. $ Days	800	1,400	1,600	1,600	1,600	2,600	3,200	3,200
Savings in Dollar Days: 6,000 (9,200−3,200)						Dollar Days Savings per Hours of Setup: 857 (6,000/7)		

of the period. For part X, the dollar days cost for period 1 is 550 units times $3 purchase cost per unit, or 1,650 dollar days. Since 550 units remain in stock at the end of period 2, an additional 1,650 dollar days accrue, and so on. In this instance, the additional setup should be given to part Y, which achieves a dollar days saving of 857 per hour of setup, higher than the saving of part X. One could calculate this ratio for every item in the schedule, and allocate one additional setup to the item having the largest. One would then subtract the setup time from the time available. If additional time exists at the bottleneck, one would repeat the procedure until capacity required equals modified capacity available.

Since the part just allocated a setup should perhaps be given still another, one must recalculate the dollar days savings from an additional setup. One would have to calculate dollar days based on three setups rather than two. One could use an optimization technique, such as dynamic programming, to determine where to place the additional setup, but the cost of calculating lot sizes might be excessive. Fortunately, simple heuristic procedures should be reasonably effective.

Once setups have been allocated, process batch sizes at the bottleneck have been determined. Transfer batch sizes and process batch sizes at non-bottlenecks will be determined as a part of the detailed scheduling.

A clearer picture of detailed scheduling within OPT exists. Fox (3) presents a conceptual overview of OPT:

> OPT's master schedule is the schedule for the bottleneck operations. Such a schedule is developed by scheduling the bottleneck operations forward in time. The reason for forward scheduling is to avoid any slack or idle time since idle time at a bottleneck operation will eventually result in lost sales. [Author's note: Due dates in the master schedule are found by forward scheduling from the bottleneck through the final operation.] . . . It may not be the best possible schedule but it certainly is a valid one and one that can be developed very quickly. Once the bottleneck operations have been scheduled forward in time, then all the operations following the last bottleneck operation also need to be scheduled forward in time. Since the bottlenecks dictate when product can be shipped, we should schedule all operations after the bottleneck so they are completed as expeditiously as possible. . . . Once the schedule for final assembly has been established, we now schedule all the remaining operations by scheduling backward in time. If there are no other bottlenecks, then all the other resources have excess capacity and we can safely schedule backward, i.e., we don't have to worry about creating an overload due to insufficient capacity.

Sometimes the process of forward and backward scheduling non-bottleneck resources turns up a resource which has sufficient capacity for most of the planning horizon, but insufficient capacity during a portion of it, causing order(s) to be late. By definition this station has now become a constraint.

OPT apparently defines this resource to be an additional bottleneck and returns to the step of simultaneously scheduling all bottleneck resources.

In performing forward and backward scheduling of non-bottleneck resources, one maximizes the amount of operation overlapping and lot splitting in order to minimize the amount of time the order spends in the shop. This reduces inventory investment. It also reduces the lead time to the customer. Since lead time may be as important as price in obtaining business, profits increase by using operation overlapping and lot splitting at non-bottleneck work centers.

APPLICATION OF THE SYNCHRONIZED PRODUCTION PHILOSOPHY

The synchronized production philosophy will now be applied to the hypothetical case given in Chapter 2. The reader may recall that War Eagle Hoists makes 432 models of hoist from four motor sizes and various combinations of cable size, hook size, and color. The winding department is very limited in capacity, requiring a level production strategy with substantial inventory accumulation during the off-peak season. All other departments—stamping, milling, sheet metal, and assembly—employ a demand chase production strategy with little accumulation of inventory. The departments, products, lead time, capacity, and demand information relevant to this discussion are given in Table 9.2.

In addition to the lead times shown in Table 9.2, there is a one-week allowance for delivery. The typical hoist sells for $500. Assume that the manufactured cost of a typical hoist is $250, the value of parts and labor after final assembly. Assume further that the value of all parts at the time final assembly

TABLE 9.2   SUMMARY OF WAR EAGLE HOISTS OPERATIONS

DEPARTMENT	PRODUCT	LEAD TIME (weeks)	PRODUCTION CAPACITY (units/week)	MAXIMUM DEMAND (units/week)
Final Assembly	Winch	2	48	48
Motor Assembly	Motor	1	80	65
Winding	Windings	Varies	40	40
Sheet Metal	Drum	4	65	65
Sheet Metal	Housing	2	70	65
Milling	Armature	1	40	40
Milling	Gears	3	56	56
Stamping	Gear Blank	1	100+	65

begins is $240 and the value of the parts when motor assembly begins is $220. Assume the value of a completed winding is $60 and the value of the rest of the components combined is $150, $100 of which is for the drum. This information can be used to graphically represent the dollar days of inventory as shown in Figure 9.2.

The dollar days calculation is shown at the top of Figure 9.2. Working from right to left, note that the value of the finished hoist is $250. Multiplying $250 by 5 days' delivery allowance yields 1,250 dollar days. The value of the parts when final assembly begins is $240. An MRP system will have all parts available at the beginning of the planned lead time. Multiplying $240 by the lead time of 10 working days yields 2,400 dollar days. In a similar fashion, all intermediate production stages are converted to dollar days using lead time and cost roll-up information. Summing the dollar days shown in Figure 9.2, one finds a total of 6,750 dollar days per hoist, excluding windings.

Windings must be treated separately, since they are the only part not produced in a demand chase fashion. Inventory projections for windings, shown in Chapter 2, Table 2.3, indicate an average inventory of 119.75 windings. Windings are valued at $60. Multiplying 119.75 average inventory by $60 average value by 365 days per year yields 2,622,525 dollar days inventory of windings. Dividing the total by 2,100 hoists produced yields approximately 1,250 dollar days per hoist.

FIGURE 9.2   DOLLAR DAYS PER TYPICAL HOIST

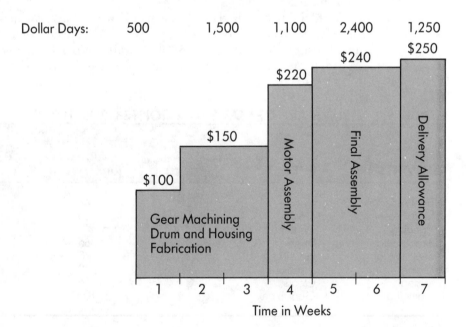

Adding the dollar days from windings to the total dollar days from Figure 9.2 yields an estimated 8,000 dollar days inventory for each finished hoist. Note that dollar days as calculated here include labor imbedded in the product at each stage. This is a departure from Goldratt's approach, which is to calculate dollar days excluding labor, a definition of dollar days that may be preferable for making product-mix decisions. The definition used here is taken from a presentation by Jim Clark of IBM to a 1987 conference (1).

The purpose of developing a graphical representation of dollar days is to convince management of the benefits that accrue from shortening lead time. Armed with such a chart, Clark was able to persuade IBM management to reduce the lead time allowance for moving a multimillion-dollar IBM 3090-class computer a distance of 12 miles from the production site to the test site from two days to half a day. The chart made it clear to management that allowing for unnecessary lead time in this case was equivalent to leaving cash equal to the value of the machine out of any interest-bearing account for the same period. Although financial managers never leave cash around not working, for some reason they seem to need aids such as Figure 9.2 to see that inventory is the same thing.

Let's see how the synchronized production concepts might be used to improve the flow of material at War Eagle Hoists. First an intermediate recommendation, which involves spending no money, is made. Then a longer-term recommendation, which involves accelerating the purchase of a fifth winding machine, is made.

Intermediate Recommendation

An intermediate recommendation which can be made is to shift the allowed lead times to reflect capacity constraints. The recommendations are summarized in Table 9.3.

TABLE 9.3 SUMMARY OF WAR EAGLE HOISTS OPERATIONS

DEPARTMENT	PRODUCT	LEAD TIME (days)	PRODUCTION CAPACITY (units/week)	MAXIMUM DEMAND (units/week)
Delivery	Delivery	2		
Final Assembly	Winch	5	48	48
Motor Assembly	Motor	1	80	65
Winding	Windings	Varies	40	40
Sheet Metal	Drum	1	65	65
Sheet Metal	Housing	1	70	65
Milling	Armature	5	40	40
Milling	Gears	3	56	56
Stamping	Gear Blank	1	100+	65

The winding operation is unchanged. It continues to produce at a level rate, averaging 119.75 units in stock over the course of the year and 1,250 dollar days per finished hoist. Since windings represent a capacity constraint, armatures need to be available to protect the winding department from unplanned idle time. Therefore, armatures might continue to be milled in batches of 40, with one week's inventory of armatures available at the winding department at all times. However, recognizing that there is some excess capacity in the milling operation, the schedule for most weeks calls for two batches of 20 armatures and two batches of gears, allowing more flexibility in the production of gears.

Changes in lead time requirements for other operations are recommended. First, the lead time allowance for delivery is reduced to two days. The allowance is an average figure. Cross-country deliveries may take three days while cross-state deliveries take only one. An average two-day delivery schedule is achievable. The dollar days inventory tied up in the delivery cycle is reduced from 1,250 per hoist to 500 per hoist.

Final assembly lead time is reduced from 10 days to 5 days. The two-week allowance was provided to minimize setups at various assembly stations and allow fairly large batches of similar hoists to be processed together. Recognizing that final assembly is not a bottleneck causes one to reexamine the possibility of reducing batch sizes. The final assembly schedule developed in Chapter 2 is reproduced as Table 9.4.

Note from Table 9.4 that in 28 of the 52 weeks, the schedule calls for less than one-shift production. Clearly, additional setups can be incurred in those weeks. In only 5 of the 52 weeks is the schedule set at the maximum level including overtime. Thus, additional setups can be absorbed in 47 of the 52 weeks with at worst some additional overtime. War Eagle's management feels that by working to reduce setup times, additional setups can be scheduled in all 52 weeks with little or no added labor expense. This change will permit final assembly to be run on a one-week rather than a two-week lead time, since the final assembly scheduler will find compatible batches run each week rather than once in a two-week cycle. Note that the one-week lead time coupled with **MRP** provides a one-week buffer of inventory in front of final assembly at all times. (MRP requires component availability at the start of the lead time.) This buffer protects the final assembly area, which is the most constrained area apart from winding. Reducing lead time at final assembly from 10 days to 5 days eliminates 1,200 dollar days inventory from each hoist.

The synchronized production philosophy calls for the bottleneck to pace non-bottleneck operations. Motor assembly is a non-bottleneck operation, having a capacity of 80 and a maximum demand of 65 units per week. There is therefore no need for a long queue of work in front of motor assembly. If the assembler is idle for a period of time from lack of work, the excess capacity allows the assembler to make up for time lost when the work does arrive. The five-day queue at final assembly protects the final assembly operation. Motor

TABLE 9.4   PROPOSED FINAL ASSEMBLY SCHEDULE, WAR EAGLE HOISTS

WEEK	DEMAND	NORMAL CAPACITY	OVERTIME CAPACITY	UNITS ASSEMBLED
1	39	40	48	39
2	28	40	48	35
3	45	40	48	38
4	29	40	48	29
5	27	40	48	33
6	41	40	48	35
7	33	40	48	33
8	31	40	48	31
9	19	40	48	19
10	15	40	48	20
11	40	40	48	35
12	35	40	48	40
13	39	40	48	40
14	52	40	48	46
15	39	40	48	39
16	31	40	48	36
17	43	40	48	40
18	42	40	48	40
19	36	40	48	36
20	16	40	48	33
21	52	55	65	40
22	60	55	65	55
23	33	55	65	49
24	45	55	65	50
25	71	55	65	50
26	26	55	65	26
27	39	55	65	50
28	52	55	65	50
29	59	55	65	50
30	51	55	65	55
31	57	55	65	55
32	60	55	65	58
33	21	40	48	40
34	54	40	48	41
35	54	40	48	48
36	44	40	48	44
37	48	40	48	48
38	34	40	48	38
39	44	40	48	40
40	23	40	48	23
41	19	40	48	19
42	31	40	48	40
43	42	40	48	40
44	47	40	48	40
45	38	40	48	39
46	41	40	48	40
47	40	40	48	48
48	45	40	48	48
49	59	40	48	48
50	26	40	48	38
51	48	40	48	40
52	44	40	48	40
Total	1,995			1,995

assembly does not need a further buffer. Reducing the lead time of motor assembly from 5 days to 1 day saves 780 dollars days inventory on each hoist.

Lead time for drum fabrication is at present four weeks. This lead time is unnecessarily large, since drum fabrication requires only 30 minutes, with a 6-hour setup when drum sizes change. There are four drum sizes. It is desired to produce some of each drum each week, necessitating four 6-hour setups, 24 hours total. In the 16 hours which remain, only 32 drums can be produced. Capacity must be maintained for 65 drums per week. Since it will take 32.5 hours to make 65 drums, the four setups must be accomplished in 7.5 hours, or just under two hours apiece. Upon investigation, it was discovered that much of the 6-hour setup was spent looking for the tools and equipment needed, and also that the setup involved much waste effort as the process had never been subjected to motion economy analysis.

The time needed to switch drum sizes was reduced to 45 minutes through the use of some ingenuity. First, the stamping machine operator, who has a great deal of idle time, was cross-trained to assist in the setup. This operator is given a schedule of times at which the setup is to occur. It is her responsibility to see that all needed tools and equipment are in place prior to that time, so that setup can begin when the last drum is completed. When the last drum is fabricated, both the drum fabricator and the stamping machine operator work on the setup. Two weekend practice sessions were held after the staff industrial engineer helped redesign the setup process.

The four setups now take a total of 3 hours, leaving 37 productive hours during which up to 74 drums can be fabricated. Since a maximum of 65 are needed in a given week, drum fabrication can be synchronized with the final assembly, maintaining the five-day buffer of material in front of final assembly. Since drum fabrication is itself not a bottleneck, no time buffer of inventory is needed in front of the station, permitting lead time to be reduced to one day.

The lead time for housings was reduced to one day simply by recognizing that it could be done. Housings are all the same size. A setup is needed when colors change (both the housing and the drum are painted). Both the drum fabricator and the housing fabricator paint at the end of each day now rather than the end of each week. This change necessitates some small setups when paint color changes, but these setups do not materially alter the capacity of the sheet metal department.

The lead time for gears is set at three days. The extra lead time for gears is needed because gear production is interrupted twice each week to produce armatures for the winding area. Lead time for stamping gear blanks is one day. The stamping operator stays one day ahead of the machine milling the gears.

Reducing the lead time for drums, housings, and gears lowers the dollar days inventory for a hoist from 2,000 (the leftmost area of Figure 9.2) to 460. The new graph of dollar days accumulation appears in Figure 9.3. Note that total dollar days per hoist from Figure 9.3 are 2,380, to which 1,250 are added

FIGURE 9.3   DOLLAR DAYS PER HOIST AFTER INTERMEDIATE
MODIFICATIONS

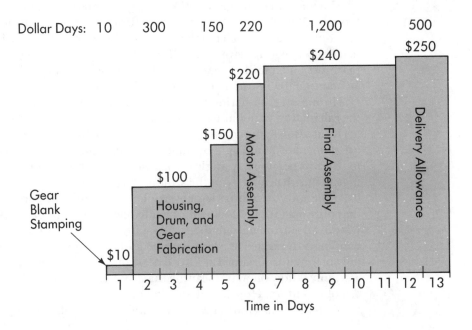

Dollar Days: 10   300   150   220   1,200   500

for windings, leaving a total of 3,630 dollar days per hoist, a reduction of 4,370 dollar days per hoist from the original 8,000.

The dollar days reduction represents working capital which is freed for periods of time to be used for other things. One way of viewing this is to note that 365 dollar days equals one dollar year, i.e., one dollar held for one year. Thus, about $11.97 is freed from inventory, year round, for each of the 2,100 hoists. About $25,000 is freed for other work. But the reduction in capital invested in inventory is just the start of the benefits.

First, the system is easier to manage because activities now work synchronously rather than independently. It is easier to determine what each station should be doing. Second, because quite a bit of inventory has been removed, problems are easier to spot when they develop. Third, reducing lead times causes subsequent operations to be performed sooner. Since often a quality problem created at station A is discovered by the subsequent station, B, having B process A's product sooner means faster feedback on quality problems. Faster feedback leads to faster identification and resolution of problems and to better quality. Finally, since War Eagle competes on quality and lead time as well as price, improving quality and reducing lead time should lead to a larger market share. Synchronous production improves War Eagle's performance on many dimensions.

Longer-Term Recommendation

Having observed the benefits which the intermediate recommendation brought, War Eagle management is willing to implement the longer-term recommendation, which involves accelerating the purchase of a fifth winding machine. The long-term plan calls for the eventual addition of two winding machines and a milling machine. The argument for immediate purchase of an additional winding machine is that it will permit the entire factory to be synchronized, eliminating the need to stockpile windings. Figure 9.4 shows the calculation of dollar days after this change is implemented.

In addition to purchasing a new winding machine and hiring and training a new operator, War Eagle expanded the maximum allowable overtime from 8 to 16 hours per week. A single worker working 56 hours can produce 14 windings. Thus the capacity of the winding department is 50 windings without overtime and 70 windings with overtime. The winding department now paces the entire operation. Moving the pacing operation from final assembly to the winding department leads to several savings. First, the constraining resource, winding, is protected by a four-day queue of work, but this queue now consists only of armatures, valued at $10 each. Second, the lead time allowed for final assembly is now one day, meaning that final assembly is buffered by only one day of inventory. However, there is a larger time buffer of inventory moving through motor assembly, gear, drum, and housing fabrication, and winding,

FIGURE 9.4   DOLLAR DAYS PER HOIST AFTER LONGER-RANGE MODIFICATIONS

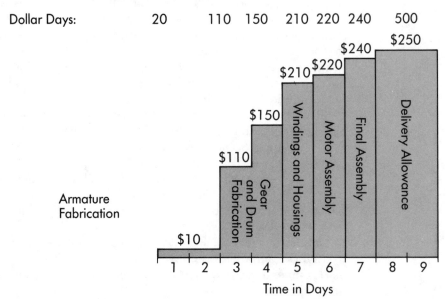

all of which move toward final assembly in synchronized sets. An advantage of synchronizing all activities is that the buffer is redefined to this larger concept. For this buffering procedure to be realistic, one must of course eliminate sources of large variation such as machine breakdowns which require long repairs. Note from Figure 9.4 that dollar days inventory per hoist is now 1,450 including windings, compared to 3,630 after the intermediate steps were taken.

MODELING MORE THAN ONE BOTTLENECK

One issue which is entirely lacking from published discussions of the synchronized production philosophy is a methodology for simultaneously scheduling more than one bottleneck. The problem can be solved by dynamic programming, but a dynamic programming approach can be very time-consuming even for relatively small problems. The following procedure is suggested by the author for multiple bottlenecks. Please note that this suggestion is untested.

First, Gantt chart the most heavily loaded station (the station with the highest activation proportion). Next, take the second most heavily loaded station. Identify all jobs which must go through both stations and set up windows on the Gantt chart into which these jobs must fit to avoid precedence constraint violations. Then schedule the second station making sure all jobs processed at both bottlenecks are within their respective windows. If a third bottleneck exists, set up windows for all jobs passing through the first two bottlenecks and schedule the third station. Continue in this fashion until all bottlenecks have been scheduled. Try to avoid overlap scheduling between bottlenecks. When all bottlenecks have been scheduled, Gantt chart the non-bottlenecks using the procedure described by Fox, i.e., first forward-schedule from bottlenecks to stock, then backward-schedule from bottlenecks to order release. Use overlap scheduling as much as possible at non-bottlenecks to reduce the lead time.

Since one need not avoid overlap scheduling at non-bottlenecks, this procedure should not be particularly difficult to carry out. A computer program which could perform the Gantt charting would be very useful. The author is not aware of Gantt charting software which supports overlapped schedules.

THE IDENTIFICATION OF BOTTLENECKS—V-A-T ANALYSIS

Many managers contend that their plants have no permanent bottlenecks, only temporary bottlenecks. Large lot sizes can create a "floating bottleneck" phenomenon. As lot sizes are decreased and inventory is removed from the system, permanent bottlenecks become more apparent. In his training courses Goldratt provides aids to bottleneck identification which he calls V-A-T analysis. At the time of this writing, no articles on V-A-T analysis had appeared. This section, which is intended to assist bottleneck identification, is based on materials obtained by James F. Cox, a colleague of the author, who attended such a training course.

The bottleneck identification procedure differs by type of plant. Goldratt identifies three basic types which he calls the V-plant, the A-plant, and the T-plant. The V-plant involves few raw materials which are converted into many intermediate products and many more end products, using parallel routings with shared, specialized machinery. An example is a carpet mill, having few basic woven styles which are dyed many colors and backed in a variety of ways. All carpets share weaving, dyeing, and backing facilities.

An A-plant produces a few end items assembled from a variety of common subassemblies and components. An example might be a microcomputer manufacturer, making a few basic PC's from a large set of boards, disk drives, and monitors, which in turn are assembled from a variety of components. A T-plant has one common manufacturing process followed by many packaging options. An example is a brewery making a few types of beer but packaging it in many different bottle and can sizes, kegs, etc. Sometimes more than one type of plant may be under the same roof.

To locate a bottleneck in a V-plant one focuses on queues. Queues awaiting the bottleneck tend to be long; those on machines downstream from the bottleneck tend to be rather short. To determine queue length, one must multiply the quantity by the time per part to convert the queue length to time required to process the queue.

In an A-plant, parts follow different routings and do not necessarily use the same resources. Parts which pass through the bottleneck tend to be late and/or expedited because of delay at the bottleneck. One can identify bottlenecks by reviewing the routings of part numbers which are consistently late and listing all stations on these routings. Next, one reviews the routings of all parts which are seldom late and removes all stations on these routings from consideration, since parts which are seldom late must not pass through a bottleneck. What remains is a set of suspected bottlenecks. The suspected bottlenecks must be checked for routing dependency (if A depends on B for parts, A may be late because it has to wait for B, not because it is a bottleneck), data accuracy, and temporary problems caused by breaking setups to expedite lots. This review process should identify the true bottlenecks. Inventory buffers in A-plants should be established at bottlenecks and also for parts that join to bottleneck parts. The objective here is to maintain the flow of bottleneck parts once produced.

T-plant packaging can sit atop either a V-plant process or an A-plant process. Bottleneck identification closely follows the procedure valid for the underlying plant. The major difference found in a T-plant is that it is common to find that parts from one order are raided in order to ship another order.

Thus, late shipments may be due to raiding rather than to passing through a bottleneck. The effects of raiding, ideally the practice itself, must be eliminated before T-plant bottleneck identification can be performed.

Regardless of the type of plant, identification of bottlenecks should lead to better management of scarce resources by inspecting parts before bottleneck time is invested in them, by buffering the bottleneck against fluctuations at other stations, and by using alternate routing whenever possible to reduce the number of items which must pass through the bottleneck.

SUMMARY

Synchronized production is a philosophy of regaining control of capacity which is likely to have as much impact on job shop planning as just-in-time, examined in Chapter 10, has had on assembly line planning. This philosophy was introduced by Dr. E. M. Goldratt with a set of software called OPT (optimized production technology) and now includes a set of principles which, when understood and applied, are a means of shop control through the scheduling of bottleneck operations. Nonconstrained resources (non-bottlenecks) are scheduled to deliver material at the appropriate time to maintain a buffer in front of bottleneck operations. It is simpler to manage a factory in which operations are synchronized than one in which activities apparently occur independently of one another. Managing an asynchronous factory is like herding cats. A certain amount of screeching and clawing occurs in both activities.

Two difficulties with the synchronized production philosophy are that it continues to evolve and that it is not completely documented. Both difficulties arise from the fact that the concept is very new. Most of Dr. Goldratt's writing on the subject is contained in two rather unusual books, *The Goal* (6) and *The Race* (7), which state general principles but offer no specific methodology. The Avraham Y. Goldratt Institute, named after Dr. Goldratt's father, began publishing *The Theory of Constraints Journal* in 1987 (8). Both E. M. Goldratt and his colleague R. E. Fox have given a number of talks which are recorded in APICS *Proceedings*, especially the annual conference proceedings from 1981 on. In addition, a number of OPT seminars have been held around the country to explain the approach.

In Chapter 11, results of a survey of early implementers of the OPT software are presented.

DISCUSSION QUESTIONS

1. Discuss the difference between a transfer batch and a process batch. Why does MRP consider only one batch size? Why does OPT consider both?

Does an assembly line environment utilize a transfer batch, a process batch, or both?

2. Why is activating a resource not synonymous with utilizing it? Does this distinction arise in actual shops? How?

3. Why is an hour saved at a non-bottleneck a mirage? Is it always or just sometimes? What should a non-bottleneck worker do when he or she runs out of work?

4. What is meant by the principle that capacity and priority must be considered simultaneously and not sequentially? How does an MRP system using rough-cut capacity planning and CRP treat capacity and priority —sequentially, simultaneously, or neither? Why? Consider how MRP systems are actually utilized as well as how they should be utilized.

5. What is meant by throughput? How does this differ from efficiency? Which is more appropriate for judging departmental performance? Why?

6. What is meant by dollar days? How does this measure differ from inventory value? Which is more appropriate for measuring manufacturing inventory? Why?

REFERENCES

1. Clark, Jim. Remarks to APICS Logistics Conference, Dallas, May 1987.

2. Fox, R. E. "OPT—An Answer for America." *Inventories & Production* (November/December 1982).

3. Fox, R. E. "OPT vs. MRP: Thoughtware vs. Software." *Inventories & Production* (November/December 1983).

4. Goldratt, E. M. Comments to APICS International Conference, Toronto, October 1985. This remark is not contained in the *Proceedings* although an article by Goldratt does appear.

5. Goldratt, E. M. Speech to faculty and graduate students, Department of Management, University of Georgia, May 1986.

6. Goldratt, E. M., and Jeff Cox. *The Goal*. Croton-on-Hudson, N.Y.: North River Press, 1984.

7. Goldratt, E. M., and R. E. Fox. *The Race*. Croton-on-Hudson, N.Y.: North River Press, 1986.

8. Goldratt, E. M., and R. E. Fox. *Theory of Constraints Journal* 1 (1987).

9. Smith, S. F., M. S. Fox, and P. S. Ow. "Constructing and Maintaining Detailed Production Plans: Investigations into the Development of Knowledge-based Factory Scheduling Systems." *AI Magazine* (Fall 1986).

10. Vollmann, T. E. "OPT: An Enhancement to MRP II." *Production & Inventory Management* (1986).

APPENDIX 9A
Results of Experiments

The output of station 2 is either 100 units or the sum of station 1 production and station 2 queue, whichever is smaller. When station 1 production plus station 2 queue is less than 100, station 2 runs out of work. Station 2 works at a fixed pace and cannot be speeded up.

In the following version, station 1's production is uniformly distributed on [80,120], averaging 100, and station 2's queue is not limited.

Day	Random Number	Station 1 Production	Station 2 Queue	Station 2 Production
1	96.56402	97	30	100
2	107.6227	108	27	100
3	115.8049	116	35	100
4	80.25815	80	51	100
5	98.17889	98	31	100
6	109.9339	110	29	100
7	106.2188	106	39	100
8	114.7907	115	45	100
9	85.20592	85	60	100
10	95.00996	95	45	100
11	107.5274	108	40	100
12	82.50718	83	48	100
13	87.14302	87	31	100
14	108.1775	108	18	100
15	117.4938	117	26	100

16	107.8992	108	43	100
17	106.5412	107	51	100
18	109.0086	109	58	100
19	98.91051	99	67	100
20	89.15598	89	66	100
21	109.8420	110	55	100
22	111.8352	112	65	100
23	111.3157	111	77	100
24	109.9478	110	88	100
25	89.81664	90	98	100
26	103.0228	103	88	100
27	100.2489	100	91	100
28	87.65717	88	91	100
29	93.98103	94	79	100
30	106.8757	107	73	100
31	103.4199	103	80	100
32	114.9282	115	83	100
33	83.36343	83	98	100
34	102.0509	102	81	100
35	83.16794	83	83	100
36	81.41308	81	66	100
37	95.99782	96	47	100
38	100.3543	100	43	100
39	84.58344	85	43	100
40	92.58697	93	28	100
41	119.5191	120	21	100
42	109.7950	110	41	100
43	108.6703	109	51	100
44	92.51012	93	60	100
45	87.23514	87	53	100
46	113.7722	114	40	100
47	99.92140	100	54	100
48	107.4089	107	54	100
49	102.0496	102	61	100
50	88.27015	88	63	100
51	97.68311	98	51	100
52	96.95316	97	49	100
53	82.61235	83	46	100
54	88.93561	89	29	100
55	90.68439	91	18	100
56	90.10256	90	9	99
57	116.0706	116	0	100
58	89.91356	90	16	100
59	84.10453	84	6	90
60	92.39989	92	0	92

61	91.79732	92	0	92
62	106.3152	106	0	100
63	98.55509	99	6	100
64	101.5834	102	5	100
65	80.47020	80	7	87
66	102.1944	102	0	100
67	110.3509	110	2	100
68	98.39523	98	12	100
69	92.87838	93	10	100
70	115.9059	116	3	100
71	112.4451	112	19	100
72	89.45932	89	31	100
73	102.8299	103	20	100
74	84.72288	85	23	100
75	85.40346	85	8	93
76	89.10566	89	0	89
77	108.5361	109	0	100
78	100.5856	101	9	100
79	117.7921	118	10	100
80	97.01408	97	28	100
81	96.84727	97	25	100
82	118.8597	119	22	100
83	85.35528	85	41	100
84	98.55363	99	26	100
85	104.7152	105	25	100
86	111.9752	112	30	100
87	108.3563	108	42	100
88	84.69229	85	50	100
89	102.2572	102	35	100
90	109.8254	110	37	100
91	96.45811	96	47	100
92	98.35191	98	43	100
93	111.7965	112	41	100
94	98.79728	99	53	100
95	100.5176	101	52	100
96	84.08354	84	53	100
97	107.2544	107	37	100
98	81.30989	81	44	100
99	80.66927	81	25	100
100	87.93800	88	6	94

Total production   **9,936**

In the following version, station 1's output is uniformly distributed on [85,125], averaging 105, and station 2's queue is limited to 60.

Day	Random Number	Station 1 Production	Station 2 Queue	Station 2 Production
1	92.73608	93	30	100
2	115.0725	115	23	100
3	89.40681	89	38	100
4	98.41460	98	27	100
5	107.5814	108	25	100
6	88.69853	89	33	100
7	122.3084	122	22	100
8	91.90040	92	44	100
9	121.7966	122	36	100
10	96.53080	97	58	100
11	96.49485	96	55	100
12	108.1168	108	51	100
13	93.09661	93	59	100
14	110.5549	111	52	100
15	87.25329	87	60	100
16	88.41151	88	47	100
17	86.16400	86	35	100
18	124.9125	125	21	100
19	124.2785	124	46	100
20	94.46535	94	60	100
21	114.6090	115	54	100
22	98.59383	99	60	100
23	97.09038	97	59	100
24	112.6457	113	56	100
25	96.56300	97	60	100
26	100.0449	100	57	100
27	118.7713	119	57	100
28	113.7112	114	60	100
29	105.7792	106	60	100
30	103.0634	103	60	100
31	94.89978	95	60	100
32	122.2423	122	55	100
33	110.1172	110	60	100
34	93.35912	93	60	100
35	94.55347	95	53	100
36	100.1745	100	48	100
37	119.2839	119	48	100
38	115.1522	115	60	100
39	90.25813	90	60	100
40	98.80752	99	50	100

41	113.7086	114	49	100
42	97.18725	97	60	100
43	123.7565	124	57	100
44	103.6659	104	60	100
45	96.42519	96	60	100
46	107.5350	108	56	100
47	124.4730	124	60	100
48	86.58687	87	60	100
49	99.83692	100	47	100
50	96.55913	97	47	100
51	97.54786	98	44	100
52	109.4087	109	42	100
53	109.2399	109	51	100
54	117.4208	117	60	100
55	88.31744	88	60	100
56	93.63694	94	48	100
57	114.9786	115	42	100
58	103.4992	103	57	100
59	100.1145	100	60	100
60	120.4607	120	60	100
61	115.1094	115	60	100
62	92.09898	92	60	100
63	112.2639	112	52	100
64	95.49722	95	60	100
65	100.4469	100	55	100
66	113.8234	114	55	100
67	115.1483	115	60	100
68	102.6361	103	60	100
69	103.8684	104	60	100
70	96.98616	97	60	100
71	89.21936	89	57	100
72	101.3619	101	46	100
73	85.75066	86	47	100
74	106.4362	106	33	100
75	104.8295	105	39	100
76	111.9271	112	44	100
77	117.4147	117	56	100
78	86.17355	86	60	100
79	89.75878	90	46	100
80	122.7520	123	36	100
81	94.45394	94	59	100
82	85.12715	85	53	100
83	101.3117	101	38	100
84	124.4263	124	39	100
85	101.8187	102	60	100

86	115.4734	115	60	100
87	109.8602	110	60	100
88	124.6870	125	60	100
89	122.5353	123	60	100
90	122.8678	123	60	100
91	110.7060	111	60	100
92	88.74811	89	60	100
93	111.9320	112	49	100
94	117.9661	118	60	100
95	111.1389	111	60	100
96	119.3566	119	60	100
97	109.2475	109	60	100
98	88.60917	89	60	100
99	109.5653	110	49	100
100	120.9507	121	59	100

Total production   10,000

In the following version, station 1's output is uniformly distributed on [95,105], averaging 100, and station 2's queue is not limited.

Day	Random Number	Station 1 Production	Station 2 Queue	Station 2 Production
1	104.2617	104	30	100
2	102.1454	102	34	100
3	104.3233	104	36	100
4	98.86906	99	40	100
5	97.89441	98	39	100
6	97.21724	97	37	100
7	104.2395	104	34	100
8	100.6899	101	38	100
9	101.7433	102	39	100
10	98.94535	99	41	100
11	96.51071	97	40	100
12	104.9000	105	37	100
13	103.2681	103	42	100
14	98.87668	99	45	100
15	98.12050	98	44	100
16	104.6427	105	42	100
17	96.47766	96	47	100
18	98.16773	98	43	100
19	95.33451	95	41	100
20	98.96236	99	36	100

21	102.6907	103	35	100
22	104.0658	104	38	100
23	98.86084	99	42	100
24	99.25103	99	41	100
25	100.3701	100	40	100
26	98.93954	99	40	100
27	97.69225	98	39	100
28	98.79164	99	37	100
29	98.87118	99	36	100
30	101.0759	101	35	100
31	102.7236	103	36	100
32	95.86513	96	39	100
33	103.4516	103	35	100
34	98.96500	99	38	100
35	103.7389	104	37	100
36	103.3910	103	41	100
37	101.3840	101	44	100
38	103.2888	103	45	100
39	95.86037	96	48	100
40	100.5698	101	44	100
41	101.5155	102	45	100
42	103.3342	103	47	100
43	104.0550	104	50	100
44	104.4962	104	54	100
45	102.1191	102	58	100
46	97.04858	97	60	100
47	96.79115	97	57	100
48	102.2118	102	54	100
49	104.3791	104	56	100
50	96.45666	96	60	100
51	102.4392	102	56	100
52	96.16552	96	58	100
53	101.3556	101	54	100
54	102.6574	103	55	100
55	104.5104	105	58	100
56	98.55186	99	63	100
57	104.7705	105	62	100
58	97.12000	97	67	100
59	104.3268	104	64	100
60	102.4941	102	68	100
61	104.4609	104	70	100
62	98.49680	98	74	100
63	102.2173	102	72	100
64	100.5423	101	74	100
65	97.84039	98	75	100

66	96.67344	97	73	100
67	100.8322	101	70	100
68	103.4545	103	71	100
69	99.21543	99	74	100
70	98.27336	98	73	100
71	96.67120	97	71	100
72	104.7295	105	68	100
73	101.2983	101	73	100
74	100.3364	100	74	100
75	98.41730	98	74	100
76	98.86105	99	72	100
77	103.7613	104	71	100
78	101.3902	101	75	100
79	103.1720	103	76	100
80	103.7808	104	79	100
81	96.17521	96	83	100
82	101.6323	102	79	100
83	104.1839	104	81	100
84	100.4598	100	85	100
85	95.17699	95	85	100
86	96.44316	96	80	100
87	96.16580	96	76	100
88	95.13720	95	72	100
89	98.20931	98	67	100
90	99.94695	100	65	100
91	96.79252	97	65	100
92	102.1436	102	62	100
93	98.67619	99	64	100
94	97.84126	98	63	100
95	95.47529	95	61	100
96	97.79064	98	56	100
97	99.85836	100	54	100
98	101.2119	101	54	100
99	103.0044	103	55	100
100	98.29167	98	58	100

Total production   **10,000**

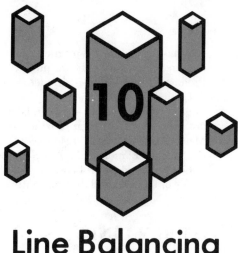

Line Balancing

An assembly line may be defined as a group of workers and/or machines that perform sequential tasks in order to assemble a product. These tasks often have precedence constraints; e.g., assembling a bolt into a predrilled hole must precede tightening a nut onto the bolt. The planning of assembly line capacity involves determination of the line structure, i.e., the number of workers/machines and the tasks assigned to each. This problem is commonly called **line balancing.**

Henry Ford is generally credited with having demonstrated the advantages of an assembly line to the manufacturing world. Recently the Japanese have greatly extended Ford's concept by increasing the proportion of a product which is built in assembly line fashion. Ideally, every component of a product is built on an assembly line, with a lot size of one unit, each worker passing the part to the next worker on a synchronized line. The result of such an arrangement is that material moves through a factory like water through a series of pipes, never standing idle. The Japanese approach has come to be called **just-in-time (JIT).** Part of the JIT philosophy is that a line should produce at the rate at which the product is sold (thus minimizing finished goods inventory). In order to maintain market rate production, line balancing is performed once a month to adjust to the most recent rate of sales. Line balancing may include adding or subtracting workers. Because of the growing interest in JIT in the United States over the past five years, this chapter will be devoted to the problem of line balancing.

Del Mar (10) lists a number of advantages of assembly line layouts over job shop layouts:

1. If there is adequate output volume, processing and assembly unit costs are low because of the high utilization rates of plant, equipment, and processes.

2. Raw materials and parts inventory control requirements are lower because inputs are required for only one product. . . .
3. Production scheduling is simpler since only one product is being made or assembled.
4. High volume of output and high labor efficiency result when the sequential tasks performed require approximately the same amount of time.
5. Material-handling costs are low because of the wide use of conveyors and other mechanical or automated transfer equipment.
6. Supervisory and control costs are low because of the repetitive and routine nature of the tasks and the uniformity of the processing results. [p. 145]

TYPES OF ASSEMBLY LINES

Del Mar's description, especially points 2 and 3, applies primarily to a single-product assembly line. There are also multiproduct assembly lines. In the United States, multiproduct assembly lines usually build a single product at a time. After some predetermined lot size has been built, the line is set up for the next product, usually incurring a fairly large setup cost. Therefore, the multiproduct assembly line-balancing problem also involves a lot-sizing decision. In JIT, the multiproduct line typically involves little or no setup between products, so the lot size of a given model may be as small as one. In this situation, the line is usually called a mixed-model line. Ghosh and Gagnon (2) have an extremely thorough discussion of the balancing of single-product and multiproduct lines. Three recent books which discuss balancing mixed-model assembly lines are Schonberger (25), Hall (13), and Suzaki (27). In this chapter all three line types—single-product, multiproduct, and mixed-model lines—will be discussed.

THE LINE-BALANCING PROBLEM

The process of balancing a single-product line, including heuristics for balancing, will be examined in detail. Multiproduct lines are discussed in less detail. A number of practical considerations are noted.

Two important considerations in defining the line-balancing problem are whether the problem is deterministic or stochastic, and whether the line is paced or unpaced. In the deterministic line-balancing problem, all task times are constants. In the stochastic version, task times are a random variable having some known distribution. A paced assembly line is one in which a conveyor is moving the assembled object, strictly limiting the time any worker has on a given part. An unpaced assembly line lacks conveyors; each worker moves at his or her own pace. Since inventory may exist between stations in an unpaced line, one must consider the optimization of interstation inventory. Figure 10.1 is a model of the 12 possible assembly line configurations.

FIGURE 10.1   TYPES OF ASSEMBLY LINE MODELS

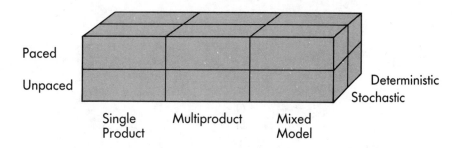

The literature on assembly line balancing is extensive. Ghosh and Gagnon (2) list 162 references. No attempt is made to discuss all of the important studies related to assembly line balancing, but the major aspects of the problem are identified and references for further reading relative to each important aspect are provided.

SINGLE PRODUCT, DETERMINISTIC TASK TIMES

A number of reasonably thorough discussions of single product, deterministic task time (SPD) line-balancing problems exist, including Niebel (20), and Adam and Ebert (1). This section draws heavily on Sawaya and Giauque (24), who have perhaps the most extensive discussion. The steps required to balance a line are as follows:

1. Identify individual tasks or activities to be performed.
2. Determine the time required to perform each task.
3. Establish the precedence constraints, if any, associated with each task.
4. Determine the required assembly line output.
5. Determine the total time available to produce that output.
6. Calculate the required cycle time, i.e., the time between product completions required to complete the output required within the time allowed.
7. Assign tasks to workers.
8. Determine the theoretical minimum number of stations.
9. Assess the effectiveness of the solution.

EXAMPLE 10.1: A DETERMINISTIC LINE-BALANCING EXERCISE

A factory desires to produce 480 widgets within each 8-hour shift. Producing a widget requires 10 operations. Task times and precedence constraints are as follows:

Operation	Precedents	Time (seconds)
A	—	42
B	—	28
C	B	18
D	A,C	39
E	B	27
F	A,E	14
G	D	41
H	F	29
I	F	32
J	H,I	11

An activity-on-node network representation of Example 10.1 is shown in Figure 10.2. In an activity-on-node network, nodes represent activities which must be performed; arrows connecting the nodes represent precedence constraints.

Note that the first five steps listed by Sawaya and Giauque have been completed prior to development of the data shown. Individual tasks have been defined. The time required to perform these tasks has been determined by some form of time study (assume that these times are constants). Precedence constraints have been developed, and the desired output and time available have been set.

Step 6, calculating the cycle time, must now be performed. Cycle time is defined to be the maximum allowable time per unit. Since the entire line will be paced by the time required at the slowest station, no station can be assigned a time greater than the cycle time. The time available per unit is found by dividing the time available by the required output. In this case

$$Cycle\ time = \frac{480\ minutes/shift}{480\ units/shift} = \frac{1\ minute}{Unit} = \frac{60\ seconds}{Unit} \qquad (10.1)$$

FIGURE 10.2   ACTIVITY-ON-NODE NETWORK REPRESENTATION OF EXAMPLE 10.1

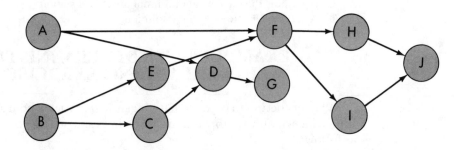

Step 7 is to assign tasks to workers. There are a number of heuristics available for this process, including giving highest priority to (a) tasks with longest operation times, (b) tasks with most followers, and (c) tasks whose operation times plus operation times of followers are greatest. For this example the heuristic based on longest operation time first is used. This heuristic is explained at length in the following paragraphs and is summarized in Table 10.1. In brief, the heuristic is to assign to the current station that job, from among those with no unsatisfied precedence constraints, which has the longest cycle time not exceeding the remaining time available at the station. If all jobs whose precedence constraints have been satisfied require operation times longer than the time available at the station, a new station is planned.

TABLE 10.1   SOLUTION USING THE LONGEST OPERATION TIME FIRST ALGORITHM

AVAILABLE TASKS	NOT EXCEEDING TIME AVAILABLE	TASK WITH LONGEST TIME NOT EXCEEDING TIME AVAILABLE	TIME REQUIRED	TIME AVAILABLE	WORK CENTER
A,B	A,B	A	42	60 18	WC1
B	—				
B	B	B	28	60 32	WC2
C,E	C,E	E	27	5	
C	—				
C,F	C,F	C	18	60 42	WC3
F,D	D,F	D	39	3	
F,G	—				
F,G	F,G	G	41	60 19	WC4
F	F	F	14	5	
H,I	—				
H,I	H,I	I	32	60 28	WC5
H	—				
H	H	H	29	60 31	WC6
J	J	J	11	20	

Using the Algorithm

At the start of the assignment process one assigns tasks to workstation 1. In Example 10.1 the only choices are tasks A and B, since the remaining tasks have unsatisfied precedence constraints. In this case one chooses task A, which has the longer operation time, 42 seconds. There are 18 seconds remaining to be assigned to workstation 1. Task B cannot be assigned because it requires 28 seconds and would bring the time at station 1 to 70 seconds. No other task can be assigned because each has unfulfilled precedents. One must therefore begin to assign tasks to workstation 2.

Workstation 2 is first assigned task B, the only task available to be assigned. Station 2 now has 32 seconds remaining to be assigned. Tasks C and E are available to be assigned now that their precedent (task B) has been assigned. Of these, E has the longer time, 27 seconds, and can be completed within the time remaining for workstation 2. Workstation 2 now has been assigned two tasks (B and E) totaling 55 seconds. As there are no tasks shorter than or equal to 5 seconds, one begins assigning tasks to workstation 3.

Once task E is assigned, task F can be added to the available list since both its precedents (A and E) have been assigned. Tasks C and F are available to be assigned. Task C has the longer operating time, 18 seconds. Workstation 3 has 42 seconds remaining after task C is assigned to it. Task D can be added to the available list since its precedents are assigned. Task D has a longer operating time than task F, so task D is assigned next, bringing the total time required at station 3 to 57 seconds. One must now begin assigning tasks to station 4.

Task G can be added to the available list, since its precedent (D) has now been assigned. The available list consists of F and G. G has the longer task time, 41 seconds. Station 4 has 19 seconds remaining. Task F requires 14 seconds and can be assigned to station 4.

Station 5 can now consider tasks H and I, each added to the available list when task F was assigned. Task I requires 32 seconds and is assigned first. Task H cannot be assigned, as it requires 29 seconds and would bring the time at station 5 to 61 seconds, one second over the cycle time.

Station 6 can be assigned tasks H and J in sequence, requiring a total of 40 seconds.

Workstation assignment using the longest operation time first algorithm has now been completed. Let's compare the results of this algorithm with the theoretical minimum number of stations. By adding up the ten task times one finds that they require a total of 281 seconds. Dividing 281 by the cycle time, 60 seconds, one finds that if one could assign 60 seconds of work to the first four stations and 41 seconds to a fifth, one could balance the line with five stations and a total of 19 seconds of idle time for each part produced. The solution reached through use of the algorithm requires six stations and a total of 79 seconds of idle time for each part.

Since the first solution did not achieve the theoretical minimum number of stations, one might consider other balancing algorithms. Note, however, that there are only 19 seconds of idle time to allocate among five workstations. There may in fact be no solution which achieves five stations.

The Algorithm Repeated Without Precedence Constraints

One way to test whether a five-station solution might be possible is to apply the longest operation time first heuristic without taking precedence constraints into account. Ignoring precedents, the five stations would be assigned as follows:

Station	Tasks	Time Required	Time Idle
1	A,C	60	0
2	G,F	55	5
3	D,J	50	10
4	I,B	60	0
5	H,E	56	4

As expected, idle time is 19 seconds. Note that while the existence of a five-station solution without precedence constraints does not guarantee the existence of a solution with constraints, it at least presents hope that such a solution may exist. If a solution could not be found which would balance the line with five stations ignoring precedence constraints, further algorithms would not be pursued. (Note: The longest operation time first algorithm does not guarantee an optimal solution to the unconstrained problem. From a practical standpoint, however, it is a waste of effort to search for better solutions to the constrained problem than the longest operation time first algorithm achieves on the unconstrained problem.)

Job Categories as a Constraint

An additional constraint to the line-balancing problem will now be considered. Often work categories limit the tasks performed by a worker. Eliminating such artificial barriers by developing multifunction workers may allow the line to be balanced with fewer workers. The single-function worker is often a result of union job categories. In many instances, such as at the new GM Saturn plant, a company has negotiated worker flexibility by giving the union concessions on job security. Such compromises are clearly win-win situations.

Operation Times Exceeding the Cycle Time

One question which undoubtedly has occurred to the reader by now is, "What does one do if a single operation time exceeds the required cycle time?" In this example, the problem would arise if an operation existed with a cycle time of 70 seconds (or any time greater than 60). The solution would be to set up two parallel stations. One station would take the first unit, the other the second unit, and so on. Since each of the pair of stations handles every second unit, the cycle time at the station would be twice as long as normal. In this case, the 70-second job would be placed in one of the two parallel stations and other jobs would be added up to a limit of 120 seconds. Two stations, each operating every 120 seconds, yield one unit every 60 seconds. Akagi, Osaki, and Kikuchi (11) have a recent paper on assembly line balancing where parallel stations are permitted.

Limitations of Algorithms

Another question which perhaps has occurred to the reader is, "Aren't there any procedures that find the minimum number of stations?" The answer to this is that such procedures do exist, but they are not always practical, especially for large lines. In an excellent review of optimum-seeking algorithms, Baybars (5) states: "In general, when the number of tasks is large, all exact algorithms fail, in the sense that the CPU times grow very rapidly. However, some limited success has been attained by Johnson [15], Wee and Magazine [30], and Talbot and Patterson [28]: Talbot and Patterson, for instance, report that their method, in general, performs well when [the number of tasks to be assigned is less than] 50." Conversely, when the number of tasks gets much over 50, the computer time required to solve the exact problem is large and grows quickly as more jobs are added. Unfortunately, most real-world problems involve far more than 50 tasks to be assigned. A further limitation of optimum-seeking algorithms is that they optimize only one criterion, efficiency, ignoring other important considerations.

Ghosh and Gagnon (11) list a number of real-world factors which are not considered in the line-balancing problem as it has been formulated. These include requirements that some tasks be done at separate stations or at the lefthand or righthand side of the line, task groupings by worker skill level, wage scale considerations, off-line repairs for uncompleted units, and job incentive/enrichment considerations.

An early 1970s survey by Chase (7) of 95 companies operating assembly lines found that only 5 percent were using published algorithms to balance their lines. Ghosh and Gagnon imply that the situation has not changed much today, perhaps because of inadequate communication between researchers and practitioners: "While many of the assembly line methodologies developed were mathematically advanced, they had not yet satisfied real-world needs."

SINGLE PRODUCT, STOCHASTIC TASK TIMES

One consideration which has been explored extensively is the variability of processing times. Given an evenly balanced line which is unpaced, and given that the time required to complete a task varies from part to part, then as the variability of the processing time increases the capacity of the line decreases.

EXAMPLE 10.2: A STOCHASTIC LINE-BALANCING EXERCISE

To demonstrate that variability in job times reduces the capacity of a balanced line, consider the following example. Assume that there exists a five-station assembly line in which each station requires an average of 300 seconds to process the part. Assume further that only *one* unit of work in process (WIP) is allowed between each station, i.e., each station may have one unit in process plus one unit in queue. There is no scrap or rework. Initially each station has one unit in queue. If there is no variation in job time, the time required to produce 500 units should be 150,000 seconds. A generalized manufacturing simulator (GEMS) model was constructed to determine the length of time required in this situation given that job times are normally distributed at all stations with standard deviations of 50, 100, 200, and 300. The GEMS code for this model appears in Appendix 10A at the end of this chapter. The mean time required to process 500 units is as follows:

Max. Queue	1	1	1	1
Process Deviation	50	100	200	300
Mean Time	156,324	168,935	202,261	237,949
Std. Dev. of Time	608	1,119	2,126	3,152
Error of Estimate	192	354	672	997

The mean time data are based on 10 simulation runs each. The standard deviation of the time required between various replications of the same model is given, as is the error of estimate associated with the estimate for the mean.

It is apparent that as variability of job times increases, the output of a line with little WIP decreases dramatically.

The Effect of Work-in-Process Inventory on Utilization

Since WIP inventory causes a station to be somewhat independent of the station upstream, the length of the queue between stations is an important issue. The following table shows the result of the same simulations except that the maximum allowable inventory is now set at 20 units:

Max. Queue	20	20	20	20
Process Deviation	50	100	200	300
Mean Time	153,564	157,359	166,236	182,236
Std. Dev. of Time	876	1,542	2,267	3,442
Error of Estimate	277	488	717	1,088

Using WIP to make stations independent is a popular technique with many North American manufacturers. The one major drawback of the technique is that quality may be adversely affected. Suppose that an inspection occurs at the end of station 3. With 20 units of WIP permissible, if station 1 begins making bad parts 40 bad parts may be built before the problem is detected. With one unit of WIP permissible, no more than four defective parts would be built before the problem is detected.

Improving quality is one of the major reasons North American manufacturers are beginning to adopt the low-WIP approach, which has come to be known as zero inventory or just-in-time (JIT). Successful JIT implementation requires that variations in job times be reduced in order to avoid slowdowns on the entire line. Example 10.2 amply illustrates this point. While a certain amount of research has been done regarding the relationship between process-time variability and the number of **kanbans** needed, very little has been done explicitly on the relationship between variance, WIP, and capacity utilization. This relationship needs to be researched in order to assist the design of JIT lines.

BALANCED VERSUS UNBALANCED LINES

The preceding examples demonstrate that where variability exists in operation times, line output is difficult to predict with small WIP because the utilization of one station depends on parts being fed from an upstream station. Goldratt (12) indicates that a balanced line is undesirable. One of the principles of synchronized production, as discussed in the previous chapter, is to balance flow, not capacity. Example 10.2 studied a line with five equally fast stations, each requiring 300 seconds to process a part, and examined the effect of increasing variance on output. Now suppose one has the opportunity to put in a very reliable machine at the first station. This machine requires 330 seconds with 0 variance. It permits the time at station 5 to be reduced to 270 seconds. Because of more consistent quality, it also permits the standard deviation of job times at the other stations to be reduced 10 percent. What happens to the capacity of this line?

The approach used in Example 10.1 would indicate that the line has lost capacity. Since the cycle time (time of the slowest station) is now 330 seconds, the time required to produce 500 parts should be 165,000 seconds, up from 150,000. But in the case in which the standard deviation of job time was 300 seconds per station and the maximum WIP was set at 20 units per station, the actual time required was over 180,000 seconds. In order to see how the newly defined line would operate it was simulated in GEMS. Across 10 replications the time required to finish 500 parts averaged 175,000 seconds with a standard deviation of 3,430 seconds. Thus the capacity of the line increased despite the fact that the theoretical capacity decreased.

What would happen in the case in which the standard deviation was 300 but WIP was set at 1? The simulation model for the case with a 330-second cycle time and no variation on the first machine indicates an average time of 218,000 seconds with a standard deviation of 4,012 seconds. This is an 8 percent decrease in time compared to the 238,000 seconds required in the original model. (One might also note that the difference is statistically significant; the t value for a hypothesis test of no difference is 15.7. Thus these differences cannot be attributed to sampling error.)

It is important to note that in this example, the bottleneck machine also had zero variance. This example illustrates that in some cases reducing variance of process time may offset increased average time.

Although Goldratt may have been the first to popularize the notion that an unbalanced line was preferable to a balanced line, he was not the first to study the phenomenon. In 1966, Hillier and Boling (14) noted that if there is an imbalance to the line, the stations with the longest times (bottlenecks) should be placed at either end of the line rather than in the middle. This effect came to be known as the "bowl phenomenon." A scholarly debate occurred concerning whether an unbalanced line having bottlenecks at either end could increase output over a balanced line. A number of researchers contributed to this debate, including Rao (22), Muth (19), and Payne, Slack, and Wild (21). Smunt and Perkins (26) summarized the results of this research as follows:

1. Unbalancing task times is optimal when the coefficient of variation (CV) is large. Unbalancing, whether by using a bowl distribution or alternating fast and slow stations, improves the output rate. [Author's note: The coefficient of variation is the standard deviation divided by the mean. A CV greater than 0.5 is considered to be large. In Example 10.2 standard deviations of 50, 100, 200, and 300 correspond to CV's of 0.17, 0.33, 0.67, and 1.0, respectively.]

2. Unbalanced allocation of buffer storage capacity can also improve line output rate when the CV is large. Allocation of buffer capacity concentrated around the most variable task times or in a bowl distribution appears to work best.

3. The output rate of a line decreases as the number of sequential workstations increases.
4. Output rate increases as more buffer storage capacity is available due to the decoupling effect.
5. Output rate decreases as the CV of service times increases.

STOCHASTIC LINE BALANCING

In balancing the line, one wishes to achieve the property that each station is equally likely to finish within the cycle time. If all stations exhibit the same distribution, this is achieved by having equal standard deviations. However, given a situation in which some of the operation times are from a skewed distribution, such as the exponential, while other operation times are from a symmetric distribution, such as the normal, equalizing the standard deviations will not equalize the probability of finishing within the cycle time. Fortunately for practical applications, when several random variables are added together the sum tends to be normally distributed even if the underlying distributions are not (this is known as the central limit theorem). This property mitigates the problem somewhat, particularly if the underlying distributions are symmetric. A distribution is symmetric if the probability of being less than the mean by some amount is the same as the probability of being greater than the mean by that amount. If an occasional rare event causes an operation to be exceedingly long, then that operation comes from a skewed distribution rather than a symmetric one. Eliminating the cause of the rare event will make the task of line balancing much easier from several perspectives.

The body of literature on stochastic line balancing is not large. Published studies include Moodie and Young (18), Reeve and Thomas (23), and Kottas and Lau (16). Ghosh and Gagnon (11) indicate that the state-of-the-art algorithm for stochastic assembly line balancing still appears to be an early (1966) algorithm known as COMSOAL, developed by Arcus (4).

MULTIPLE-MODEL LINES

Analysis of multiple-model lines is quite complex because in addition to the factors mentioned in the previous section, one must consider the length of the production run. Thomopoulos (29), Dar-El (9), and Chakravarty and Shtub (6) are among those who discuss this problem.

The traditional Western assembly line tends to involve a large setup time between models, and hence a large run length. A typical pattern might be 1,000 A's, 500 B's, and 500 C's and then back to A's. In contrast, with such a product mix the ideal just-in-time line would be AABCAABC repeated indefinitely, or perhaps even ABACABAC repeated. The advantage of the just-in-time approach is that it greatly simplifies the problem of capacity planning in the areas which fabricate components for the assembly line. Large batch sizes create lumpy demand in the fabrication area which must be carefully coordinated with assembly. With a mixed-model line and a lot size of 1, a level load is created throughout the fabrication area, so that the same amount is produced each day and large inventories of WIP are eliminated.

Some Western assembly lines have always handled mixed models. For example, automobile manufacturers have plants which produce custom-ordered models on assembly lines on which no two adjacent vehicles are alike. However, Japanese manufacturers are far more likely to operate true mixed-model lines. The key to a mixed-model line is short setup times. Monden (17) and Suzaki (27) have excellent discussions of setup-time reduction.

PRACTICAL ASSEMBLY LINE BALANCING

Given that the assembly line-balancing problem is so complex, one might ask how the Japanese manage to rebalance lines once a month. The answer is that the Japanese view the problem in a different light. Americans seem to assume that process times are immutable and that a line must be laid out once for all time. The Japanese treat any solution as an approximation to be refined. They recognize that some workers are more experienced than others. They recognize that improvements may be made in the production process. In a Japanese shop, a worker who is not able to complete the task within the required cycle time is required to turn on a warning light. When the light goes on, supervisors and/or engineers address the problem. Perhaps the worker needs additional training or an additional tool. Perhaps a more experienced worker needs to be shifted to this task, moving the less experienced worker to a less demanding task. Perhaps a part of the task needs to be moved to another station. Line balancing continues dynamically as problems appear.

If one views the line-balancing problem as an approximation procedure, with final details to be worked out on the line itself, then the simple deterministic model is sufficient for the single-product case. Where excessive variance causes delay, engineers will be called to reduce the variance or to adjust the balance of the line. Such an approach would seem to be necessary if the line is to be adjusted once a month to produce to the current market. Schonberger (25) has an excellent discussion of how problems are identified and solved in order to reduce variance. His list includes simple techniques such as good housekeeping and having the worker keep a list of the frequency of problem occurrence so that the most frequently occurring problems may be attacked first.

JUST-IN-TIME SYSTEMS

Just-in-time involves much more than simply rearranging the workplace into a series of assembly lines. It is really a manufacturing philosophy. The

APICS Dictionary (3) defines the JIT philosophy as "an approach to achieving excellence in a manufacturing company based on the continuing elimination of waste (waste being considered as those things which do not add value to the product)." Crawford (8), who summarizes 220 JIT-related articles, identifies 12 common elements of the JIT philosophy:

1. Pull method of production. The worker signals when delivery of more work is needed. Work cannot be pushed forward to the next station before it is needed.
2. Quality. The goal is zero defects. Defect rates as small as a few parts per million have been obtained.
3. Preventive maintenance. The goal is no lost productive time due to unexpected failures.
4. Multiskilled workers. JIT requires flexible workers to maximize line balance.
5. Level schedule. Parts are not produced in large batches in order to minimize changes in day-to-day activities.
6. Setup-time reduction. Small setup times are needed to support small batch sizes.
7. Revised plant layout. Ideally, each family of parts has a dedicated assembly line.
8. Reduced lot sizes. Small lots minimize both WIP inventory and hidden quality problems.
9. Supplier involvement. *After* a shop has control of its own operations (level schedule, no breakdowns, good quality) the JIT concept is extended to suppliers. This involvement goes beyond requiring the supplier to make frequent deliveries of small batches. The JIT philosophy must be used internally by the supplier to eliminate excess inventory from the system.
10. Workplace organization. All parts and tools must be in their assigned location. The worker is responsible for cleanliness within his or her work area.
11. Small-group improvement activities. The most widely known small-group activity is the quality circle. Small groups also work on productivity improvements and the resolution of other problems.
12. Management commitment. Any system fails unless top management both understands the system and conveys support for the system to the work force.

A number of American companies are already experiencing tremendous success with JIT. Chapter 11 includes a review of some JIT case studies. Three excellent books on JIT implementation in the United States are Schonberger (25), Hall (13), and Suzaki (27).

SUMMARY

In this chapter the problem of line balancing is examined, including both single and multiproduct lines. A simple heuristic for achieving a rough line balance, longest operation time first, is presented. Although more-sophisticated techniques are examined, it is noted that the Japanese approach of achieving a rough balance and adding refinements on the shop floor is likely to be more effective than expending additional effort to achieve a theoretical balance before putting the solution into practice. Finally, it is noted that just-in-time is much more than simply moving to assembly line style production; it is a manufacturing philosophy of continuous improvement via identification and elimination of waste.

REFERENCES

1. Adam, Everett E., Jr., and Ronald J. Ebert. *Production and Operations Management Concepts, Models, and Behavior.* Englewood Cliffs, N.J.: Prentice-Hall, 1986. Pp. 322–331.
2. Akagi, Fumio, Hirokazu Osake, and Susumu Kikuchi. "A Method for Assembly Line Balancing with More Than One Worker in Each Station." *International Journal of Production Research* 21, no. 5 (1983): 755–770.
3. *APICS Dictionary.* Falls Church, Va.: American Production and Inventory Control Society, 1987.
4. Arcus, A. L. "COMSOAL: A Computer Method of Sequencing Operations for Assembly Lines, I—The Problem in Simple Form; II—The Problem in Complex Form," in *Readings in Production and Operations Management,* ed. E. S. Buffa. New York: John Wiley & Sons, 1966.
5. Baybars, Ilker. "A Survey of Exact Algorithms for the Simple Line Balancing Problem." *Management Science* 32, no. 8 (August 1986): 909–932.
6. Chakravarty, Amiya K., and Avarham Shtub. "Balancing Mixed Model Lines with In-Process Inventories." *Management Science* 31, no. 9 (September 1985): 1161–1174.
7. Chase, R. B. "Survey of Paced Assembly Lines." *Industrial Engineering* 6 (February 1974): 14–18.
8. Crawford, K. M. "An Analysis of Performance Measurement Systems in Selected Just-in-Time Operations." Ph.D. dissertation, University of Georgia, 1987.
9. Dar-El, Ezey M. "Mixed-Model Assembly Line Sequencing Problems." *Omega* 6, no. 4 (1978): 313–323.
10. Del Mar, Donald. *Operations and Industrial Management: Designing and Managing for Productivity.* New York: McGraw-Hill Book Co., 1985. P. 145.
11. Ghosh, Soumen, and Roger Gagnon. "A Comprehensive Literature Review and Hierarchical Taxonomy for the Design and Balancing of Assembly Lines." Working Paper Series 86–4, College of Administrative Science, Ohio State University, 1986.
12. Goldratt, Eliyahu M., and Jeff Cox. *The Goal.* Croton-on-Hudson, N.Y.: North River Press, 1984.

13. Hall, Robert W. *Attaining Manufacturing Excellence*. Dow Jones-Irwin/APICS Series in Productivity Management, 1987.

14. Hillier, F. S., and R. W. Boling. "The Effect of Some Design Factors on the Efficiency of Production Lines with Variable Operation Times." *Journal of Industrial Engineering* 17, no. 12 (December 1966): 651–658.

15. Johnson, R. V. "Assembly Line Balancing Algorithms: Computational Comparisons." *International Journal of Production Research* 19 (1981): 277–287.

16. Kottas, John F., and Hon-Shiang Lau. "A Stochastic Line Balancing Procedure." *International Journal of Production Research* 19, no. 2 (1981): 177–193.

17. Monden, Yasuhiro. *Toyota Production System*. Industrial Engineering and Management Press, Institute of Industrial Engineers, 1983.

18. Moodie, C. L., and H. H. Young. "A Heuristic Method of Assembly Line Balancing for Assumptions of Constant or Variable Work Element Times." *Journal of Industrial Engineering* 16 (1965): 23.

19. Muth, E. J. "The Production Rate of a Series of Work Stations with Variable Service Times." *International Journal of Production Research* 11, no. 2 (April 1973): 155–169.

20. Niebel, Benjamin W. *Motion and Time Study*. Homewood, Ill.: Richard D. Irwin, 1982. Pp. 148–158.

21. Payne, S., N. Slack, and R. Wild. "A Note on the Operating Characteristics of 'Balanced' and 'Unbalanced' Production Flow Lines." *International Journal of Production Research* 10, no. 1 (January 1972): 93–98.

22. Rao, N. P. "A Generalization of the 'Bowl Phenomenon' in Series Production Systems." *International Journal of Production Research* 14, no. 4 (July 1976): 437–443.

23. Reeve, N. R., and W. H. Thomas. "Balancing Stochastic Assembly Lines." *A.I.E.E. Transactions* 5 (1973): 223.

24. Sawaya, William J., Jr., and William C. Giauque. *Production and Operations Management*. New York: Harcourt Brace Jovanovich, 1986. Pp. 374–386.

25. Schonberger, Richard J. *World Class Manufacturing: The Lessons of Simplicity Applied*. New York: The Free Press, 1986. Ch. 2.

26. Smunt, Timothy L., and William C. Perkins. "Stochastic Unpaced Line Design: Review and Further Experimental Results." *Journal of Operations Management* 5, no. 3 (May 1985): 351–373.

27. Suzaki, Kiyoshi. *The New Manufacturing Challenge: Techniques for Continuous Improvement*. New York: The Free Press, 1987.

28. Talbot, F. B., and J. H. Patterson. "An Integer Programming Algorithm with Network Cuts for Solving the Single Model Assembly Line Balancing Problem." *Management Science* 30 (1984): 85–99.

29. Thomopoulos, Nick T. "Mixed Model Line Balancing with Smoothed Station Assignments." *Management Science* 16, no. 9 (May 1970): 593–603.

30. Wee, T. S., and M. J. Magazine. "An Efficient Branch and Bound Algorithm for Assembly Line Balancing—Part 1: Minimize the Number of Work Stations." Working Paper no. 150, University of Waterloo, Waterloo, Ont., 1981.

EXERCISES

1. Discuss the advantages an assembly line layout has over a process layout. Discuss the circumstances in which a process layout is preferable.
2. Discuss the difference between a multiproduct assembly line and a mixed-model assembly line. Why does a just-in-time system utilize the latter?
3. Discuss the difference between a paced and an unpaced assembly line. Which type is most commonly found in a just-in-time system? Why?
4. Define cycle time. In a JIT system, how should the manufacturing cycle time compare to the rate of sales of the item? Why?
5. Is a rough approximation to a balanced line sufficient for a JIT line? Why or why not?
6. Balance the line in Example 10.1 by assigning task B to workstation 1 first and thereafter applying the largest operation time first algorithm.
7. Given the set of tasks shown below, balance the line using the largest operation time first algorithm (breaking ties using the task letter which is lower in the alphabet first). The line is to produce 300 units each 8-hour shift. Determine the cycle time, the minimum number of stations, and the amount of idle time involved per unit.

   When the station has been balanced using a deterministic algorithm, determine the standard deviation of the time at each station (assume all task times are independent of the preceding task and are normally distributed). Comment on the adequacy of the solution from a stochastic viewpoint.

Task	Precedents	Mean	Standard Deviation
A	—	10	5
B	—	40	15
C	—	22	11
D	A,B	31	14
E	B	18	8
F	B,C	26	19
G	D	15	10
H	E	18	6
I	A,F	23	15
J	D,E	11	4
K	F	35	14
L	I	15	8

M	K,L	17	12
N	L	29	15
O	M	13	7
P	N	26	15

8. *Advanced.* Simulate the line created in Exercise 7 with each station having 2 units in queue at the beginning of the simulation and with one unit released to the system every 96 seconds. Each station has a maximum queue of 5 units with a preceding station blocked whenever a queue is full. Determine how many units are actually produced in an 8-hour day.

9. Repeat Exercise 7 with the following data. Desired output is 400 units per 8-hour shift.

Task	Precedents	Mean	Standard Deviation
A	—	52	58
B	—	26	30
C	A,B	39	41
D	A	65	70
E	D	23	25
F	C	11	15
G	E,F	37	40
H	F	29	35
I	G	46	50
J	I	27	32

10. *Advanced.* Repeat Exercise 8 using data from Exercise 9. Compare the results of this exercise with those of Exercise 8. Discuss the effect of increasing variance on the output of the line.

APPENDIX 10A
GEMS Code for Example 10.2

```
$run idrun=2,mentry=200,natrib=2,netrl=500,npass=20,nbox=8,
npars=1,iseed=12479,que=t,inq=-2,-3,-4,-5,-6,
finish=1,1,1,1,1,$end
$par psn=1,itype=2,param=300,50,1000,100,$end
$box id=1,nfrl=0,nprl=1,dur=300,ifoll=1,2,$end
$box id=2,psn=1,ifoll=3,qbox=t,blkq=t,maxq=1,jbalk=8,$end
$box id=3,psn=1,ifoll=4,qbox=t,blkq=t,maxq=1,$end
$box id=4,psn=1,ifoll=5,qbox=t,blkq=t,maxq=1,$end
$box id=4,psn=1,ifoll=6,qbox=t,blkq=t,maxq=1,$end
$box id=6,psn=1,ifoll=7,qbox=t,maxq=1,$end
$box id=7,dur=0,sink=t,nprl=1,$end
$box id=8,dur=0,nprl=1,$end
$stat in=-1,8,2,0,$end
```

For those not familiar with GEMS, it uses a format-free input with key words separated by commas.

The $run card says the following: this is run 2, there can be a maximum of 200 entities in the system at once, each entity may have 2 attributes, we will simulate until 500 entities have completed the network, we will make 20 iterations, there are 8 boxes, there is 1 parameter set in the network, the seed value for the random number generator is 12479, there are queues in the network, and boxes 2, 3, 4, 5, and 6 initially have one item in queue.

The $par card says parameter set 1 is normal (itype 2) having mean, minimum, maximum, and standard deviation as shown.

The $box cards define the 8 boxes. Five (boxes 2–6) are queues, box 7 may be viewed as finished goods inventory. The first box is not a queue as it is a source box, starting a new entity whenever it completes the previous one. The statement maxq=1 limits queue length to 1 (plus 1 in service). The statement blkq=1 says that if the following queue is full, this station must go idle.

The $stat card collects statistics.

Note: The model as shown requires 4 minutes, 5 seconds CPU time on an 8-MHz IBM PC–AT with 80287 coprocessor. The simulation was run again with no statistics collected at queue boxes. Eliminating these statistics reduced running time to 2 minutes, 59 seconds.

Case Studies

Very few case studies in capacity management exist. The few that do exist are due to the efforts of the American Production and Inventory Control Society (APICS) and will be briefly reviewed in this chapter. Additional sources of information on capacity management systems in use at a number of different companies are given in the bibliography at the end of the chapter, a listing of papers presented at APICS International Conferences during the period 1980–1987 and published in the APICS *Proceedings*.

REVIEW OF *CASE STUDIES IN CAPACITY MANAGEMENT*

The most complete case studies relating to MRP systems are three contained in an APICS monograph entitled *Case Studies in Capacity Management*, by Wemmerlov (13). The three companies that Wemmerlov studied were apparently selected to represent three different types of capacity management processes. The first company discussed is engineer-to-order, having one schedule which is both a master production schedule (MPS) and a final assembly schedule (FAS). The second company is assemble-to-order, high volume, and repetitive, the typical assembly line situation. The third company is assemble-to-order, with fairly low volume and a complex product, typical of situations in which the master production schedule is used to plan component availability and the final assembly schedule is used to meet deliveries.

In all three cases Wemmerlov presents the complete manufacturing planning and control process, so that capacity management can be seen in its proper context. He presents 55 exhibits, most of which are reproductions of documents actually used in the capacity management process.

CAPACITY MANAGEMENT PROCESSES: 3 CASES

Motter Printing Press Company

The Motter Printing Press Company manufactures rotogravure printing presses and accessories to customer specifications. The company employs over 300 people, has sales of approximately $25 million, and operates solely according to a backlog, which is usually one to two years. The manufacturing plant occupies 145,000 square feet and consists of three machining and two assembly departments. Total lead time, engineering and manufacturing, is about one year. There is only one schedule, with no differentiation between the master production schedule and the final assembly schedule.

Customer delivery date is determined by the backlog and capacity constraints in engineering and manufacturing. As is typical of engineer-to-order plants, it is just as important to plan engineering capacity as it is manufacturing capacity. An engineering and purchasing schedule (EPS), in the form of a Gantt chart, is constructed before the design process begins and is used to manage both engineering and purchasing. As parts are designed, information concerning them is entered into the computer system for use during MRP and CRP.

A detailed assembly schedule is created, allowing ample time to complete the design process and to obtain purchased materials for each job entered into the schedule. This schedule serves as the master production schedule, i.e., it is input into the MRP system, which then determines the schedule to be used in the machining departments.

Motter uses two techniques for capacity management. One is a form of rough-cut capacity planning, documenting cumulative capacity available in machining and assembly to capacity already scheduled. This process is used in setting order promise dates. The second technique is CRP, which is used to manage queues and planned lead times. The rough-cut technique is performed manually; the CRP technique is performed by computer, using a modified IBM IPICS program on an IBM System 3. Wemmerlov presents 14 exhibits for this case.

Steelcase, Inc. – Panel Division

The Steelcase Panel Division manufactures panels used as wall dividers in offices. Customers of this division typically order desks, chairs, and files from several other divisions of Steelcase at the same time. A centralized order entry system places a promise date on multidivision orders, based on the last date any single division can deliver.

The panel division employs 400 direct and 60 salaried workers, occupying 750,000 square feet of manufacturing area. Final assembly is organized like a flow line, with conveyors and continuous production. Although the product is high volume and the final assembly area is repetitive, the fabrication area is organized like a job shop, with groups of similar machines organized into departments. Total manufacturing lead time is 23 workdays, 15 days for fabrication and 8 days for final assembly and packing.

Steelcase analyzes capacity requirements across three time horizons. They perform resource requirements planning annually, using a 5- to 10-year horizon. A 12-month production plan is prepared once every 6 months. A 24-week sales operation plan is updated every 4 weeks. Once a shipment date has been arranged (coordinated with other divisions for multidivision orders), backward scheduling is used to schedule final assembly and fabrication. Rough-cut capacity planning is performed using the capacity planning using overall factors (CPOF) technique. The technique is applied manually and is used for medium-term labor force planning.

CRP is used to control capacity in the fabrication area. This report is generated centrally on Steelcase's IBM 3081 mainframe. The program was developed internally. It has a simulation capability which examines the impact tentative MPS would have on the fabrication area. MRP is regenerative, the weekly run requiring 2.5 hours while CRP requires 0.25 hours.

Wemmerlov reports that Steelcase's data accuracy is quite good. One aspect that contributes to data accuracy is that there are few engineering changes (about one major change a week) and the product is not very complex. Wemmerlov presents 23 exhibits for this case.

Trane Company – Commercial Air Conditioning Division

The Trane Company is a multinational manufacturer of heating and air conditioning equipment. Several plants make air conditioning equipment. Wemmerlov's case seems to be based on several plants, primarily four located in La Crosse, Wisconsin.

The planning and control system consists of several interrelated stages. Trane performs resource requirements planning once a year using a 5-year horizon. The MPS has a 52-week horizon and is composed of both actual orders and forecast orders. Forecast orders are exploded through the use of planning bills of material. There is no overplanning utilized in planning bills for optional items, and hence there is no overplanning of capacity. The FAS has a one-month horizon, is prepared monthly, and is very close to the master production schedule. The execution of the schedule is monitored daily; production personnel meet with the plant manager several times a week to discuss performance to the schedule.

Rough-cut capacity planning is performed using the bill of labor approach, which Trane calls a capacity bill, using monthly planning buckets. Capacity requirement planning reports are produced weekly using a 12-

week horizon. A detailed report is available specifying order numbers and part numbers associated with each work center. The traditional machine load report is also produced. Input/output control is used to level loads at gateway work centers and to control labor force planning at other stations.

The programs run on an IBM 370/168, requiring 20 hours for the MRP portion and 7 hours for the CRP. (Both programs are apparently run centrally and cover multiple plants; Wemmerlov mentions one CRP report covering 1,100 work centers.) Input/output was manual at the time Wemmerlov studied it. He reported plans to computerize the input/output report and to add a daily priority dispatch list. Wemmerlov presents 18 exhibits for this case.

REVIEW OF *MASTER PRODUCTION SCHEDULING: PRINCIPLES AND PRACTICE*

The monograph *Master Production Scheduling: Principles and Practice* (2) grew out of a seminar held at Indiana University in the late 1970s. The eight firms participating in the seminar were selected for their preeminence as MPS practitioners. Three of the firms are process industries; the rest represent fabrication and assembly operations. Make-to-stock, assemble-to-order, and engineer-to-order operations are all represented. Although the focus of the monograph is on the creation of the MPS, the cases of necessity also describe the rough-cut process used to verify that there is sufficient capacity to carry out the plan. Often the cases also describe other aspects of capacity management. The eight cases are reviewed very briefly in the following subsections.

MPS: 8 CASES

Pfizer, Inc. – Easton (Pa.) Plant

The Pfizer Easton plant produces iron oxides used for coloring in paints, plastics, and cosmetics and for magnetic properties in magnetic inks, recording tapes, etc. The plant has annual sales of $15 million and employs 250 people. It produces approximately 50 end items. The operation is make-to-stock.

The planning system consists of resource requirements planning, master production scheduling, and detailed equipment scheduling. Resource requirements planning is performed annually on a divisional basis using a

10-year horizon. The master production schedule is prepared on a general basis for a quarter and on a detailed basis for a month. It is updated every two weeks. The MPS is also the final assembly schedule. Pfizer uses the CPOF approach to estimate capacity requirements at all work centers. A more detailed analysis based on a bill of labor approach is used for bottleneck work centers. A detailed equipment schedule, essentially a Gantt chart, is prepared for each major piece of equipment and is used in lieu of capacity requirements planning.

The performance of the system is evaluated in terms of late shipment frequency, capacity utilization, inventory, and performance to the MPS. The case includes 8 figures.

Ethan Allen Inc. – Case Goods Division

The Case Goods Division has annual sales of $120 million manufactured in 14 plants. Finished product is shipped from the 14 plants to five consolidation warehouses which ship either direct to one of 287 stores or to field warehouses. There are approximately 1,000 end items manufactured from 40,000 components. The deepest bill of materials is 5 levels.

The master production schedule is stated in weekly buckets, covering an 18-week horizon. It is revised monthly. The MPS is firm for the first 8 weeks. The MPS is done at the final assembly stage, one MPS for each assembly line. MPS preparation involves both corporate headquarters and each factory. Corporate inputs include forecasts, running the software, and monitoring plant performance. Plant inputs include adjustments which must be made because of problems, setting lot sizes, and executing the schedule.

Ethan Allen does not use a formal rough-cut capacity planning procedure. However, each assembly line is loaded to its capacity based on established rates of output. Planning of component availability for final assembly is not discussed; apparently it is not a problem. The case includes 12 figures.

Black and Decker Manufacturing Co. – Hampstead (Md.) Plant

The Black and Decker Hampstead plant produces electric tools such as drills, circular saws, and accessories for such tools. The plant has annual sales of $200 million. It employs 2,500 people and occupies about one million square feet of plant space. The company produces 3,100 end items which are sold to 3,500 customers, mostly distributors, with a one-week delivery time. Customer orders are filled by warehouses; all finished goods inventory is owned by marketing.

The master schedule is stated in end items (all 3,100!!) in weekly buckets over a 12-month horizon. Both marketing and manufacturing are involved in master scheduling. The MPS has three fences: 8 weeks, 13 weeks, and 26 weeks. The first 8 weeks are considered the final assembly schedule.

The company uses rough-cut, CRP, and input/output analysis, although none are discussed in detail in the case. The case includes 9 figures.

Abbott Laboratories Ltd. of Canada

Abbott Laboratories produces pharmaceuticals, hospital supplies, and nutritional products for infants. The company is make-to-stock, having sales of $50 million to 2,000 customers. About 200 of these customers account for 90 percent of sales. These customers expect one-day delivery. Abbott maintains approximately five weeks of finished goods inventory. Some of the finished goods have limited shelf lives. Manufacturing lead time is about 8 weeks.

About 750 end items are master scheduled. Abbott was the first company to extend MRP logic to distribution, a process which is now called distribution requirements planning (DRP). Although the term DRP is not used, the process was in place at the time the case was written and is briefly described.

The MPS goes out two years. The MPS and the FAS are the same thing. An interesting aspect of this case is that the company uses CRP for both medium- and long-range planning, performing CRP for the entire two-year horizon and using CRP as the rough-cut technique. A negative aspect of this approach is that limited "what if" capability exists, since preparation of the capacity plan requires 12 to 14 hours of computer time. This is viewed as a minor problem by management, one which was to be corrected by changing from regenerative to net change MRP. There are 10 figures presented with the case.

Dow Corning Corporation

Dow Corning produces silicone materials for industrial and commercial applications. The plants studied in this case (which include only the domestic market) produce 4,000 end items for about 20,000 customers. Gross sales for the corporation were about $450 million. There are about 16,000 component items; the typical bill of materials contains 7 levels. The company is approximately 85 percent make-to-stock, 13 percent make-to-order, and 2 percent engineer-to-order.

There are 12 master schedulers, each of whom is assigned approximately 300 products, divided by product line. The MPS covers a 26-week horizon in weekly time buckets. The MPS is considered firm for the first 4 weeks.

Like many other process companies, Dow Corning uses a manual rough-cut approach which apparently is similar to the CPOF technique. This case contains very little information on capacity management.

Elliott Company, Division of Carrier Corporation – Jeannette (Pa.) Plant

Elliott builds air and gas compressors and steam turbine devices for industrial uses. The products are generally engineer-to-order. Typical lead time is 40 to 60 weeks. The plant employs 2,100 people and occupies about 635,000 square feet. The shipping dates are usually specified by the customer. Products are very large, averaging 50 tons in weight.

A particular customer order may consist of three or more end items, each having its own bill of materials. Each item is master scheduled separately, although some master scheduled items are not usable by themselves. The MPS is stated in weekly time buckets, covering about a two-year planning horizon, depending on the amount of customer backlog.

Elliott uses a bill of labor approach to perform resource requirements planning once each year. The horizon was not stated in the case. Rough-cut capacity planning is manual, using a technique similar to the resource profile approach. Since each item is engineer-to-order, time standards in the true sense do not exist and the analysis is therefore crude. Capacity analysis focuses on fabrication and machining.

Final assembly scheduling is used to control assembly and test operations. Orders are entered onto the FAS once all components have been completed and taken to stock.

One problem is that since the business is predominantly engineer-to-order, bills of material do not exist at the time the order is booked. Elliott compensates by using one of 100 generic bills of material which represent typical final configurations. The case contains 8 figures.

Hyster, Inc. – Portland (Ore.) Plant

The Hyster Portland plant manufactures lift trucks, straddle carriers, and towing winches. The plant has roughly $55 million annual sales, employs 520 people, and occupies a total of 275,000 square feet of floor space. Because of a wide variety of options, the number of end items is virtually unlimited; 2,600 end items make up 90 percent of the sales volume. The company is assemble-to-order for certain standard configurations and engineer-to-order where necessary. Quoted lead times are 4 weeks for standard configurations and 16 to 20 weeks for engineer-to-order items.

Hyster's MPS uses a planning bill approach. Planning bills contain percentage forecasts for each of the product options. The MPS covers a one-year horizon. Firm orders for standard configurations usually cover about 5 weeks. Planning bills cover the remaining 47 weeks and are useful in planning options. Readers unfamiliar with this approach should consult Orlicky (10) or the APICS *Bill of Material Training Aid* (1).

Hyster has 1,400 master scheduled items, a total of 30,000 part numbers. MRP is run daily on an IBM 370/115 computer. CPU times for MRP are not reported in the case.

The capacity planning activities consist of three levels. Hyster uses a modified CRP program once a year to perform resource requirements planning over a five-year horizon. An MPS is used to schedule delivery of standard units. The first uncommitted unit is promised to the customer. A formal rough-cut capacity planning procedure is not in use, but informal checks are made on certain bottleneck workstations.

A final assembly schedule, issued weekly, is used to plan and control assembly operations. The case contains 15 figures.

Tennant Company

The Tennant case describes two plants which make industrial floor maintenance equipment and chemical products. The plants have about $70 million in annual sales and employ 1,200 people. Sales are about 60 percent basic machines and 40 percent spare parts. Customers expect delivery in 1 to 6 weeks; production lead time is 14 weeks. Thus, Tennant is largely make-to-stock.

Two capacity planning activities, the MPS and the FAS, are described in the case. The MPS covers two years. There are 600 master scheduled items representing 30 product families. A long-range load report, developed by CRP, showing labor hours for the full two-year planning horizon, is run once every two weeks. The run time required precludes running the report weekly. The order backlog is typically 4 weeks, so 100 weeks of this report is based on a forecast. Rough-cut capacity planning is not performed at Tennant, since CRP is used for this task.

A final assembly schedule, considerably more detailed than the MPS, uses daily buckets for two weeks and weekly buckets for two additional weeks. The FAS is prepared manually by master schedulers, who have responsibility to ensure that the FAS and MPS are synchronized. The case includes 7 figures.

REVIEW OF PROCESS INDUSTRY CASES

Process industries are so named because at some stage of manufacture the product is made as a continuous process. Examples of process industries include chemicals, textiles, rubber and plastic products, and magnetic tape. Many process industry firms contend that because they are different from traditional fabrication and assembly plants, traditional production planning and control processes do not meet their needs. Many other practitioners disagree, seeing the difference between process industries and other industries as primarily one of terminology.

Consider, for example, a plant that makes a number of brands of laundry detergent powder. The powder is typically compounded in a large vat, transported over a conveyor, and packaged into boxes of various sizes. The same vat may be used for several different detergent compounds. One might consider the packaging process, at which the product becomes discrete rather than continuous, to be the final assembly operation. Both the detergent and the package are fabricated elsewhere. Fabrication must be controlled by some sort of master production schedule which is coordinated with the final assembly schedule so that the right packages and the right compound will be available simultaneously.

The study of six process industry plants described in Finch (7) and Finch and Cox (8) was undertaken to determine how the plants accomplished the fundamental tasks of master production scheduling, capacity planning and control, and priority planning and control.

One of the companies, Company P, is discussed in Chapter 8. The remaining five case studies are reviewed here.

PROCESS INDUSTRIES: 5 CASES

Company B - Textiles

Company B is a producer of denim fabric used by clothing manufacturers. Denim is made in several colors, yarn contents, and weights. The customers of Company B have rather inflexible capacity, resulting in a fairly stable, predictable demand. Company B typically knows 6 weeks before any given quarter the production plan for the entire quarter.

The manufacturing process for Company B starts with raw cotton which is fluffed, blended with synthetic fibers, placed on cards, cleaned, spun into yarn, dyed, woven on looms, treated, shrunk, cut into rolls, and shipped.

The bottleneck operation for Company B is the loom department. Since restringing the warp threads is a rather lengthy process, an effort is made to minimize the need to change from one product to another. There are 480 looms which are run 24 hours per day, 7 days per week. Because of differences in weight of cotton fiber it is not possible to predict in advance how much denim will be produced from one pound of cotton. This problem, called yield variability, is common to most process industries.

Marketing determines the loom schedules for all 480 looms. Scheduling a loom involves assigning blocks of looms to produce denim of a specific style and color. There are more looms than denim combinations. Since all other departments have higher capacities than the looms, capacity management is merely a matter of forward and backward scheduling of operations based on the loom schedule to keep them in synchronization with the looms. Simple, manual capacity planning is used.

Company F - Fruit Juices

Company F produces several products from natural fruit juices. The production process involves two phases: conversion of whole fruit to juice and then conversion of juice into the desired product and packaging it. The basic process for producing juices is unloading, removing stems, heating, pressing, filtering, pasteurizing, and storing. Four basic product lines, each with its own production process, are fed by the basic juice.

In developing its master production schedule, Company F uses a combination of rough-cut and detailed capacity planning to produce load profiles of each of the four production lines. There are no overall bottlenecks in the system, although temporary bottlenecks due to periodic sales promotions require occasional stockpiling of inventory.

Company C - Carpets

Company C markets two product lines through 40 distributors. The company employs 500 people. It typically works two shifts 5 days a week, although during the summer peak season it sometimes works 7 days. In producing carpet, Company C blows yarn into the air to deliberately entangle it and then warps, tufts, dyes, cuts, and coats the carpet. Company C produces 5,000 end items from approximately 500 raw materials. A common characteristic of process industries is having more end items than raw materials or components. This situation is the inverse of that at wood and metal fabrication plants, which usually have tens of thousands of component part numbers.

Company C maintains large in-process and smaller finished goods inventories because long production runs are needed at the tufting stage. The company is largely make-to-stock. Some items are made for special orders; when special orders are processed, however, the company usually produces an economic order quantity and places the residual in stock. When a customer order is received, the company checks to see if it can be filled from finished goods inventory. If the item is not in inventory, the company next determines whether there is in-process inventory at any stage of production and uses such material if it exists. This procedure serves to minimize delivery time to the customer.

Because demand is seasonal, peaking in the summer when schools are replacing their carpets, inventory must be accumulated prior to the summer peak. Tufting is the bottleneck operation. Rough-cut capacity planning is performed when the MPS is generated (weekly). No detailed capacity planning is performed. Capacity control is performed manually. The volume of orders is small enough so that few queues exist.

Company M – Molded Products

Company M produces rubber and vinyl floor mats for the automotive industry. The business has two peaks, one in the fall with orders from automotive manufacturers and one in the spring with orders from consumers who are sprucing up their cars.

Company M compounds a bag of rubber, weighing approximately 3,000 pounds. The rubber is then extruded into 6" × 4" × 1/2" slugs. The slugs are placed in molds, on presses. Each press can operate with up to 8 molds. Each mold has from one to eight cavities. Daily output is approximately 55,000 mats per day.

Molding of different colors is sequenced to minimize the need for mold cleaning. Lighter colors are followed by darker colors. Red, which stains the molds, is always used immediately prior to cleaning. Company M strives to produce one month ahead of the automotive manufacturers' market. The company is sensitive to the fact that the automotive manufacturers produce just-in-time and that lack of a mat can shut down an assembly line.

The company does capacity planning at the time the MPS is created. The MPS typically goes out one month. The company usually works 5 days a week. Capacity shortfalls are corrected by adding a sixth or seventh day to the MPS. Company M continuously monitors output from extrusion, molding, and trimming to spot any trends which would indicate loss of capacity.

Company Z – Magnetic Tape

Company Z produces magnetic tape for video, audio, and instrumentation markets. Although some items are produced for individuals, the majority of sales are to commercial and government customers. Government orders are large, perhaps 100,000 tapes, and unpredictable, as they are often awarded on a bid basis. The company produces a liquid having magnetic characteristics which it applies to rolls of polyester film. The rolls are then slit to an appropriate width, burnished, tested to mark defects, and cut and loaded onto reels or cassettes.

The MPS, updated monthly, contains 13 weeks of production in weekly buckets. A separate 26-week plan is used for metal components (metal reels), which have a 24-week lead time. Rough-cut capacity planning is done manually, once a month, for critical work centers. CRP is done manually whenever a new production schedule is released or a large, unanticipated government order has to be added to the plan. Because of yield variability capacity has to be carefully monitored.

REVIEW OF JIT CASES

In 1986 APICS published a set of case studies of early implementers of just-in-time in North America. This monograph, *Just-in-Time, Not Just in Japan*, by Mehran Sepehri (12), is extremely well written. Although they provide few details of capacity management per se, the cases make very interesting reading. The companies and plants studied include Hewlett-Packard plants in Cuppertino, California, and Fort Collins, Colorado; Apple MacIntosh; Omark Industries; Harley-Davidson; John Deere; New United Motor Manufacturing, Inc.; and IBM Raleigh, North Carolina.

The most complete description to date of a JIT implementation process is found in Burnham (3), a detailed study of how implementation has been carried out at ALCOA. This case includes some discussions of capacity planning, scheduling, redesign of work flows, setup time reduction, and other capacity-related matters. Schonberger (11) presents 26 short cases on just-in-time and total quality control implementation. These cases are intended for training and classroom use and therefore do not contain a great deal of detail on capacity. Two cases are particularly interesting. Hewlett-Packard Computer Systems Division discusses the transition from batch manufacturing to flow (JIT) manufacturing, and Kawasaki, in Lincoln, Nebraska, discusses mixed-model assembly lines.

Crawford, Blackstone, and Cox (6) surveyed a number of firms which were among the early JIT implementers in the United States. Although many of the firms were still in the implementation process, they reported an average 41 percent inventory reduction, 40 percent lead time reduction, 30 percent warehouse space reduction, and 54 percent increase in profit margin. These results are impressive, comparable with reductions achieved by mature MRP systems. One of the most commonly mentioned difficulties with JIT implementation found by this survey was a conflict between JIT and existing performance measurement systems, particularly systems which measure the utilization of individual work centers or which provide incentives to maximize production at individual stations. The problem with providing such incentives is that (1) they emphasize quantity over quality, and (2) non-bottleneck stations simply create excess inventory which piles up at bottlenecks.

Crawford (5) reports on six firms which had altered their performance measurement systems to accommodate JIT. It is interesting to note that all six firms are using performance to schedule rather than output maximization as the principal criterion for judging capacity management. One of Crawford's propositions is that performance to schedule must be measured on the basis of the entire group rather than on an individual basis.

Thus, JIT and Goldratt's optimized production technology (OPT) are similar in that they both emphasize group productivity rather than individual productivity. Both focus on capacity management as a whole rather than on management of individual work centers. As a result, they focus on teamwork rather than individual output. The theme for capacity management in the 1990s seems to be the encouragement of group productivity rather than individual productivity.

OPTIMIZED PRODUCTION TECHNOLOGY (OPT) SOFTWARE

To date, no case studies of OPT software implementers have been published. The initial issue of *Theory of Constraints Journal* (9) contains a discussion of a firm in the midst of implementing the synchronized production philosophy without the software. Cox, Blackstone, and Fry (4) surveyed all firms which had purchased the OPT software as of the fall of 1986. The results were similar to those of Crawford et al. (6) on JIT in both magnitude of improvement and type of implementation problem. One of the major problems with OPT implementation was found to be failure to change to an appropriate performance measurement system prior to implementation.

SUMMARY

This chapter discusses case studies which relate to capacity management in MRP, JIT, and OPT systems. Since few case studies devoted exclusively to capacity management exist, the review includes a number of case studies which, though focused on some other issue, do contain some information on the company's capacity management system. The bibliography which follows lists a number of other sources of information.

REFERENCES

1. American Production and Inventory Control Society. *Bill of Material Training Aid.* Falls Church, Va.: APICS, n.d.
2. Berry, William, Thomas Vollmann, and D. Clay Whybark. *Master Production Scheduling: Principles and Practice.* Falls Church, Va.: American Production and Inventory Control Society, 1972.
3. Burnham, John M. *Just-in-Time in a Major Process Industry.* Falls Church, Va.: American Production and Inventory Control Society, 1986.
4. Cox, James F., John H. Blackstone, Jr., and Timothy D. Fry. "Survey of OPT Implementers." Working Paper, University of Georgia Department of Management, 1987.

5. Crawford, Karlene M. "An Analysis of Performance Measurement Systems in Selected Just-in-Time Operations." Ph.D. dissertation, University of Georgia, 1987.

6. Crawford, Karlene M., John H. Blackstone, Jr., and James F. Cox. "A Study of JIT Implementation and Operating Problems." *International Journal of Production Research*, forthcoming.

7. Finch, Byron J. "Production Planning and Control in Process Industries: A Study of Methods Used to Accomplish Planning and Control Functions and Characteristics Instrumental in Method Selection." Ph.D. dissertation, University of Georgia, 1986.

8. Finch, Byron J., and James F. Cox. *Production Planning and Control: A Case Study Approach to Identifying Techniques and Impacting Factors in Process Oriented Companies.* Falls Church, Va.: American Production and Inventory Control Society, 1987.

9. Goldratt, E. M., and R. E. Fox. *Theory of Constraints Journal* 1 (1987): 1–37.

10. Orlicky, Joseph. *Material Requirements Planning.* New York: McGraw-Hill Book Co., 1975. Chapter 10.

11. Schonberger, Richard J. *World Class Manufacturing Casebook.* New York: The Free Press, 1987.

12. Sepehri, Mehran. *Just-in-Time, Not Just in Japan.* Falls Church, Va.: American Production and Inventory Control Society, 1986.

13. Wemmerlov, Urban. *Case Studies in Capacity Management.* Falls Church, Va.: American Production and Inventory Control Society, 1984.

DISCUSSION QUESTIONS

1. Select any two cases involving material requirements planning systems and compare and contrast the systems with respect to master schedule horizon, master schedule freezing, final assembly schedule usage, type of rough-cut technique utilized, and utilization of capacity requirements planning. Discuss the environmental factors which are likely to have caused any difference in approach.

2. Select any single case involving material requirements planning and suggest improvements to the overall system, e.g., adding a rough-cut technique. Discuss reasons the suggested technique is not utilized.

3. Select any case involving material requirements planning and discuss the applicability of JIT to that company. Discuss the applicability of OPT.

4. Process industry firms often contend that because they are different from traditional fabrication and assembly plants MRP will not work for them. Choose any process industry case and compare and contrast its situation with that of War Eagle Hoists as presented in Chapter 2.

BIBLIOGRAPHY

Case Studies Presented at APICS International Conferences, 1980–1987

1980

Clauson, James R. "A Capacity Tool Using MRP." Pp. 342–345. (Hill-Rom Division of Hillenbrand Ind.)

McCormick, Robert. "Master Production Scheduling—The Fundamental Concept." Pp. 400–403. (Crane Co.)

Motwane, Aman A. "Capacity Planning and Control." Pp. 327–331. (Power Transmission Division of Western Gear Corp.)

Warren, Charles R. "Capacity (Not Materials) Planning—A Must for Process Industries." Pp. 349–352. (Laclede Steel Co.)

1981

Blumenau, Rod. "FORCAPS—A Resource Requirements Planning System." Pp. 236–239. (Eastman Kodak Co.)

Bolander, Steven F. "Capacity Planning with TPFS." Pp. 207–209. (Rockwell International)

Hoffman, William C. "MRP II at a Paper Goods Plant—Case Study." Pp. 226–228. (Paper Goods Plant)

Muegel, A. L. "Planning, Controlling, and Executing the Production Plan in a Make-to-Stock/Make-to-Order Environment." Pp. 242–246. (Timken Co.)

Thoren, Stanley A., Jr., and Drake Sheahan. "A Unified Approach to Capacity Planning and Marketing Strategy—A Case Study." Pp. 224–225. (Sheahan/Dougall, Inc.)

1982

Ahrens, Roger. "Capacity Management—Who Is Accountable?" Pp. 396–400. (Owatonna Tool Co.)

Bartholomew, Gary L. "Controlling the Shop Floor from MRP to CRP—A Case Study." Pp. 410–413. (WABCO Construction and Mining Equipment Group)

Gould, Ralph R. "Capacity and Manpower Planning Are Easier in Repetitive Manufacturing." Pp. 319–321. (RTE Corp.)

Rowley, Thomas. "Multiplant Capacity Planning—A Case Study." Pp. 373–375. (Sperry Univac Division)

Stickler, Michael J. "Capacity Management—A Case Study." Pp. 376–378. (Machine Tool Co.)

1983

Busby, Linda G., and Michael S. Spender. "Successful Closed-Loop Education at John Deere: A Case Study." Pp. 528–533. (John Deere Engine Works)

Njus, John. "Resource Requirements Planning: The Sunstrand Model." Pp. 480–483. (Sunstrand Hydro–Transmission)

1984

(Note: The 1984 *Proceedings* were split into several volumes. This case is from *Readings in Material and Capacity Requirements Planning.*)

Carmody, Richard H. "Finite Capacity Management Using OPT in the Nuclear Fuels Industry." Pp. 82–84. (Westinghouse)

1985 and 1986: No cases

1987

Mirto, Lawrence J., and Stewart J. Lehman. "Tools for the Future." Pp. 568–570. (United Technology)

Additional References from APICS International Conferences

1979

Clark, James T. "Capacity Management." Pp. 191–194.

1981

Anderson, Samuel R. "Data Requirements for Capacity Requirements Planning." Pp. 219–223.

Hoffman, James G. "Capacity Management and Valid Schedules." Pp. 200–202.

Sari, F. John. "Resource Requirements Planning and Capacity Requirements Planning—The Case for Each and Both." Pp. 229–231.

Van DeMark, Robert L. "Adjust Your Capacity, Do Not Reschedule Your Shop Orders." Pp. 148–151.

1982

Bechte, Wolfgang. "Controlling Manufacturing Lead Time and Work-in-Process Inventory by Means of Load-Oriented Order Release." Pp. 67–71.

1983

Groen, Jerome J. "A Microcomputer-Based Rough Cut Resource Planning System." Pp. 138–141.

Kalonda, Dennis J. "Using CRP Output: What Have You Done for Your Plant Manager Lately?" Pp. 224–326.

1984

Abair, Robert A., and Philip F. Helle. "Capacity Planning: A Commonsense Approach to Manufacturing Planning." Pp. 65–67.

Lankford, Ray, and Stephen D. Smith. "The Beginning of the Post-MRP Era." Pp. 50–53.

Russell, Richard K. "Rough-Cut Capacity Planning—The First Step in Managing Capacity." Pp. 70–73.

1985

Blackstone, John H., Jr. "Tutorial on Capacity Management." Pp. 105–107.

Goddard, Walter E. "Practical Principles of Capacity Planning." Pp. 81–86.

Heilweil, Norman L. "Do You Actually Control Your Capacity?" Pp. 108–110.

Miller, Chuck, and Olin Thompson. "Forget Materials—Plan Capacity First." Pp. 76–80.

Quillen, L. D. "Repetitive Manufacturing Assembly Scheduling." Pp. 73–75.

Reinhart, Leroy D. "Delineation of Capacity Planning Responsibility." Pp. 92–95.

Russell, Stephen P. "Capacity Planning for Preventative Maintenance: Pay Me Now or Pay Me Later." Pp. 96–100.

1986

Blackstone, John H., Jr. "Rough-Cut Capacity Planning Using Spreadsheets." Pp. 190–191.

Bruun, Richard J. "Operation Sequencing: Scheduling for On-Time Delivery." Pp. 192–193.

May, Neville P. "The Major Issues of Capacity Requirements Planning." Pp. 170–172.

Nelson, Mel. "Capacity Planning and Execution: The Other Half of the Equation." Pp. 173–177.

Thorne, Frederick L. "Capacity Management: Managing Today While Planning for the Future." Pp. 182–185.

1987

Sari, F. John. "How to Master Schedule If Your Problem Is Capacity Not Materials." Pp. 582–584.

Taylor, Sam G., and Steven F. Bolander. "Processor Dominated Scheduling." Pp. 571–572.

Additional References from Other Sources

Classen, Ronald J., and Eric M. Malstrom. "Capacity Planning as a Productivity Tool in the Automated Factory." *Industrial Engineering* 14, no. 4 (April 1982): 73–81.

Gaw, William H. "Capacity Planning—A Key to On-Time Deliveries." *Operations Scheduling Seminar Proceedings*, San Francisco, Calif., APICS, January 29–30. Pp. 7–10.

Internicola, Philip. "The Master Schedule as a Capacity Management Tool." *Production and Inventory Management Review* 2, no. 6 (June 1982): 48–49, 51.

Johnson, Bruce P. "Controlling Capacity Is the Only Thing." *Process Industries Seminar Proceedings*, Las Vegas, Nev., APICS, April 22–24, 1981. Pp. 1–10.

Karni, R. "Capacity Requirements Planning—A Systematization." *International Journal of Production Research* 20, no. 6 (November/December 1982): 715–740.

Lunz, Alfred G. "The Missing Factors—The Real Keys to Effective Capacity Requirements Planning and Control." *Production and Inventory Management* 22, no. 2 (1981): 1–12.

Stickler, M. "Capacity Planning—A Case Study." *Proceedings of the Canadian Association for Production and Inventory Control*, 1982. Pp. 197–207.

Thurwachter, William A. "Capacity Driven Planning." *Proceedings of the Canadian Association for Production and Inventory Control*, 1982. Pp. 282–290.

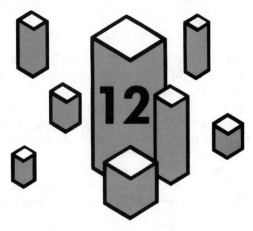

Performance Measures and Future Directions

This text considers capacity from three distinct perspectives—the traditional material requirements planning viewpoint, the synchronized production (OPT) viewpoint, and the just-in-time (JIT) viewpoint. Implementers of JIT and OPT have consistently found that traditional performance measures are not appropriate for these new environments. In the sections that follow, performance measures appropriate for the three environments are discussed, followed by some brief thoughts on future capacity management–related research.

PERFORMANCE MEASURES

Consultant Jack Gip tells a story which dramatically illustrates the impact of performance measurement on actual performance (3). A one-time client operated two plants, the first a fabrication plant, the second an assembly plant. The parts fabricated at the first plant were assembled at the second. Both plants were evaluated on the basis of tonnage shipped from the plant. The fabrication plant was perennially exceeding its quota of shipped tonnage; the plant's management enjoyed nice bonuses each year. The assembly plant never met quota, in spite of several managerial changes. Gip was called as a consultant to suggest better capacity management procedures at the assembly plant.

Gip found that the real culprit lay in the performance measurement system. Because fabrication was measured on tonnage shipped, as every evaluation cycle drew to a close, fabrication expedited heavy, simple parts, delaying light, intricate parts. This action helped fabrication exceed its quota. Naturally, assembly was chronically short of light, intricate components, especially toward the end of each evaluation cycle. The assembly plant had even set up a small machine shop to create needed components from surplus heavy components! When Gip informed general management that the problem was really at the fabrication plant, they refused to believe him. The fabrication plant was their pride and joy.

One must exercise extreme caution in establishing performance measures. Old performance measures such as work center efficiency have been shown to be counterproductive. What will replace them?

Efficiency and Utilization

Efficiency is defined as standard hours of output divided by clock hours actually worked. Efficiency needs to be measured for information purposes in capacity planning. It is necessary to transform the standard hours of output required into the clock hours needed to produce that output. As a performance measure, efficiency is useful only in identifying workers who cannot perform to standard and should be assigned different responsibilities. Efficiency should not be used to determine pay.

Utilization is defined as the hours actually worked divided by the hours scheduled to be worked. As such, it is not a useful measure, because downtime may be due to far different causes—absenteeism or machine breakdown, which one always wants to avoid, or lack of work, which one does not always want to avoid. Therefore, utilization should be split into two components, availability and activation. The definitions of availability and activation, and a rationale for their use, are given in Chapter 3. Availability would measure the proportion of time the work center was *available* for service. Activation would measure the proportion of *available time* the station was actually utilized. Both availability and activation are useful performance measures. *Target availability* is 100 percent. *Target activation*, as explained in Appendix 1A, is a function of planned queue length. The appropriate performance measure is absolute deviation from target in both instances. Making this change in performance measure would greatly improve MRP system performance.

Performance to Schedule

Performance to schedule is a crucial performance measure. As inventory is removed from the shop floor, work centers lose the independence of operation made possible by inventory buffers, so that station B's deviation from schedule may cause station A to go idle. To exist in a low-inventory environment, performance to schedule must replace efficiency as the crucial performance measure.

Consider the milling operation at War Eagle Hoists as described in Chapter 2. Recall that this operation produces an armature which goes into windings and three types of gear sets, one gear set being part of each hoist assembly. The milling machine operator could raise his or her efficiency by producing type A gears for an entire week, then B gears for an entire week, then C gears for an entire week, and then armatures for a week. However, this increase in departmental efficiency has several adverse consequences for the plant. First, winding, which is the bottleneck department, is forced to go idle for three weeks for lack of armatures. Second, as the supply of windings is exhausted, motor assembly and final assembly will also go idle. Finally, once all components are available and work resumes at all stations, the level of inventory held in gears and armatures has risen. The additional inventory represents a real cost, whereas the increase in departmental efficiency represents a fictional improvement since the milling operator is able to complete all necessary tasks without overtime under the present arrangement of milling all parts each week. By measuring the milling operator on performance to schedule rather than efficiency, one eliminates an incentive for actions which benefit the individual to the detriment of the group.

Zero Defects

An affluent world demands high-quality products. American products at one time enjoyed a reputation for high quality. This reputation has eroded steadily since the early 1960s, largely because of better quality control in countries such as Japan. Even in the United States, Japanese products are often preferred to competing American products for their higher quality. From a capacity management viewpoint, time spent building a product which is ultimately scrapped is time wasted. Time wasted at a bottleneck is especially costly. Goldratt (4) recommends that quality inspection be performed prior to the bottleneck to remove all defective units before expending any bottleneck time on them. He even suggests that parts which have passed the bottleneck be marked with gold ribbon to symbolize the value they represent in expensive time saved.

For a long time American managers believed that higher quality meant greater production costs. This belief was challenged by a flood of Japanese imports which not only were of higher quality than their American counterparts but were also cheaper. Managers now accept that good quality control at every station, making the product right the first time, can help to improve productivity as well as quality. This changing awareness is exemplified by the title of one of the more popular quality control books, *Quality Is Free*, by Philip Crosby (1). Many managers now argue that the title does not go far enough; they assert that quality is not just free, it pays!

Dollar Days

Dollar days are defined as the dollar value of a good multiplied by the days until expected sale. This measure is strongly advocated by Goldratt (4) for the following reasons:

1. The traditional way of treating inventory, as an asset on the P&L statement, provides a disincentive to reduce inventory and masks the true state of a plant. Building inventory during a recession is reflected on paper as an increase in assets and profits, but the plant is really worse off than if the workers had been assigned cross-training or maintenance duties rather than unnecessary production duties.
2. It makes sense to treat inventory as a loan given to the manufacturing unit.
3. Using dollar days as a measure encourages plants to write off obsolete inventory. Operations are streamlined. Problems become more visible.
4. The measure encourages purchasing to acquire material just-in-time. There are several disincentives to just-in-time purchasing given standard performance measures.
5. It penalizes premature release of orders to the shop floor.
6. It encourages sale of finished product. Today, slow-moving products and poor forecasts are accepted as inevitable.
7. Getting faster flow through the plant forces management to find ways to reduce disruptions such as breakdowns and long setups, scrap and rework.

Goldratt summarizes his argument as follows:

> All of these actions will have a direct bearing on the competitive position of the plant. Focusing attention on the inventory of the plant will force the plant to analyze implementation of these policies and process improvements. What we need is a way to evaluate quantitatively the impact of any proposed action. The dollar days measure of inventory provides us with such a measure. Every proposed action should be analyzed for its impact on the inventory as measured in dollar days. The proposed improvements can then be prioritized. [p. 16]

An example of how dollar days are calculated is presented in Chapter 9.

Stability of Schedule

An absolute requirement for good capacity management is a stable schedule. Frequent schedule changes disrupt shop floor coordination. The Japanese freeze their schedule for a month. American manufacturers can too. If just-in-time or synchronized production techniques are used to dramatically reduce lead times, customers will find that even with a schedule which is frozen one month out, a plant is very responsive to changing needs.

Longer-term schedule stability should be used to evaluate marketing, which is responsible for forecasts. Better yet, let marketing own all finished goods. Evaluate its performance partly on the basis of dollar days held in inventory.

Capital Acquisition

Acquisition of capital equipment should be evaluated on the basis of *throughput* as defined by Goldratt, i.e., goods produced and *sold*, rather than increased production at the work center. In the past, direct labor input has been used to measure performance of capital equipment. Consider the following. A plant currently has a manually operated lathe, operated two shifts. This lathe can produce 100,000 widgets per shift per year. Total sales are 150,000 widgets per year. The bottleneck operation is heat treat, where an expensive oven is used to capacity. The two lathe operators make a combined $60,000 per year. There is thus $0.40 labor per widget at the lathe. The old lathe has a 10-year useful life. The supervisor would like to buy a new numerically controlled lathe at a cost of $200,000. This lathe would have a capacity of 300,000 widgets per shift. Industrial engineering calculates that direct labor cost will now be $0.10 per widget, saving $45,000 annually, and strongly recommends purchasing the machine.

Throughput analysis reaches another conclusion. The lathe is *not* the bottleneck. Buying a new one will not increase sales. At best, the new lathe will replace the second-shift operator, saving $30,000 annually. It is more likely, however, that some second-shift production will continue to be needed because of expediting or timing considerations, so savings will be less than $30,000.

Analysis of capacity expansion at the bottleneck itself becomes quite difficult. When one bottleneck is eliminated, one must determine what the next bottleneck will be. In most cases one must employ computer simulation to determine what the new throughput and bottleneck are.

The reason computer simulation is necessary is that since there is a direct correlation between activation and WIP (and hence lead time), one must simulate the plant to determine the level of throughput achievable with the new machine *without increasing WIP*.

All things considered, computer simulation is the most underutilized tool in capacity management.

FUTURE DIRECTIONS IN CAPACITY MANAGEMENT

Assembly Shops

Kenneth McGuire (5) best expressed the future of capacity management in assembly shops with the following:

In Japanese companies the product is designed with the production process already in mind. The product design is not viewed as separate from the process with which it will be manufactured. Engineers design with an understanding that leveling and balance are the predominant control mechanisms in manufacturing. Therefore, a product that does not flow well through the manufacturing process is considered to have not been well designed. Constraints on capacity are thus considered from the outset and confirmed regularly by adhering to a goal of constant leveling.

When the design of the product and the design of the process are accomplished together, the capacity can more easily be determined and expressed in terms of a unit rate of output. The production rate is then geared to flexibly match the consumption rate of the end product. Production engineering concentrates on reducing the manufacturing cycle time to below the sales cycle time. The market rate of demand, including the susceptibility to demand fluctuation, is the primary manufacturing time cycle mandate for the ultimate design of the production process. Flexibility of response is an important criterion from the start. Achieving flexibility in the capacity eliminates the need for speculative production. Since the lead times and manufacturing cycle times are designed to be very short, the question of how much to produce is quite dependent on how much will be sold or consumed. The balance between consumption and production rates is altered only to provide specific levels of finished inventory. In the production process inventories accumulate only where there is imbalance in the flow. These imbalances can then be corrected with additions or reductions in people resources at each of the many points throughout the process. This movement of flexible resources to the work, instead of attempting to move the workload to the resources, helps achieve the desired rate with a balanced flow. Where several product groups or different products exist they are intermittently mixed into the production process to balance resource consumption on a daily, weekly, or monthly basis. Demand fluctuations then become a simple matter of what rate is being produced, and how much less or extra time will be required to produce the specific quantity of goods. Also, with the lead times between production and consumption remaining very short, demand fluctuations over short cycles are less likely to result in large quantity variations as a result of extended lead times, frozen schedules, and large lot sizes.

Simply *achieving* the conditions described by McGuire will keep assembly shops busy for the next decade.

It is critical that all American manufacturers begin to recognize capacity constraints and machine limitations at the time a product is designed. Before a design for any part is accepted, process engineering should certify that the part can be built within tolerance at a stated cost. If process engineering refuses to certify it, the part should be redesigned or the production process changed so that the design can be certified. The identification of problems after a new part has been given to the floor to build is one of the most expensive continuing mistakes made by American management. The Japanese have shown us a better way.

The Japanese have also shown us the advantages of a flexible work force. It is often argued that American unions will refuse to accept work-force flexibility. Recent settlements indicate most unions are willing to trade work-force flexibility for job security. This is a reasonable trade-off, particularly if workers are cross-trained during recessionary periods.

Flexible Manufacturing Systems

Whether flexible manufacturing systems (FMS) become a major force in American manufacturing by the turn of the century remains to be seen. Their impact depends heavily on the development of artificial intelligence software capable of providing good real-time capacity management. This software will be developed, but to have an impact by the turn of the century such development efforts probably need additional support.

Job Shops and Fabrication and Assembly Shops

The directions that job shops will take in capacity management over the next decade is subject to speculation. A number of experts think MRP must be entirely replaced by some new approach, such as OPT software. Others feel MRP will work perfectly well if minor changes, such as recognizing the relationship between activation, lead time, and tardiness percentage, are made. Detailed finite loading should be added to MRP software, using the synchronized production approach of loading the bottlenecks first.

RESEARCH DIRECTIONS

Two major research needs in the capacity management area are case studies and simulation studies. Case studies are needed because very few detailed cases exist, particularly from plants using just-in-time or synchronized production techniques. Very detailed information concerning what works, what fails, and why needs to be shared. Simulation studies are needed to test proposed changes in capacity management practice. Recent research suggests that lot-sizing rule and sequencing-rule performance are sensitive to the number of levels of the bill of material and the bill of material shape, and that an interaction between lot sizing and scheduling exists (2). Other likely influences are demand seasonality and work-force flexibility.

Information concerning the trade-off between activation, in-process inventory, lead time, tardiness percentage, and schedule stability needs to be developed through simulation studies. If we are to truly manage capacity to become world-class manufacturers, we must have more sharing of information among companies and better research from academic institutions.

REFERENCES

1. Crosby, Philip. *Quality Is Free.* New York: New American Library, 1979.
2. Gardiner, S. C. "A Simulation Study of Lot Sizing and Dispatching Techniques in a Material Requirements Planning Environment with Master Production Schedule Instability." Ph.D. dissertation, University of Georgia, 1987.
3. Gip, Jack. Presentation to Chattahoochee Valley APICS chapter, Columbus, Georgia, May 1983.
4. Goldratt, Eliyahu. Epilogue to *The Goal*, draft, 1986.
5. McGuire, Kenneth. *Impressions from Our Most Worthy Competitor.* Falls Church, Va.: American Production and Inventory Control Society, 1987.

DISCUSSION QUESTIONS

1. Discuss the advantages and disadvantages of the following performance measures to a single department: utilization, efficiency, dollar days, throughput, inventory investment, average cost per unit, overall profit.
2. Discuss a set of performance measures which would suffice to correct the problems found by Jack Gip as described in the chapter.
3. Define utilization, activation, and availability as discussed in the chapter. Show that utilization is the product of activation and availability. Discuss the applicability of activation and availability as performance measures.
4. Discuss performance to schedule as a performance measure in a MRP environment. A JIT environment. An OPT environment.
5. Discuss zero defects as a performance measure in a MRP environment. A JIT environment. An OPT environment.
6. Discuss the importance of master schedule stability to MRP, JIT, and OPT. Discuss the costs of freezing the master schedule for 4 weeks, 8 weeks, and 6 months. How long should the master schedule be frozen, if at all?

USE OF WORKSHEETS

On the diskette which accompanies the Instructor's Manual is a Lotus worksheet called RCCP.WKS and a compiled FORTRAN program called RGHCUT.EXE. The worksheet will work with either Version 1A or Version 2 of Lotus 1-2-3. It is too large to use with the student version of Lotus. The worksheet allows one to perform rough-cut computations using the bill of labor, CPOF, or resource profile approach. The software is easy to use and assumes only minimal knowledge of Lotus 1-2-3.

For anyone having access to Lotus 1-2-3, the Lotus worksheet is recommended. For those lacking access to Lotus, RGHCUT.EXE is available. The documentation provided in this appendix is intended merely to document how to get started using the software. It is sufficient for most uses of the software. More extensive documentation is provided on the diskette itself in the files RGHCUT.DOC and RCCP.DOC, documenting the FORTRAN and Lotus versions, respectively. To obtain a printed copy of either of these files, place the diskette in the default drive. At the DOS prompt, key TYPE [filename]>PRN and press ENTER. For filename, key either RGHCUT.DOC or RCCP.DOC.

RCCP.WKS

To use the software, first boot Lotus and place the diskette containing RCCP.WKS in a floppy drive. Issue the command sequence / FD (file directory). Lotus will tell you which drive it uses for retrieving and saving files. This drive should be the drive containing RCCP.WKS. For example, if Lotus is in drive A and RCCP.WKS is in drive B, the command / FD (file directory) should indicate that the default drive is B:\. If it does, press the ENTER key and go on; if not, type B:\, press the ENTER key, and go on. Next enter the command sequence / FR (file retrieve). The name RCCP should appear on the second line. If it does not, return to the definition of the default drive given earlier in this paragraph. Assuming RCCP appears, press the ENTER key while RCCP is highlighted to retrieve the worksheet. Because RCCP is a large worksheet, it takes a while to load. Be patient.

When RCCP is loaded, a title screen displays. Near the bottom of the screen is a message to press ALT M to go to the main menu. While holding down the ALT key, press M. A menu of options appears. Move the cursor across the row of options. Notice that an explanation of what each menu choice can do appears on the line below the menu. Options in order are (1) MPS, (2) CPOF, (3) BILL OF LABOR, (4) R-PROFILE, (5) LOOK, (6) EXECUTE, (7) SAVE, and (8) QUIT. To execute you must define the master schedule and the rough-cut procedure options you wish to execute.

When you select an entry from the main menu you will go to a submenu which allows you to enter data, save data, modify data, calculate the requirements, or print any of the above. The submenus also contain explanations of the choices available. To go from a submenu back to the main menu, press the ESC key. When you select a submenu item, the worksheet is split, with the top of the screen giving you a message explaining what to do in that section and also explaining how to get back to the various menus. Please read and follow these directions.

RGHCUT.EXE

The program RGHCUT.EXE executes from the DOS prompt level. If the DOS prompt reads A>, place the diskette containing RGHCUT.EXE in the A drive, key RGHCUT, and press ENTER. A menu will appear which will allow you to create and save data, retrieve previously created data, or complete the rough-cut calculations. RGHCUT.EXE will handle much larger problems than the Lotus version. The program is entirely menu driven. Simply choose menu options and respond. The program is not quite as easy to use as the Lotus software, because spreadsheets are inherently easier for data creation and editing.

GLOSSARY

Definitions marked with an asterisk (*) are taken from the *APICS Dictionary*, 6th ed., 1987.

***assemble-to-order** designating a make-to-order product where all components (bulk, semifinished, intermediate, subassembly, fabricated, purchased, packaging, etc.) used in the assembly, packaging, or finishing process are planned and stocked in anticipation of a customer order.

bill of capacity. See *bill of labor.*

***bill of labor (BOL)** a listing of the capacity and key resources required to manufacture one unit of a selected item or family. Often used to predict the impact of the item scheduled on the master production schedule and load of the key resources.

***bill of material (BOM)** a listing of all the subassemblies, intermediates, parts, and raw materials that go into a parent assembly showing the quantity of each required to make an assembly. There are a variety of display formats of a bill of material, including the single-level bill of material, indented bill of material, modular (planning) bill of material, transient bill of material, matrix bill of material, costed bill of material, etc. May also be called "formula," "recipe," or "ingredients list" in certain industries.

***bottleneck** a facility, function, department, etc., that impedes production—for example, a machine or work center where jobs arrive at a faster rate than they can be completed.

***capacity** 1. in a general sense, refers to an aggregated volume of work load. It is a separate concept from priority. 2. the highest reasonable output rate which can be achieved with the current product specifications, product mix, work force, plant, and equipment.

***capacity requirements planning (CRP)** the function of establishing, measuring, and adjusting limits or levels of capacity. The term capacity requirements planning in this context is the process of determining how much labor and machine resources are required to accomplish the tasks of production. Open shop orders, and planned orders in the MRP system, are input to CRP which "translates" these orders into hours of work by work center by time period. See also *closed-loop MRP; resource requirements planning; rough-cut capacity planning.*

***closed-loop MRP** a system built around material requirements planning and also including the additional planning functions of sales and operations (production planning, master production scheduling, and capacity requirements planning). Further, once this planning

261

phase is complete and the plans have been accepted as realistic and attainable, the execution functions come into play. The term "closed-loop" implies that there is feedback from the execution functions so that the planning can be kept valid at all times.

cost over time (COVERT) a dispatching procedure which selects the job having the higher ratio of total cost to time remaining until due date.

critical ratio (CRR) a dispatching rule which calculates a priority index number by dividing the time to due date remaining by the expected elapsed time to finish the job.

$$\frac{Time\ remaining}{Work\ remaining} = \frac{30}{40} = 0.75$$

Typically ratios of less than 1.0 are behind, ratios greater than 1.0 are ahead, and a ratio of 1.0 is on schedule. See also *least slack per operation*.

deterministic model a model where no uncertainty is included. Examples include inventory models without any safety stock considerations. Cf. *stochastic model*.

dispatching the selecting and sequencing of available jobs to be run at individual workstations and the assignment of these jobs to workers.

earliest job due date (EDD) a dispatching procedure in which the job which has the earliest date to complete the final operation is selected.

earliest operation due date (ODD) a dispatching procedure in which the job which has the earliest date to complete the current operation is selected.

economic order quantity (EOQ) a type of fixed order quantity, which determines the amount of an item to be purchased or manufactured at one time. The intent is to minimize the combined costs of acquiring and carrying inventory.

efficiency standard hours produced divided by actual hours worked. Efficiency for a given period of time can be calculated for a machine, an employee, a group of machines, a department, etc.

end item a product sold as a completed item or repair part; any item subject to a customer order or sales forecast.

engineer-to-order designating products whose customer specifications require unique engineering design or significant customization. Each customer order then results in a unique set of part numbers, bills of materials, and routing.

expediting the "rushing" or "chasing" of production or purchase orders which are needed in less than the normal lead time. See also *dispatching*.

FIFO (first in, first out) a method of dispatching. The assumption is that oldest inventory (first in) is the first to be used (first out).

final assembly schedule (FAS) a schedule of end items to finish the product for specific customer orders in a "make-to-order" or "assemble-to-order" environment. It is prepared after receipt of a customer order as constrained by the availability of material and capacity, and it schedules the operations required to complete the product from the level where it is stocked (or master scheduled) to the end item level.

Gantt chart the earliest and best-known type of control chart especially designed to show graphically the relationship between planned performance and actual performance, named after its originator, Henry L. Gantt. Used for machine loading, where one horizontal line is used to represent capacity and another to represent load against that capacity, or for following job progress where one horizontal line represents the production schedule and another parallel line represents the actual progress of the job against the schedule in time.

*heuristic a form of problem solving where the results or rules have been determined by experience or intuition instead of by optimization.

highest-value job first (HVF) a dispatching procedure which selects the job having the highest value.

*input/output control a technique for capacity control where actual output from a work center is compared with the planned output as developed by capacity requirements planning and approved by manufacturing management. The input is also monitored to see if it corresponds with plans so that work centers will not be expected to generate output when work is not available. See also *closed-loop MRP.*

*job shop a form of manufacturing organization in which the productive resources are organized according to function, such as drilling, forging, spinning, or assembly. The jobs pass through the functional departments in lots and each lot may have a different routing.

*just-in-time in the broad sense, an approach to achieving excellence in a manufacturing company based on the continuing elimination of waste (waste being considered as those things which do not add value to the product). In the narrow sense, just-in-time refers to the movement of material at the necessary place at the necessary time. The implication is that each operation is closely synchronized with the subsequent ones to make that possible.

*kanban a method of just-in-time production which uses standard containers or lot sizes with a single card attached to each. It is a pull system in which work centers signal with a card that they wish to withdraw parts from feeding operations or vendors. *Kanban* in Japanese, loosely translated, means "card," literally "billboard" or "sign." The term is often used synonymously for the specific scheduling system developed and used by Toyota Corporation in Japan.

least slack per operation (OPS) a dispatching procedure which directs the sequencing of jobs based on the time from today until the due date minus the remaining processing time.

*least total cost a dynamic lot-sizing technique that calculates the order quantity by comparing the carrying cost and the setup (or ordering) costs for various lot sizes and selects the lot where these are most nearly equal.

*line balancing the assignment of tasks to workstations so as to minimize the number of workstations and to minimize the total amount of idle time at all stations.

*load the amount of scheduled work ahead of a manufacturing facility, usually expressed in terms of hours of work or units of production.

*make-to-order designating a product which is finished after receipt of a customer order. Frequently components with long lead times are planned before the order arrives in order to reduce the delivery time to the customer. Where options or other subassemblies are stocked in advance of customer orders, the term "assemble-to-order" is frequently used.

*make-to-stock   designating a product which is shipped from finished goods, "off the shelf," and therefore is finished before a customer order arrives.

*master production schedule (MPS)   the anticipated build schedule for those items assigned to the master scheduler. The master scheduler maintains this schedule and, in turn, it becomes a set of planning numbers which "drives" material requirements planning. It represents what the company plans to produce expressed in specific configurations, quantities, and dates. The master production schedule is not a sales forecast which represents a statement of demand. The master production schedule must take into account the forecast, the production plan, and other important considerations such as backlog, availability of material, availability of capacity, management policy and goals, etc. Synonym: master schedule. See also *closed-loop MRP.*

*material requirements planning (MRP)   a set of techniques which uses bills of material, inventory data, and the master production schedule to calculate requirements for materials. It makes recommendations to release replenishment orders for material. Further, since it is time phased, it makes recommendations to reschedule open orders when due dates and need dates are not in phase. Originally seen as merely a better way to order inventory, today it is thought of as primarily a scheduling technique, i.e., a method for establishing and maintaining valid due dates (priorities) on orders. See also *closed-loop MRP.*

modified operation due date (MOD)   a dispatching procedure which modifies operation due dates by taking the larger of the original due date and the earliest time a job can be completed. Jobs are selected on the basis of smallest modified due date.

nominal capacity.   See *rated capacity.*

optimized production technology (OPT)   a production philosophy which emphasizes maximizing the total amount manufactured and sold while minimizing inventory and operating expense. The philosophy centers on the management of bottleneck resources.

*period order quantity   a lot-sizing technique under which the lot size will be equal to the net requirements for a given number of periods (e.g., weeks) into the future.

*planned order   a suggested order quantity, release date, and due date created by MRP processing, when it encounters net requirements. Planned orders are created by the computer; exist only within the computer; and may be changed or deleted by the computer during subsequent MRP processing if conditions change. Planned orders at one level will be exploded into gross requirements for components at the next lower level. Planned orders, along with released orders, also serve as input to capacity requirements planning, to show the total capacity requirements in future time periods.

*priority   in a general sense, refers to the relative importance of jobs, i.e., the sequence in which jobs should be worked on. It is a separate concept from capacity.

*queue   a waiting line. In manufacturing, the jobs at a given work center waiting to be processed. As queues increase, so do average queue time and work-in-process inventory.

*rated capacity   capacity calculated from data such as utilization and efficiency, hours planned to be worked, etc. Synonym: theoretical capacity.

resource requirements planning   very long term planning, primarily concerned with plant expansion and the acquisition of major equipment.

*rough-cut capacity planning (RCCP)   the process of converting the production plan and/or the master production schedule into capacity needs for key resources: labor force, machinery, warehouse space, vendors' capabilities, and, in some cases, money. Product load profiles are often used to accomplish this. Synonym: resource requirements planning. See also *capacity requirements planning*.

*routing   a set of information detailing the method of manufacture of a particular item. It includes the operations to be performed, their sequence, the various work centers to be involved, and the standards for setup and run. In some companies, the routing also includes information on tooling, operator skill levels, inspection operations, testing requirements, etc.

*safety stock   1. in general, a quantity of stock planned to be in inventory to protect against fluctuations in demand and/or supply. 2. In the context of master production scheduling, safety stock can refer to additional inventory and/or capacity planned as protection against forecast errors and/or short-term changes in the backlog. Sometimes referred to as "overplanning" or a "market hedge." Synonym: buffer stock.

*sequencing   determining the order in which a manufacturing facility is to process a number of different jobs in order to achieve certain objectives. See also *dispatching*.

*shortest processing time (SPT)   a dispatching technique which directs the sequencing of jobs in ascending order by processing time. Following this rule, the most jobs per time period will be processed. As a result, the average lateness of jobs is minimized, but some jobs will be very late.

Silver-Meal algorithm   a lot-sizing procedure which determines order quantities sequentially but uses as its criterion minimization of the sum of setup and inventory carrying costs per period. The basic idea is to compare order quantities Q_n and Q_{n+1}, forecast demand for periods n and $n + 1$, for increasing values of n. When the cost per period for Q_{n+1} exceeds the cost of Q_n for the first time, Q_n is selected as the order quantity.

*stochastic model   a model where uncertainty is explicitly considered in the analysis. Cf. *deterministic model*.

*summarized bill of material   a form of multilevel bill of material which lists all the parts and their quantities required in a given product structure. Unlike an indented bill of material it does not list the levels of manufacture and lists a component only once for the total quantity used.

*throughput   the total volume of production through a facility (machine, work center, department, plant, or network of plants).

*utilization   a measure of how intensively a resource is being used. It is the ratio of the direct time charged for production activities (setup and/or run) to the clock time scheduled for those production activities for a given period of time:

$$Utilization = \frac{Direct\ time\ charged}{Clock\ time\ scheduled}$$

For example, to calculate labor utilization, the direct labor hours charged are divided by the total clock hours scheduled for a given period of time. Similarly, to calculate machine utilization, the total time charged to creating output (setup and/or run time) is divided by the total clock hours scheduled to be available for a given period of time.

zero inventory.   See *just-in-time.*

INDEX